Even in Andrews

Janice Harshbarger

ISBN: 9781691027965
Imprint: Independently published

Contents

Introduction

Only in Andrews told the story of a small town in Huntington County, Indiana, from its founding in 1853 to the middle of 1916. Stories about the early pioneers, the railroad, Civil War veterans, local politics, and the development of the town schools filled the volume. During those early years, things happened that truly could have taken place "Only in Andrews."

The book ended on a good note. Andrews had overcome its loss of the division point for the Wabash Railroad, and there was a good-sized factory in town, the Wasmuth-Endicott Company, that provided jobs for many of the men. Although a war raged in Europe, the conflict had minimal impact at that point on the life of Andrews. A huge "Booster Days" celebration had just taken place, a festival that attracted thousands of people and, yes, gave a boost to Andrews's many businesses.

Soon, though, life changed in Andrews. "Only in Andrews" gradually became "even in Andrews." County, state, and national events affected Andrews more and more. First came "The War to End All Wars" and the epidemic of "Spanish Influenza." National Prohibition was in force—but that didn't keep alcohol from entering town life. The Ku Klux Klan had a local chapter here in the 1920s. After suffering through the Great Depression, Andrews sent many men off to World War II, and then again to the Korean "conflict." All too soon, Vietnam also called many men, and some women, into military service. Even in Andrews, we were not immune to national problems.

But Andrews also still had its own life. Businesses came and went, and as the years went on, mostly they left. Several factories came and went, sometimes staying long enough to make a real impact on the town. The schools kept operating, turning out people who achieved beyond what could be expected of a typical small school. Clubs and lodges continued, and churches flourished. And there was still time for youngsters to make precious childhood memories, of wading and fishing in the creek, playing under the street lights, helping with chores, gardening with grandparents, and enjoying the freedom of small-town life.

Yet several of the factories closed. The high school consolidated with all the other public schools in the county, and the local school became an elementary school only. Andrews was not the same after these changes, so let's look at the town during those special years when life was good, even through the bad times, in Andrews, Indiana.

Chapter One
1916-1919

NATIONAL

Andrews in 1916 was not totally isolated. It was only eight miles to the outskirts of Huntington and about 32 miles to Fort Wayne. A few automobiles drove the streets of town and the roads of the county, although buggies and wagons were still the most common forms of transportation. There was a train depot in Andrews, and people rode the Wabash Railroad to work in Huntington, or Wabash, every day. Another option was the "trolley," or interurban. That was not quite so convenient to reach, because it was located just north of the Wabash River, but it did get a lot of local usage and could take one to Fort Wayne or Logansport, or points in between, as needed. Yet another option was the "Dumbauld Transit Company," which picked people up at Shinkel's Shoe Store five times a day, and dropped them off there five times a day. This provided transportation to downtown Huntington and, with a transfer, to College Park, still not really part of Huntington. The Wasmuth-Endicott Company attracted vendors and suppliers, job applicants and salesmen, and soon there were other factories, so the transportation business was booming, even before considering more personal modes of transportation.

As 1917 arrived, America was beginning to realize the nation would, like it or not, be going to war. The war against

Germany was officially declared on April 6, 1917, but Andrews men had already enlisted and were in various stages of training. The draft, set up on May 18, 1917, initially called men aged 21 to 30 and later expanded to include those 18 to 45. (Few of the youngest and oldest men were actually drafted for the military, but they had other duties). By November 10 of 1917, 1,120 men from Huntington County had been drafted, and the number continued to increase. In one draft call of 160 men, it appears that only four had Andrews addresses. It is hard to determine who volunteered, who was drafted, and who actually served from Andrews, but we know there were many men who went overseas.

Men who avoided military service were not home free, however. They were assigned extra work in the farm fields. Andrews alone was responsible for providing 68 men for 331 days of labor in the farms of Dallas and Polk townships, during the summer months of 1918. This work was organized by the Farm Labor Reserve Board, a department in the fairly new Department of Labor. Apparently the men did their duty, helped harvest the crops, and kept our soldiers fed.

While the men were away, or working jobs they were not accustomed to working, the women were at home doing much as they had done during the Civil War. They ran their homes, farms, and businesses as needed, and took over jobs in the churches of the town. They rolled bandages, knit sweaters and socks for the "boys" overseas, and sewed hospital garments. They also raised gardens, and learned to cope with government-requested "meatless," "fatless," and "wheatless" days each week. Soon the American Red Cross began encouraging the women to take "home nursing" courses, and women responded. It was a good thing that they accepted this challenge, for soon every available nurse was needed, not for service on the war front, but here at home. Women didn't have the right to vote yet, and they were still wearing long skirts, but they were vital to the community, and the war.

Everyone contributed to the war effort in one way or another. There were countless campaigns to buy war bonds or assist financially in other ways, no matter the income level of the home. Each home was actually assessed a certain amount to "contribute." If a family wished, for whatever reason, not to contribute, they had to turn in a "yellow card" as an appeal, and it would be reviewed and either accepted or declined. In the "War Chest" campaign that was concluding in June 1918, only four "yellow cards" were received from Andrews residents. The employees at Wasmuth-Endicott (and undoubtedly others) purchased war stamps, which were a smaller investment than a savings bond but still contributed to the war effort. Even schoolchildren contributed, by "adopting" a French war orphan and providing for his or her needs. Andrews supported the war effort in every way possible, and was changed because of the war.

The town was fortunate in counting casualties of the war. Although there were certainly men who were injured and others who caught the influenza known as the "Spanish flu," only one man from Andrews was killed, and that was an accident and not a battle death. Louis Haller was 35 years old and had lived in the West for the six years preceding his entry into the service. He was killed at Camp Meade, Maryland, when he tried to jump from one train to another and slipped. He was the son of Mrs. Thad Hart of Andrews. It touched the hearts of Andrews when people learned he had married just one day before entering the service on July 2, 1918.

The international epidemic of influenza, sometimes called the "Spanish flu," also affected Andrews, although later in the pandemic than many other towns. This timing was fortunate, because as the disease continued, the virus mutated and became less virulent. Still, people died, and people suffered. The life of all of Andrews was affected, because public meetings were forbidden for a time. The theater, the churches (not sure this was enforced here), stores, and workplaces were officially closed, and even family gatherings were discouraged. The funeral of one of our Andrews pioneers, Joseph Baker, was private "owing to the ban on gatherings due to influenza." It is hard for us to imagine the hardship that just complying with the state and county health department requirements meant for Andrews. The streets would have been very quiet, the merchants would have worried about their businesses, schoolteachers would have been fretting about the time the students were missing. Schools were intermittently (I think) closed from October 1918 through March 1919, although it's hard to keep track of the days missed because so many authorities (state, county, local) closed the schools at different times.

Andrews was hit the hardest during the month of March 1919, when at one time 200 of the 1,071 (1920 census figures) inhabitants were ill. When you add the ones who had been ill earlier and the ones who became ill later, it seems that at least 20 percent of the town suffered from flu, which in about 10 percent of cases led to pneumonia. Doctors and nurses responded, but the caseload was almost too much for them. At one point, there was a discussion about setting up a hospital for flu cases, as Huntington had done, but that idea was not carried out. I located three obituaries of Andrews people who died of influenza or pneumonia during the period of October 1918 to March 1919, and there may well have been more. In addition, there were several obituaries of nephews or other relatives of Andrews residents who had died of influenza, sometimes in Army camps, sometimes elsewhere. Many families, therefore, grieved.

By 1919 the war was over and the men were home, although some had a difficult time getting here. Wilbur Beeks was one of those men. He had volunteered, or had been volunteered, to join a group that became famous as the "Michigan Polar Bears." This unit went to Russia to open a small "second front" but ended up fighting Russians, not Germans. When the war ended, that group was not brought home immediately. It took a congressional investigation to get the soldiers deployed home and discharged, and Beeks finally got home in the summer of 1919. Other men had stories to tell of their service in France, Germany, or other parts of the world. It must have been interesting to hear firsthand accounts of what the soldiers had seen and done.

TOWN GOVERNMENT AND INFRASTRUCTURE

Life in town continued, and elections were held. I found little about town council members or decisions during this time period, but there was discussion about the town's infrastructure, including telephone service and production of electricity. The Lagro-Andrews telephone company was granted a rate hike in October 1918; it could charge as much as $1.35 a month for a party line or $1.80 for a private line, with a 15 percent discount for paying on time. The Huntington Light and Power Company came to Andrews to demonstrate the "Hoover Suction Cleaner." There would be a drawing for a $7.00 universal iron and an $8.00 electric table stove at the Saturday night demonstration. They were hoping to take over the Andrews electric utility, but those hopes were misplaced.

FACTORIES

A huge center of influence in Andrews was the Wasmuth-Endicott Cabinet Company, already famous for their Kitchen Maid cabinets. By 1916 the factory was running on a regular basis; in fact, the company was doing quite well. In 1916 they were producing 20,000 Kitchen Maid cabinets a year, and the factory employed about 100 men (no mention of women). In 1918, despite wartime restrictions, the company was able to state that they were national in scope, thanks to the success of their advertising in trade magazines. They also advertised in national women's magazines and, on the whole, seem to have had a very good public relations department, which could have been just one person. The company added on to their original building in 1918 and again in 1919. The 1919 addition was about 6,000 square feet and enabled the workforce to be increased.

As the war continued, the company had to find replacement employees for the men who were now in the service of their country. One of these new employees was Miss Ila Hefner. She was operating a buzz saw in the factory and somehow got her hand caught. Unfortunately, she suffered the loss of three fingers and her thumb on her left hand. I found this interesting because a woman was being permitted to work with the machines (in December 1918), because it shows that guards and other safety precautions were not yet required, and because, as nearly as I can determine, she was not quite 15 when this accident took place. Her father and her brother were also working for the company in 1920. Perhaps they thought they could keep an eye on her there, and she was contributing both to the war effort and to the family income. It's a reminder that school was not available to everyone.

Andrews was a bustling town in the late years of the decade. The Gets factory, which at first made spark plugs, was started and soon grew to be national in scope. O. K. Gleason, who had published the Andrews newspaper *The Signal* for 19 years, sold the newspaper to the *Lagro Reviewer*, retired from newspaper work, and gave his full-time attention to his position as secretary of the Gets factory.

OTHER BUSINESSES

The Wasmuth Elevator was sold to the Farmer's Equity Exchange, and the transaction included control of a warehouse "on the north side of the tracks" that gave the equity a large storage facility. Howard Dunn repaired jewelry at "Lee Thompson's old stand." The Kilty Brothers, who had established a furniture and undertaking business in Andrews, sold their business, leaving only Park & Son as furniture dealers in the town, and no undertaker for the time being. There were several grocery stores, restaurants or lunch counters, and other businesses, but we don't have a complete list of them. Events at the opera house were still mentioned, but it's not known whether these were special events, or how often the opera house was being used. Movies may have been shown there.

A reminder that these were different times is the news that Sam Pressler purchased the Sprowl blacksmith property and also the Wohlford blacksmith property. He planned to wreck the Wohlford building and replace it with a cement-block building. He is listed as a blacksmith in the 1920 federal census.

The Andrews Hotel was apparently in and out of business during much of the decade, but we know that there was at least something going on there in 1918, when "Mary A. Rose," "noted healer," was to appear at the hotel.

Following the complete story of "Mary A. Rose" is outside the scope of this book, but she has quite a story. Although there were many claims in the advertising, mentioning all the people she had "healed" without medicines or surgery, she of course was a fake, apparently controlled by her husband. Both Mr. and Mrs. John Braun (these seem to be their legal names) were several times convicted of fraud, practicing medicine without a license, and other crimes. The people of Andrews didn't know this, however. (Neither did the people of Huntington, where "Mary A. Rose" appeared several times.)

Andrews had a "Booster Days" celebration in October 1917, with such attractions as "Madame Pontefex and Midget, the diving pony"; Professor Thompson, the handcuff king and ventriloquist; and the Minstrel Maids. The merchants even gave a car away at the close of the two-day celebration. It is likely that war rationing prevented having a similar 1918 event, and I've not found a newspaper mention of "Booster Days" in 1919, either.

SCHOOL

Despite the war and despite the influenza epidemic, school must go on. At the school, which was still almost new and was located in the current city park, 9 students graduated high school in 1917, 6 in 1918, and 10 in 1919. For the 1919-20 school year, 89 students were enrolled in the high school, The high school offered some sports, and there were class plays, "operettas," and the beginnings of a yearbook. The school was one of the important town centers, as parents united in making sure their children had the best possible education.

CHURCHES

The churches were the Methodist Episcopal Church, the Christian Church, and the Church of the Brethren. There is frequent mention in the Huntington newspapers of election of officers, social events, and special meetings or activities. For instance, the young men of the Methodist Episcopal Church agreed to put out the *Andrews Signal*, the town newspaper, during the absence of the editor in 1917. R. O. Bixby, D. R. Alpaugh, D. C. Kilby, F. L. Gurtner, Earl Hughs, and Harry R. Wasmuth were the young men in charge. There was a Boy Scout troop, which may have been associated with the M. E. Church. The Christian Church had a revival, with 50 persons joining the church during the three-week-long revival. All of the churches had ladies' groups that sponsored "markets," selling crafts and food to raise money for church and mission projects.

LODGES AND CLUBS

The main lodges were still the International Order of Odd Fellows and the Masonic Lodge, each with its own auxiliary, as well as the Knights of Pythias. There were frequent news stories about the installation of officers and the social gatherings of the lodges, but nothing about the work they may have done in the community.

Men home from the war soon formed an American Legion post, somewhat in emulation of the Grand Army of the Republic post that the Civil War veterans had formed. Those Civil War veterans had done much for the town of Andrews and had enjoyed rich relationships with each other, and the World War I veterans probably expected some of the same things. In fact, they met in the original GAR room and formed the Haller Post number 163, named after the only Andrews soldier who had died in the service of his country. The original members of the organization were Howard Dunn, Paul Haller, Mr. Wiley, Earl Stephan, Vernice Stephan, William Ross, Bert Ross, Wilbur Beeks, Chester Beeks, Edgar Keefer, Roy G. Declan, Homer Ellison, Henry Kingsley, John Hefner, Joseph Schmalzried, Earl Brenaman, Eugene Wire, and Delmar Chubb. The men had fund-raisers such as an oyster dinner, and formed a band. They were active in town for a few years, but they seem to have been absorbed into the Huntington post sometime after 1926.

Even after the war ended, women continued their contributions to the town. A women's group was formed in 1918, called the Franchise League, which was one of several in the county. It operated for just a short time, because the purpose was to get women the right to vote. Two short years later, the women of Andrews, and of the nation, were voting, many for the first time. The Women's Christian Temperance Union continued to meet and continued to work to keep Indiana, and Huntington County, dry.

The Library Club, also a women's group, contributed greatly to town life during this time. They operated a library and had many fund-raisers to buy books and make improvements to the room that was used. Although I found no record to support this, the library likely was closed during the flu epidemic of 1918-19, as was required by the state or county health department. The location of the books changed from time to time, and we don't have enough information to track all of those locations. We do know that in 1919 the library was forced to find a new location quickly, The article I found was a little ambiguous but stated that the town library and a garage had been condemned by the deputy state fire marshal, and that the wiring in the hotel had to be repaired within 30 days or the hotel would be forced to shut down. I'm not sure whether the library was operating out of the hotel, or whether they had a separate location. However, the article in the October

21, 1919, *Huntington Press* said, "It is understood that the town authorities will remove the books in the library as quickly as possible to a new location in compliance with the report of the inspector." I would just guess that it was the ladies who did the "removing," since they probably had a catalog system of some sort and the books would have needed to be packed and unpacked in a certain order.

CRIMES

Andrews always had its own share of "interesting characters" and, of course, crimes both major and minor. James Murray, who ran a "soft drink place" in Andrews, was raided by the county sheriff, a deputy, and a member of the Huntington police force. They were looking for a blind tiger (drinking establishment, illegal under state law of the time), and as they raided the beverage shop, the smell of whiskey was obvious, but no evidence was found. Five men were arrested on a charge of gaming, however, and at least one, James Murray, pled guilty to the charge and paid a fine of $15.05. The other men, C. H. Lyons, J. L. Steele, V. R. Kelsey, and Elmer Burtnet, perhaps had a bit of explaining to do when they got home. It would be interesting to know the whole story surrounding this!

Then there is the case of Donald VanDolson, or Mahoney. His crime was a bit more serious and is one of those that likely made his mother want to say "What were you thinking?" Donald had lived in Andrews with his grandparents, James and Sarah Mahoney, since at least 1900, when he was 11 years old. When he was a bit older, he must have developed an "eye for the girls," as the phrase goes. Like many young men, he was attracted to an older woman, Mary Hubric, who was variously listed at age 32 or 44 when they married. Donald left, but we don't know the circumstances that led to the separation. Next he married, without the benefit of divorce, Gladys Zoll of Hammond, Indiana. Her age is given as 17, but it's not clear whether that was her age when she married him or when she divorced him in 1916. Finally, there was the wife in Andrews, Oca Poling. He was found and arrested at the home of her parents, two weeks after a grand jury indictment charged him with bigamy. There was a trial, he was found guilty, and the sentence was expected to be two to four years. However, I've not found a newspaper article that reported the sentence. I did locate a record of a marriage license for Donald Van Dolsen in 1922 in Huntington. He reported that he had had two previous marriages (not correct), when he married Edna Schneider, who had three previous marriages. I hope they lived happily ever after.

Finally, there is the sad case of Firmer Shearer, who was found guilty of killing his father-in-law, Newton Stevens, in 1915. He was apparently not a fan of prisons. Shearer was a trusty at the Michigan State Prison when he escaped in January 1919. He was eventually found in May, on a farm near London, Ontario, Canada, and returned to the state prison, facing additional charges. His chances of an early release were gone, unless he did something to help himself. That he did. He escaped again, this time in September 1919. I've been unable to trace his steps after that, but reportedly he went to Kansas, where he changed his name, married, had children, and took some of his family to Colorado. He was eventually captured in Oregon, where he had come to the attention of authorities for selling liquor to Indians on their reservation. Sent back to Michigan City, he later ended his life by taking some kind of poison. There was more than one way to escape Michigan City.

PASSINGS

From time to time Andrews had to say goodbye to people to whom they owed much. Some were pioneers of the town and others had shorter histories, but they contributed to the town's growth and prosperity. John Kahl, a veteran of the Civil War, was hit by a train at the Main Street crossing and died November 10, 1917. He had been active in town politics, commander of the Andrews GAR post for many years, and a member of the Methodist church and the Masonic lodge.

Mrs. Almira Clingel, who had lived in Andrews since 1860 (actually, the town was named Antioch for 22 years), died at age 93.

Joseph Baker had lived in Andrews for just about 80 years when he died at 84 in 1918. All of these people had seen much and done much for the town, and I would love to have heard their stories.

Andrews at the end of 1919 was thriving, and the Roaring Twenties were right around the corner. The new decade would bring new challenges and opportunities, but at the end of the decade that had seen the Great War and the influenza epidemic, Andrews was looking forward to whatever would come next.

Chapter Two
1920-1929

NATIONAL

On the whole, the 1920s seem to have been good years for Andrews, just as they were for the rest of Indiana and the rest of America. Not only was the Wasmuth-Endicott Company booming, but the Gets Manufacturing Company, with a different set of leaders and an entirely different market, also was expanding. Businesses changed hands in Andrews, but it was a rare event for a business to totally close its doors. Until the last few years of the decade, the school system was stable, and families could live their lives with only the normal (pre-antibiotic) fears of disease, accident, or job loss.

There was still work to be done in Andrews that was international in scope. Much of Europe was still in ruins from the Great War, and Herbert Hoover was leading the efforts to feed those who needed help. Andrews had its own "Hoover dinner" in 1921, raising several hundred dollars for the cause. Fund-raisers to help Europe recover, to support the veterans, and for the Red Cross were part of life in the 1920s, even in Andrews.

As another follow-up to the war, the Huntington post of the American Legion received bronze markers to erect at the graves of World War I veterans on Decoration Day in 1923. One grave was located in Riverside Cemetery, that of

Ralph Cassady. He had died in action in France on October 27, 1918, just a few days before the Armistice, but his body wasn't returned until 1921. Ralph was born in Andrews but had moved to Wabash as a young boy.

Nationally, the main memories of the 1920s include political corruption, Prohibition, financial excesses, and the Ku Klux Klan. Even in Andrews, we dealt with Prohibition and the KKK, at least. Prohibition still resulted in blind tigers, and the marshal spent at least some of his time looking for them, but possibly he turned a blind eye, at least some of the time.

Andrews definitely did jump on the KKK bandwagon, however. From at least 1923 to 1927, there was a Klan active in or around Andrews, and some say that it was still active until sometime in the 1940s, although activities were quieter after the initial few years. The first newspaper mention is on June 3, 1923, when "several" Andrews residents attended a Ku Klux Klan parade at North Manchester. Another mention is in September of that year, when the *Huntington Press* printed a small article stating that the attendance at the free moving-picture show on the streets of Andrews was conspicuous by the absence of the middle-aged, who were well represented at the KKK parade and speech at Lagro. An elderly resident of Lagro said that he had never seen such a crowd in Lagro as was present that night.

Soon enough, it was our town's time in the KKK spotlight. The town council gave permission for the members of the Ku Klux Klan to have access to the streets of Andrews for the parade to precede a meeting that would include initiation of Klan members and "to enjoy the privilege of hearing a national speaker of the organization." On October 16, 1923, a Tuesday, the Klan led a meeting and parade through the town of Andrews. It included 500 "masked" Klansmen and a crowd of about 3,000 others.

The Andrews population couldn't account for 3,000 onlookers, so surely many of the number were family members of those marching, the curious from other communities, and perhaps some who were planning similar events elsewhere. The rally was held "on the lawn diagonally across the street from the vacated post office building," which would have been somewhere on South Main Street, perhaps where the library is now.

The *Huntington Press* of October 18, 1923, indicated that for many, this was the first time they had heard a Klansman speak (this is before nationwide radio) and that it was a very well-behaved crowd. Later in the year, "consecration services" were held at seven towns in Huntington County, including Andrews. The last mention that I found that probably includes Andrews was a notice on July 15, 1926, of a Klan meeting to be held at Gunther Park. Each Klan was to be responsible for organizing its part of the parade and furnishing its own regalia.

One story indicates how many men may have joined, for at least a short time, the local Klan. A middle-aged citizen passed away rather suddenly, and the widow noticed at the funeral and burial that very few of her late husband's friends attended either service. Normally, there would have been church, lodge, and business men there, because that's the way Andrews did things. It was only later that she realized that all those white-robed men who stayed at the rear of the cemetery included the missing friends. They had stayed back apparently out of respect for her strong feelings against the KKK. The friends were there, but not in a way that was a comfort to the widow.

The KKK was not seen at the time as only an anti-black organization, although that was surely a large part of it. Many men joined because it appealed to what we still call "old fashioned values": that men should support their families financially, should love and not abuse them, and should attend church and generally support "Christian" behavior. I was told of one person who admitted to a grandson's wife that he had gone on "missions" for the KKK. A description that she remembered was that several Klansmen, including the gentleman speaking, had gone to a farm in southern Indiana, where they burned a barn belonging to a man who had been repeatedly warned to stop beating his wife. Almost 100 years later, we are aghast that such things would happen, but if we think for a few minutes, there are probably analogies to some of today's news stories.

Another movement that was national in scope and local in influence was the Chautauqua. The original Chautauqua Assembly was at a fixed location. An event held every summer in New York state, it started out as a "summer Sunday school" for the family. "Daughter" Chautauquas arose in various areas, again each at a fixed time and location. In 1904, the idea was conceived that a cultural, entertainment, and religious event could be taken across the country, and the tent Chautauqua event was born. It grew throughout the first decades of the 20th century until the Great Depression took hold.

In Andrews, the first Chautauqua spanned three days in 1923. It was held in a large tent at the school grounds (the current town park location). We're not given a program, but we know that it was free to the public, that there were two sessions a day for three days, and that Francis M. Leaman gave a lecture the last evening. One of his publicized topics was the stories of O. Henry, but we don't know if that was his topic on this evening. This was part of the Radcliffe Chautauqua, which had an extensive list of both musicians and lecturers in 1922. The Radcliffe group was set up well, with lecturers and musicians, advance workers, persons responsible for putting the tents up and taking them down, and a national office in Washington, DC. It sounds like the townspeople came up with the money and the Chautauqua did most of the rest of the work. The Wasmuth-Endicott Company, along with many other town businesses, contributed the funds for this first event, and many businesses closed so their employees could attend. We don't know whether the cabinet company closed for the afternoons, but it's possible. Attendance on the last evening was reported at over 1,000.

The 1924 Chautauqua program was even more of a success. The program ran from Saturday to Tuesday, with local talent; a hastily acquired speaker presented the Sunday evening program. There was a parade on Saturday, with Mutt and Jeff (Richard Bixby and Jack Endicott) winning first prize for best costume, and the Saturday evening program included Swiss musicians, who sang and yodeled, along with the first of three lectures on human progress that were inspirational, if not necessarily religious. Other featured acts included an accordionist, a crayon artist, and a three-act play.

The Andrews board of directors for this event included Carl Endicott, Edgar Keefer, Ford Goodale, R. O. Bixby, Bruce Glaze, Rev. C. C. Wilson, Rev. C. C. Wischmier, Rev. L. Goodmiller, Rev. T. Eisen, and Charles Hegel. Most of those men are also mentioned elsewhere in this book, as they were "movers and shakers" in Andrews.

Chautauquas were held each summer until at least 1931, and possibly longer. Some of the older residents of Andrews remember attending as young children, but the last mention I found in the newspaper was 1931. The town looked into employing a different company for a "Lyceum" in 1932, but there's no further mention of that. For however long it lasted, Chautauqua was looked forward to and enjoyed by residents of the town and those who lived nearby. One just couldn't get entertainment like that anywhere else, and "free" is always a good word.

TOWN GOVERNMENT AND INFRASTRUCTURE

Through all of this, various aspects of government were working to keep the town running. D. R. Alpaugh, a lifelong resident of Andrews, was appointed postmaster, and when he died suddenly, S. E. Ellison was appointed in his place. A new post office was built, the first to be located north of Jefferson Street. This was the north part of the current Sports Bar and was a separate building at the time. Pauline Wilson told me that it was one of her happy chores as a child to roller-skate up the street to get the mail each day, and this was the building she referred to as the post office. The location was chosen partly to be convenient to the two factories in town, although it was still necessary to cross the railroad tracks to get from either factory to the post office. In 1923 there were three rural routes, and the mail carriers were Glynn Rudig, C. E. Knee, and Edgar R. Keefer.

The town installed a new water well in 1923, with extensions to the north and east ends of town now made possible. One wonders if this was the advent of running water for these parts of town. The small notice I found about it is confusing, but I think that's what it says.

People must have been content with the town government in 1923. There were three positions up for election, with no opposition, and all candidates were elected with a total of 30 votes each. Elected were O. K. Gleason, from the third ward; R. O. Bixby, treasurer; and C. E. Hefner, clerk. Four years later, the Democrats put up a slate nominating Pearl James for town clerk and Benjamin Prillman for treasurer. Bruce Glaze ran for the town board from precinct one and John W. Grace ran from precinct three. Committeemen were William F. Wise, William Priddy, and A. E. Mattern. However, Republicans took a clean sweep that year, with about 157 votes being cast, in total. R. O. Bixby was elected treasurer, Lawrence Cross trustee (town council member), and E. H. Roberts town clerk. The two holdover town board members were Charles Long and Roy Krontz, also Republican.

The fire department was active. Although there is infrequent mention of fires, and no real coverage of local fires, the town remembered the fires earlier in the century and ordered a new fire truck, which was to be delivered about December 15, 1924. It was a "combination chemical and hose cart fire truck," built by a firm in Logansport, Indiana. In 1928 a change was put in place that would affect the townspeople for years to come. The old fire bell was retired, and a whistle system was installed instead. Signals would still be needed, to indicate which ward of town the fire was in, but the sound of the whistle would carry farther than the bell's tolling did. The whistle would be tested twice a day, at 6:00 a.m and 6:00 p.m. I've been told often, "When that whistle went off, I'd better be home for supper!" Firemen at the time the whistle was installed were Vanis Willets, Robert Notter, Verne Clark, Charles Clark, Merle Denny, Archie Knee, Elmer Finkle, and Lawrence Merriman.

The Wabash Railroad, which was heavily used by Andrews citizens, stopped offering express and passenger service at Andrews for a short time in 1925. Express service was returned in about three weeks. I didn't find a specific date that passenger service was resumed, but subsequent events would show that it, too, was resumed. Since there was talk in the newspapers of appealing to the ICC, the Wabash may have backed down. The Wabash Railroad in 1925 was under severe financial strain, and cutting service to small communities may have seemed to them to be one way to improve their situation.

FACTORIES

The Wasmuth-Endicott Company, already known to everyone in town as "Kitchen-Maid," continued to grow throughout the 1920s. A look at the 1920 and 1930 US Census shows that many of the men and some of the women and girls who lived in Andrews worked at the "cabinet factory" in one position or another. This is not to say that only Andrews people worked there, but it must have been the first company that many Andrews residents applied at, when a job was needed.

In 1920 the job applications might have been a little more sparse than usual, for there was a typhoid outbreak in the county and it hit the cabinet company particularly hard. Two of its employees, Myrtle Dolby and Clifford Fisher, one 18 and one 20 years of age, died on March 8, 1920, each after having been ill about four weeks. The company had all of its employees vaccinated after these sad events. We know that others of the employees were also ill, because two of them, Albert Ross and Clarence Karst, asked for compensation through the Indiana Industrial Board, claiming that their illnesses had been caused by infected water at the plant. I haven't been able to locate a decision, but my guess would be that was a hard charge to prove.

Other than that, and the occasional industrial accident, the cabinet company was a good place to work. The company supported local sports teams for several years, made contributions when the businesses were having booster days or when Chautauqua assemblies occurred, and brought businessmen and vendors to town who would not otherwise have been here.

During the 1920s, reports of the company's growth were frequent in the newspapers. In 1920 the office was moved into new quarters, apparently above the factory. Fifteen telephones were installed, operated by "their own switchboard." Two new employees joined the office force at this time, Mrs. V. T. Fox and Miss Paula Stoeppelwerth, and it was expected that more office employees would be added.

One notable event, also involving the Ladies Library Club, was a banquet held at the factory. Ten cabinet company salesmen were honored guests, and the Rotary Club and the Kiwanis Club of Huntington also attended, so that in all there were 150 guests. The Library Club prepared and served the meal, although we are not told exactly where the banquet was held.

The Wasmuth-Endicott Company hired a national firm for its public-relations and advertising campaigns. The advertising was so good that several samples were included in an exhibit of international advertising held in London, England. The publicity, the quality of the cabinets, and good leadership and salesmanship all worked together so that at the end of 1922, the company said their sales had increased 50 percent over 1921 sales and were 10 times greater than when the Wasmuths took over the company several years earlier. The location of the semiannual sales meetings changed to Huntington in 1924, where the banquets were held at the Country Club or the Hotel LaFontaine.

The cabinet company added a new boiler room and a new tool room by 1926. They had introduced a new product in 1922 and now had about 100 dealers all over the country, who were showing the new Kitchen Maid line. It was no longer a single, stand-alone unit, but was now a wall unit, incorporating cabinets, a sink, and a broom closet. This was a first step toward our modern kitchen, with cabinets on two, three, or even four kitchen walls.

And still the plant grew. At the end of 1926, a two-story addition was under construction, 50 by 60 feet in size. The company also bought three lots between the factory and

Main Street; there were no immediate plans to use them, but they were available if needed. Production was expanded into locations other than Andrews, also. The company bought a plant located in Waterloo, Ontario, Canada, and had dealers all over that dominion, and in 1927 they purchased the Goodrich Cabinet Plant in Peru, Indiana, making Wasmuth-Endicott the largest kitchen cabinet company in the country at the time.

Still, with growth one can expect problems. One was that other companies "copied" the company's designs or used similar designs for their kitchen cabinets. Wasmuth-Endicott sued one such company in Richmond, Indiana, but lost that suit. And in 1929, Donald W. Thornsburgh, the sales manager for the company, was called to testify in a criminal case in Chicago. The case involved the painters' union there, and Thornsburgh's testimony revealed that the company had been forced to pay a "tribute" of $2 per cabinet for all cabinets shipped to Chicago. (Many Kitchen-Maid cabinets were designed for and installed in apartment buildings, and the market was quite large in Chicago.) The union was charged with conspiracy to violate the Sherman antitrust act. The defense moved to have the charges dismissed, and that motion was quashed, but apparently the jury could not agree on a verdict. I don't know whether the "tribute" stopped or not, but even in Andrews, big-city issues became small-town issues.

Wasmuth-Endicott was not the only factory in town. While Kitchen Maid concentrated on cabinets for homes and apartments, another company, Gets Manufacturing, was involved with the brand new automobile industry. Bruce Glaze, C. E. Endicott, and W. O. Taylor, who each loaned the initial letter of his surname to form the name of the company, began the company in 1919 with an idea for a new kind of automobile spark plug, developed by Glaze. It was a small company at first, but it gradually grew because of the innovations the company made during the first years after its founding. By 1923, it had become so well-known that it received an inquiry from a Swedish firm asking to become the company's foreign representative. That same year the first real factory building was constructed for and by the firm. It was located on the east side of Main Street, just north of the railroad tracks, on the site of the Philo Willets mill that had the fatal boiler explosion in 1907.

The building was constructed of all steel and featured 1,505 panes of glass, each 13 by 19 inches. It covered 6,000 square feet of floor space. Bruce Glaze seems to have been the one who envisioned the building, which utilized as much natural light as possible. He also invented the spark plug that the company manufactured and the machines that did the work. The Gets company continued to grow, and by the end of 1926 it was planned to add two additions to the plant, each 2,800 square feet. In 1919 the company produced 32,000 plugs. In 1926 they produced 600,000 spark plugs and were expecting to double that number in 1927. George N. Barcus of Andrews filed another patent for a spark plug in 1927, and the records show that even as late as 2003 other patent applicants were using his design in reference to their improvements. By 1927, Bruce Glaze was the president of the company, George N. Barcus was vice president, O. K. Gleason was vice president, and W. O. Taylor was treasurer. The company was set for great things.

OTHER BUSINESSES

Andrews was a bustling town in the 1920s. There were several grocery stores, and there were places to eat, a bank, an equity exchange, feed dealers, a building and loan association and later a realty company, a lumberyard . . . Even the hotel reopened and was immediately filled to capacity. The following businesses were listed in the 1926 Polk County Directory, all under the town of Andrews.

- Post Office, David Alpaugh, Postmaster
- Fire station, John Abernathy, Chief
- American Railway Express John J. Doren, Agent
- *Andrews Capital*, William Walker, Publisher
- Andrews Equity Exchange, J. E. Elward, Manager
- Andrews Feed Mill, Brice L. Bailey, Proprietor
- Andrews Garage, Earl Props, Ralph Notter
- Andrews Library, Mrs. Olive Glaze, Librarian
- Anna Baker, Dressmaker
- David Bolinger, Real Estate
- Brown's Cement Works, Frank C. Brown, Manager
- Albert Chenoweth, Physician
- Cloverleaf Creameries, Inc., Simon S. Beauchamp, Manager
- Roy J. Coss, Dentist
- Frank E. Fults, Grocer
- Emery C. Garretson, Agent, Standard Oil Company
- Gets Manufacturing Company, Bruce Glaze, President; George Barcus, vice president; O. K. Gleason, secretary; W. O. Taylor, treasurer; spark plug manufacturer
- Ford N. Goodale, Drug store
- John J. Gretzinger, Dry goods
- John E. Hemmick, Barber
- Indiana Service Corporation, Ora A. Ross, Agent
- Isenbarger & Smith, Barbers, John R. Isenbarger and Carl C. Smith
- Charles L. Jacobs, Monuments
- Charles H. Keefer, Garage
- Benjamin J. King, Grocer
- Knight Brothers (Ben F. and Roy J.), Broom Manufacturers

- Lagro and Andrews Telephone Company, W. O. Taylor
- George G. Leverton, Barber
- James P. Murray, Soft drinks and restaurant
- George V. Nichols, Hardware Store
- Lewis W. Pratt, Veterinary Surgeon
- James S. Pressler, Blacksmith
- Carl E. Richards, Grocer
- Alvin Schenkel, Stock Keeper
- William Shinkel, Shoes and Harness Maker
- Edw. E. Shoup, Furniture and Undertaker
- J. R. Small & Company, Coal
- State Bank of Andrews, E. M. Wasmuth, President; C. E. Fults, V-Pres; R. O. Bixby, Cashier
- Emanuel H. Stephan Groceries
- Lewis H. Strevey, Junk and Justice of the Peace (really!)
- Edward L. Taylor, Live Stock
- John W. Tucker, Chiropractor
- Wasmuth & Sons Builders Supplies, Harry Wasmuth, Manager
- Wasmuth-Endicott Company, E. M. Wasmuth, President; D. W. Thornburgh, Vice President; A.F. Wasmuth, Vice President; C. E. Endicott, Secretary Treasurer; Mfg Kitchen Cabinets
- S. Rollin Wintrode, Timber Buyer

This list is probably incomplete, and perhaps I've included someone whose business was actually elsewhere. Any and all errors are mine alone. However, this gives us a good idea of the businesses that the town of 1,200 supported, in addition to the four churches (Church of the Brethren, Methodist Episcopal, Christian, Holiness), the school, and the lodges.

Not long after this directory was published, the Andrews Equity Exchange went into receivership, and the land and building were advertised for sale. Samuel Gerard's grocery store was in receivership, and Roy Hanselman's grocery was also in receivership with stock and fixtures for sale. It seems that these businesses failed not because of lack of business, but because they were too generous in extending lines of credit to farmers and households.

Edgar Keefer operated the Flower Gardens, but the only notice I saw of this business was one advising their customers that they were already rebuilding their greenhouses and service building that had been destroyed by fire. (In the 1926 city directory previously referred to, Keefer is listed as a mail carrier, so his business, which continued to grow, was just getting started.) I have found no further mention of what must have been a spectacular fire, in late October 1928.

In February 1928, E. M. Wasmuth, A. F. Wasmuth, and E. V. Hughes, all of Huntington, filed to incorporate the Wasmuth Realty Company, "which will acquire and manage certain real estate in the town of Andrews." And finally, H. R. Wasmuth, E. L. Taylor, and R. O. Bixby were officers in the newly incorporated Andrews Water Company. I don't know whether this was related to town business, or whether it was set up in competition to the town, or whether the town eventually took this company over.

Mysteries abound, regarding the history of Andrews. For instance, there was no specific mention of the opera house in the directory, but it was still being used on an occasional basis, at least. Who owned it at this time? Some events that one would expect to have been held at the opera house, such as a memorial service for President Harding, were held at the Methodist church, and some that one would expect to have been held at the school were held at the opera house. We don't know what entertainment from outside the area might have still been appearing at the opera house, either. We do know this was the location for high school basketball games until 1931.

The *Andrews Signal* was sold to a gentleman from Texas, which makes one wonder whether it was still operating, or whether the *Andrews Capital* mentioned in the list above had driven the *Signal* more or less out of business. We are sadly lacking in knowledge about the newspapers of the day after 1912. The *Andrews Signal* ceased publication in 1919, although it seems to have been resurrected, sometimes with different names, several times during the coming decades. There are very few copies of any Andrews newspaper known to be in existence after 1912, although I have seen an issue of one in 1925, one in 1951, and one in 1954. It's believed each of the later publications was short-lived, but one always hopes to find more in someone's attic, someday.

SCHOOL

No account of the 1920s would be complete without the story of the schools. At the start of the decade, the Andrews school was quite small. Seven students, Udah B. Haley, Ruth M. Hefner, Marie Sharp, Ivan E. McDaniel, Earl L. Stouder, Leslie G. Streit, and William Earl Taylor, graduated from high school that year. The speaker was Dr. Wirt Lowther, who had spoken in earlier years. He had been the pastor of the Methodist Episcopal church in Logansport but had resigned to become a speaker on the Chautauqua circuit. During the off-season, he was called on to speak at many graduations and similar ceremonies, so he must have been an inspirational speaker.

There were 10 high school graduates in 1922, and by the fall of 1923 a total of 260 students attended the school, 145 in the grade school and 115 in the upper grades. At this time, there were at least three other schools operating in Dallas Township, but that was soon to change. By 1926, the graduating class had dwindled to 6, but 16 graduated the following year. This was the largest graduating class to date. School enrollment at Andrews at the end of the 1928-1929 school year was 237 for the elementary grades and 78 for the high school. Enrollment had increased. There was a reason for that, and there were repercussions. The high school had 78 enrolled and graduated 14 seniors that year.

It's hard to get an idea of all the extracurricular activities the school had, but in 1922 the 10 members of the Andrews High School girls glee club went to Noblesville, to entertain at a three-day conference of the State Young People's convention. I believe this was a part of the Prohibition movement, sponsored by the Women's Christian Temperance Union. The *Andronian*, the school yearbook, was published in 1924 under the editorial leadership of Gerald Mygrant. We have seen some other issues of the yearbook but don't know whether it had been published earlier, or how long it was published. Musical programs were presented by the music department as a whole, including the orchestra at the end of the school year and sometimes at Christmas. "Operettas" were also frequently presented. (Today, we would call these musicals.) The senior class presented a play in December 1924 at the opera house. The cast included Lucile Thurman, Dorothy Ulery, William Bellam, Herbert Abernethy, Lavana Simons, Nondas Bitzer, Clarence Wisner, Noel Keefer, Frances Fields, and Ernest Fields. (Some of these names are not listed as graduates the following spring. Some were underclassmen.)

There was a drama club in the high school during the 1926-27 school year, and it presented a play on February 23 and 24 in the opera house. The cast included J. D. Miller, Clyde Vickery, Samuel Wasmuth, Howard Wisner, Robert Warfel, Clarence Hegel, Ernest Fields, Dan Roser, Edith Priddy, Mildred Yentes, Mildred Gard, Swanora Bellam,

Mary Ulrey, Harriet Bailey, Edith Reiff, and Mabel Anson. There was a band or orchestra, or perhaps both, at the high school during most if not all of the 1920s. In 1928 there was a fund-raiser at the opera house for the school fund, and musical performances included a violin quartet by Nina Shenefield, Mary Margaret Parker, Clara Wade, and Charles Taylor and a wind quartet by Robert Bixby, Richard Bixby, Claude Garretson, and Jerome Cole. There were also various academic contests, speaking contests, and other events to keep the students challenged and learning, and there may well have been other groups that we don't know about.

For instance, we know there was a debate club in Andrews in 1927. We know that because it resulted in a lawsuit that made the newspapers. I don't know how the debate club fared, and I don't know how the lawsuit turned out, but I do know that the teacher who was charged with criminal slander still had his job the next year. (Actually, he turns out to be an interesting person, an Andrews native who helped found Kokomo Junior College a few years after this story.) The alleged incident was a trip to Wabash, Indiana, to debate that town's team. The trip was taken in a school hack (bus) with the students (unnamed), their instructor, George Beauchamp, Mrs. Minnie Zintsmeister, and three other women. Presumably the women were mothers or school boosters, accompanying the team to cheer them on. At least, that's what Beauchamp thought. Instead, when the women got to the school, they inspected the Wabash high school and did not attend the debate. Beauchamp at this time was only about 21 years old, and perhaps can be forgiven for telling the women, according to the affidavit, that "words couldn't express" the contempt he held for them and that he "considered them low-down, disgraceful specimens of humanity." My guess is that cooler heads prevailed and the "criminal slander" charge, which had been filed in Wabash city court, was dropped. Beauchamp seems to have moved on by 1930 and was teaching at Manchester College. Mrs. Zintsmeister was still in Andrews.

The school building had serious issues during this time period. It was a time of growth, change, and challenge. Progress doesn't usually come without a fight, and sure enough, Andrews had a few legal issues to contend with. The first one didn't directly involve the school, but it did affect it. In 1927 Dr. Fry, the county health officer, condemned five schools, three of them in Dallas Township. These were the Maple Grove school, the Sauerkraut school, and the Stephan school. None of the school buildings were in good condition, but each school was allowed to finish out the remaining eight weeks of the school year. In the fall, the students would be attending school in Andrews, like it or not. Some did not like it, and a lawsuit eventually went to court. Edward J. Garrison wished to continue to send his children to the Maple Grove school, saying it was in better condition than the Andrews school building, and Ari O. Garretson, as trustee for the school, was the defendant. Eventually, of course, the suit was settled and the Garrison children came to Andrews.

The specifics of the suit are pretty grim. The Andrews school was overcrowded, and while plans for a new school were being drawn up, children of at least two grades were being educated in the basement of the old Stouder Hotel in downtown Andrews. The suit charged that were was no playground provided for the children, the basement was not deep enough, the first floor was not high enough from the ground, the light didn't come down from one side into the rooms. Furthermore, there was not sufficient air capacity in the rooms, there was inadequate ventilation, the toilets were not sanitary and were obsolete, and the hotel was infected with lice and bedbugs. The lawsuit was filed before heat became an issue, but some women who remember going there said there was one stove in the middle of the room and that at every seat in the room, it was either too hot or too cold, once heating season started. The suit was eventually dismissed, and the students survived their very rough fifth- and sixth-grade years, but finding a solution for these students, as well as the ones in the school building that had outlived its usefulness, was not going to be easy.

The school was designed by January 1929. It would be a two-story building with 14 rooms, a large gymnasium, and a stage, built of brick and trimmed with stone. The projected cost was $95,000, and construction was to start as soon as contracts could be let. Even then, there was paperwork to do, and government regulations had to be obeyed. The contracts were finally let and the school was built, but details will need to wait until the next chapter in this book. The school location was greatly improved, in the eyes of many, when State Road 24 was turned into the "Old Andrews Road" and a new US 24 was built and paved, just north of the river and the traction depot and tracks.

CHURCHES

The churches of Andrews were active during the 1920s, but nothing drastic (except the saving of souls) seems to have happened. The Christian Church installed a new furnace, but that is about the extent of improvements. The stories that were reported to the newspapers were mostly of the meetings, fund-raising efforts, and dinners conducted by the various ladies' groups. The city directory used to compile the list of businesses in this chapter referred to four churches, indicating that one had been added to the list of the "Big 3." The earliest mention I find of the Pilgrim Holiness Church is in 1924, when it met in the town hall and then held tent meetings at the Hefner lot. It was a small church, but it grew at a steady pace for several years. A combined Sunday worship service of all the churches during the summer months was held in a tent, but the location isn't given. The churches also united in local charity work, although each church also supported its own causes in addition.

To give an idea of the families of Andrews and their church affiliations, I've found the following names: In August 1927, there was a birthday celebration for members of the Berean class of the Christian Church. Those celebrating birthdays were Mrs. Hazel Reiff, Mrs. Susie Hahn, Miss Tracy Kaufman, Mrs. Beulah Rudig, Mrs. Carrie Chronister, Mrs. Agnes House, Mrs. Lucille Nichols, and Mrs. Minnie Zintsmeister. Also in attendance were Mrs. India Small, Mrs. Elva Knee, Mrs. Pearl Isenbarger, Mrs. Letha Tomlinson, Mrs. Prudence Klotz, Mrs. Amy Haley, Mrs. Eva Heslet, Mrs. Winifred Notter, and Mrs. A. O. Garretson, serving as hostesses. Others present were Mrs. Maymie Ross, Mrs. Lynn Cline, Mrs. Grace Brewer, Mrs. Charlotte Brewer, Mrs. Inez Knight, Mrs. Ethel Ross, Mrs. Viola Caster, Mrs. Fanny Glaze, Mrs. Abbie Wiley, Mrs. Emma Bowles, Mrs. Sue Stouder, Mrs. Mabel Brown, Mrs. Alta Roberts, Mrs. Elizabeth Gleason, Mrs. Edith Gretsinger, Mrs. Lottie Wintrode, Kathryn Ross, Betty Gretsinger, Alda Isenbarger, Margaret Knee, Nellie House, Margaret Roberts, and Verne Bowles.

In May 1927, the ladies of the Methodist church spent the afternoon doing "fancy work" for the Easter Market, to be held March 31 and April 1. Attending this event were Mrs. George Stephan, Mrs. Samuel McKeever, Mrs. Samuel Wintrode, Mrs. Jacob Rudig, Mrs. R. O. Bixby, Mrs. Boyd Park, Mrs. Arnold Spencer, Mrs. John Schmalzreid, Mrs. Arthur Fults, Mrs. Frank Fults, Mrs. C. E. Endicott, Mrs. Alice Iry, Mrs. Edith Piety, Mrs. John Resler, Mrs. Warren

Xickery (probably should be Vickery), Mrs. Graham Thompson, Mrs. John Parrot and daughter, Mrs. Charles Hegel, Mrs. Chester Heslet, Mrs. Charles Long, Mrs. William Shinkel, Mrs. Lewis Strevey, Mrs. Laura Cummings, Mrs. Jeff Wire, Mrs. F. W. Hart, Mrs. E. E. Shoup, Mrs. Hannah Alpaugh, Mrs. Pearl Bailey, Mrs. John Blose, Mrs. B. E. Prilliman, Mrs. Elizabeth Minnich, Mrs. Joseph Alford, Mrs. Lewis Snider, Rev. and Mrs. R. C. Caylor, Miss Anna Baker, Miss Eldon, and Dessie Morris.

The Church of the Brethren held an annual meeting near Hanging Rock in 1929, and those who attended were Rev. and Mrs. Howard Dickey and sons James, John, Burton, and Galen; Mr. and Mrs. Ivan McDaniel and daughter Ellen; Mr. and Mrs. Monroe Keel and son James; Mrs. Nondas Parker and daughters Helen and Mary Margaret; Mr. and Mrs. Charles Anderson; Mr. and Mrs. Fred Byerly and daughter Wava and son Arthur; Mr. and Mrs. Howard Jeffrey and daughter Marguerite and sons Charles, Lloyd, Eldon, and Mark; Mr. and Mrs. Roy Frushour and daughter Donna; Mr. and Mrs. Jacob Milliner; Mr. and Mrs. Homer Poe; Mr. and Mrs. Frank Poe; Mrs. Catherine Shaffer and son Kenneth; Mr. and Mrs. Everett Bigelow and daughter Phyllis and son Lewis; Mr. and Mrs. Evan Bigelow and sons Edwin and Robert; Mr. and Mrs. Fred Griffith; Mr. and Mrs. Ralph Follis; Mr. and Mrs. Willard McIlrath and sons James and Junior; Mrs. Jane McDaniel and daughter Opal and son Clarence; Mrs. Haynes and daughter Ruth Ann; Mrs. Myrtle Ervin and daughter Sarah Elizabeth; Mr. and Mrs. John Slagel and sons Russell, Dean, Kenneth, and Oscar; Charles Eckman and son Junior; Joseph Slagel; John Leedy; Mrs. Etta Poe; Mildred Dinius; Melvin Dinius; Evelyn Sutton; Buff Brindle; Glen Hosler; Leonard Keel; Walter Overhiser; Lucile Osborn; Martha Plasterer; Mary Fulhart; Lucile Misner; Howard Truitt; Homer Truitt; and Garl Truitt.

36

For the Pilgrim Holiness church, which may have still been busy organizing, I wasn't able to find any kind of listing of members or attenders. However, none of these are complete lists, and some of those listed may have been visitors at the events mentioned. It does show that the churches were actively involving their members, who in sum probably made up a good portion of the town's population.

LODGES AND CLUBS

Lodges and clubs continued their importance in town. The Free and Accepted Order of Masons, the Eastern Star, the International Order of Odd Fellows, the Daughters of Rebekah, the Knights of Pythias, and the Pythian Sisters were all organizations that encompassed fraternal, recreational, and charitable aims. They were nonsectarian although religious, and nonpolitical in nature. In Andrews, there were regular meetings, banquets, and fund-raising activities. These groups undoubtedly also helped in charity work, but that is not mentioned in the newspaper articles. (As the Great Depression hit, the need for charity was perhaps not as evident when the New Deal programs took hold. Also, membership in lodges and clubs declined because fewer people could pay the membership fees. During the 1920s, however, membership was strong in Andrews.) Some years, the names of the new officers were printed in the newspaper. Most of those names are the same as in the church listings mentioned above, or at least they were members of the same families.

By far the most active club in Andrews, judging by the newspaper content I found, was the Andrews Library Club, known for a time as the Ladies' Library Club. Besides regular meetings, and staffing regular library hours, the club had numerous fund-raisers. They had a vision of obtaining a separate building in which to house their books, a place of their own that welcomed readers. It took a lot of fund-raisers such as plays, "markets" (which seem to have been like bazaars), bake sales, homecomings, and probably some events that didn't make the newspapers, to raise the money first to purchase the vacant lot just south of the hotel, and then to actually construct the building. One husband is said to have moaned during this time "Oh, no . . . Not another bake sale!"

The land was purchased in October 1923, and then the serious fund-raising began. The club formed three committees, one for fund-raising, one for the building itself, and one for grounds beautification, and it was decided that the committees would have complete charge of their duties, with no need to return to the club for approval of their decisions.

The 1924 *Andronian*, the school yearbook, acknowledged the support of the Library Club for school activities and noted that the club had provided the playground equipment for the school, so the library was not the Library Club's only focus, but it was certainly their prime focus.

By October 1926, plans for the building were in place, and the club planned a huge homecoming celebration, which involved "virtually every citizen of the town." The foundation for the library had been constructed, and part of the celebration would include the laying of the cornerstone. Congressman Albert Hall of Marion gave a speech, the community band played some numbers, and schoolchildren also presented several songs. Several hundred people attended the ceremony.

Less than a year later, on October 15, 1927, the library was officially dedicated. Again a day-long celebration occurred, and here mention is made that after the speech by C. E. McNabb, a Fort Wayne attorney, some of the program took place in the opera house. There had earlier been a parade by the schoolchildren and a band concert, and events continued throughout the day. The library was not debt-free. Of the $7,000 building cost, $4,200 had been raised. Fund-raising would continue.

In addition to the official lodges and the Library Club, there were other clubs and organizations in the Andrews during the 1920s. The Women's Christian Temperance Union had regular meetings, often in churches but sometimes in homes. There is brief mention of the Boy Scouts. In 1925 the troop had two patrols, known as the Beaver and the Eagle, and they formed a basketball team. I found only one other mention of the Boy Scouts in the papers during the 1920s, and I'd love to know more. No Girl Scout troops were mentioned during this time, but in 1924 the Camp Fire Girls organized under the leadership of Mrs. E. E. Shoup, guardian of one group, and Mrs. Carl Endicott, guardian of the other group.

One article, in the *Huntington Press* of September 22, 1922, announced the formation of an Andrews chapter of the National Delphian Society. The first members were Mrs. R. O. Bixby, Mrs. D. V. Williams, Mrs. Bruce Glaze, Mrs. H. R. Wasmuth, Mrs. A. C. Chenoweth, Mrs. A. J. Fults, Miss Treva Hefner, Miss Thelma Wisner, Miss Edna Shinkel, and Miss Marie Sharp. The purpose of this group, a chapter of a national organization, was to promote the education of women. The national society published a series of books, which apparently each local chapter was to study. Some of the women mentioned above were college-educated, but I don't think all of them had the benefit of higher education. This course was designed to give the women a background in history and literature. It's unknown how many women joined, or how long the club lasted, or how diligently the women worked at their studies.

There was also a gun club, which held shooting matches at the Thad Hart farm, where the club had a field gallery. In

1924 the club's officers were Dr. Coss, president; G. V. Nichols, treasurer; and John Abernathy and D. W. Cross, field captains. Early members were L. H. Boone, Luther Ricks, H. T. Cross, D. W. Cross, John Abernethy, Alvin Schenkel, Boyd Park, F. Akers, A. Ferris, A. Campbell, George Stephan, Paul Liggett, Ralph Kellam, Walter Gradeless, H. Park, R. Chesman, R. Notter, C. M. Long, O. Waid (Oliver Wade, perhaps?), C. A. Willets, A. R. Stouder, Earl Owens, Ed Vaught, Rol Kennedy, B. Shoemaker, G. Nichols, John Isenbarger, E. Garretson, Don Finlayson, Ed Rusher, Lewis Knight, Guy Garshwiler, Carl Smith, Frank Fults, W. A. LaRue, Arlin Bodkin, R. L. Wenter, Jake Rudig, Roy Hausman, "Dutch" Millman, "Bill" Ramer, Frank Rudig, John Chronister, Earl Stouder, Harold Stouder, "Bill" Bellam, Brice Bailey, L. P. Bailey, Lloyd Gerard, Charles Petre, Roy Krautz, Paul Wire, A. E. Wire, H. R. Wintrode, P. E. Bailey, L. M. Gerard, E. E. Shoup, Elmer Finkey, Charles Hegel, Earl Props, Bob Wintrode, Guy Scott, Byron Scott, and W. O. Priddy. The club was active in at least 1924 and 1925, but after that the trail goes cold.

A final group that deserves mention is the Andrews Band. Down through the years, ever since the Ladies Cornet band in the 1880s, there had been on-again, off-again community bands, and sometimes even an orchestra, in Andrews. The band of 1923 presented free outdoor concerts for about eight weeks during the summer. A bandstand was constructed in downtown Andrews, but I have been unable to date it or give a definite location. Perhaps this band used it. As some of the young men headed off to college, the band membership dwindled, but 23 members presented a fund-raising concert on Christmas night of that year. For the 1924 season the band included four trombones, four altos, four cornets, seven clarinets, five saxophones, three basses, one baritone, and two drums. This band was available for hire. There was mention of the reorganization of the band in 1927 and a further mention in 1928, so we know that there were at least efforts to keep the band going this long.

CRIMES

Sometimes, the town "bustled" with unwelcome visitors. Early in the morning of January 27, 1926, the Tip Top Garage, owned by Archie Knee, was burglarized. Andrews had a night watchman at this time, but he had apparently gone off duty. A number of "outer tires" and "inner tubes" and a box of "sparks" were taken. It was believed the thieves would have taken more, had they not been surprised by the lights of the bakery coming on, as the baker (unnamed in the account) began preparations for his day.

A few months later, the marshal was on duty when he encountered a highly intoxicated man. He summoned help from the sheriff and the prosecuting attorney, hoping to find where the man had acquired the wine he had in his possession. It was stated that a quantity of wine was seized and taken to Huntington for analysis. The marshal and friends visited one or two places in Andrews, and perhaps they were looking for a connection with the wine that had intoxicated the man in question. The man in question, Jesse Dilley, was arrested and taken to Huntington.

When a marshal did do his job, he was not necessarily rewarded for it. Marshal John Tidrick arrested William J. Barlier of Delphos, Ohio, on a charge of peddling without a license. Barlier claimed he was not peddling, merely taking orders for future delivery, and he sued the marshal for $10,000, which would seem to be maybe a little out of line, considering that Barlier spent an hour in the Andrews jail.

OTHER TOWN NEWS AND HAPPENINGS

During the 1920s, radio became widely available in Andrews. It was a hobby at first, with stations being listened to from New York City to San Francisco, and even Havana, Cuba. (The FCC wasn't yet regulating the frequency and strength the stations were allowed to broadcast, and early in the 1920s there was no local programming.) At parties and club meetings, sometimes the entertainment or program was announced as "Radio." When I've asked some of the older residents of our town what they did in the evenings for entertainment, I've heard "listening to the radio" and "making music" as two of the most common responses. Radio brought the news of the day, music, comedy shows, and the forerunners of "soap operas" to anyone who could afford a radio, or who had a friend who had one. This whole concept was so important that 1930 US Census asked whether or not the household had a radio, and it looks like at least half of Andrews residents did have a radio in their home. By the middle years of the decade, boys especially had crystal radio sets, and the goal was to maintain a log of all the different stations one had been able to hear. In 1924, one unnamed youth had 64 stations to his credit. Radio was a wonderful addition to Andrews, but it did have its downfalls. Why would one go out to support the community band when one could stay home and listen to music in the comfort of the living room, with no shoes required?

Andrews had bad weather from time to time, of course. Storms came and went, blizzards came and went, and life continued. But March 1925 delivered a one-two punch. First there was a "tornado," which sounds more like strong straight-line winds, which first hit just west of town and then hit the town itself. Some farm buildings and sheds were destroyed, trees were down, and a car lost its top, but no dwellings were destroyed, so the town was counting itself lucky, or blessed. Just a week later, the worst flood since 1913 pummeled Andrews. There was the usual trouble along Loon Creek, but even homes on the north end of town were affected. Basements and cellars had 18 inches of water, which meant no heat for those homes with furnaces in the basements, and some homes were completely surrounded by water for a time. Potentially serious damage was done to the interurban tracks and to state road 7 (now known as State Road 105), which was closed until it could be repaired.

Weather was not the only threat to Andrews. This was still the time before antibiotics, and before everyone understood the necessity of good hygiene. During these years, besides the typhoid centered around the Wasmuth-Endicott factory, there was a diphtheria outbreak. Consumption (tuberculosis) was still common. Scarlet fever, mumps, and measles were all part of childhood for many, with the potential for complications that had no real medical cures. Women died in or following childbirth, although not in the numbers they had in the previous century. Publicized quarantines were not as common as they had been, but quarantines still occurred.

Young people in Andrews had many opportunities for fun, for learning, and for physical activity. For instance, one young woman took up a dare and roller-skated from Huntington to Andrews, to a relative's home, got a quart of tomato juice to prove she had been to Andrews, and turned around and skated back. Ice skating was also common, although it seems to have been more of a men and boys' sport. There is a story about a 55-year-old man, Elmer Owens, figure skating on an icy rink and showing some "fancy skating," including figure 8's and circles, to "the boys" in February 1924.

Many children and youth took piano lessons, so in many years there was a recital. Mrs. Lewis Burget was a local instructor in August 1929, and the recital by her students included pieces played by Mary Margaret, Annis, and Richard Ellison; Rosemary Keefer; Lowell Jennings; Betty Gretzinger; Margaret and Matilda Meyers; Verna Bickel; Helen Parker; Pauline Campbell; Kathryn Rose; Isabelle Schenkel; and Charlotte Taylor.

Adults also had hobbies, in addition to working, running a household; belonging to churches, clubs, and organizations; and perhaps becoming part of an athletic team. Music was one hobby, as evidenced by newspaper mentions of community band members, church pianists, and music instructors. Andrews also had its share of artists. Mrs. Sue Stouder had a painting depicting the Wabash River west of Andrews on display at the Midway restaurant, and Clyde Gordon also was mentioned as having painted a good rendition of fishing on Loon Lake. Other men enjoyed "coon chases," and several were held around Andrews. One such event, on March 28, 1925, was expected to draw between 50 and 100 participants, each one likely hoping to win one of the cash prizes to be awarded by Andrews merchants. This doesn't appear to be a function of the gun club, although probably some of the hunters were also members of the club. We should not forget that hunting and fishing still played an important role as a recreational activity.

Another joy of Andrews life was movies. Starting in about 1923, the Andrews merchants provided free movies on the downtown streets, one evening a week in the summertime. Everyone, young and old, was invited to come watch the movies, bringing chairs or blankets to sit on. For a time, there were also movies during the colder months, but this was a business and not a town function. As of 1929, movies were shown every Wednesday during the summer, and there were free band concerts on Monday night. The downtown was bustling.

I wonder what "almost the main corners" of Andrews refers to. The April 17, 1924, *Huntington Press* tells us that Frank Fults, who "without doubt, according to the best information, lives in the oldest house in Andrews," was remodeling. The rear part of the building had already been razed, the main part was to be moved east and south of its present location, and a new part of frame structure would be built in front. A basement would be dug under the entire building, and the porch in front would be of brick columns and side rails. The home was on "Almost the main corners" of Andrews.

No history of Andrews in the 1920s would be complete without a tribute to Carl Endicott. He was involved in almost everything Andrews had to offer during the 1920s. He was a cashier at the bank when he first arrived in Andrews (his wife was Elizabeth Wasmuth) and then left the bank to help found the Gets Manufacturing Company. He left that company to establish the Trust and Bond Department at Citizens State Bank in Huntington, and then slowly he disengaged from the life of Andrews. For the 20-plus years Endicott lived here, he was an outstanding citizen and a member of the Methodist church. He served on the school board and the town council and appeared in plays and musicals put on by one group or another. He was an excellent musician. He was frequently asked to be a speaker at this function or that, and his sphere of influence expanded to include not just Andrews, but Huntington and beyond. He was elected state governor of Kiwanis in 1926 and later, in 1932-33, was the International President. These were illustrious honors for a man from Andrews.

PASSINGS

During the 1920s, the town continued to say goodbye to many of its early pioneers and businessmen. S. M. Minnich was one such person. He operated a grocery and dry goods store in Andrews for years and frequently wrote articles that were published in the local newspapers.

Henry Kautz died in 1925, at age 92. He had settled in Antioch (the former name of Andrews) when he returned from the Civil War in 1865, and had lived here the rest of his life. He was a member of the Christian Church and the Masonic Lodge, as well as the Grand Army of the Republic, and had served as postmaster at Andrews at the turn of the century. To the people of Andrews, his death probably felt like the end of an era.

Frank Todd also died in 1925, in California. He had been a druggist in Andrews for several years in the 1900s and operated the Todd and Butterbaugh drugstore then.

Mrs. Lessel Long, widow of one of Andrews's most famous men and thus a link to Andrews of bygone days, sold her household goods and went to live with her son. She died two years later.

Andrews also grieved for young people. Philip Wasmuth, son of Mr. and Mrs. Harry R. Wasmuth, died in the Battle Creek, Michigan, sanitarium just a week after he graduated from Andrews High School in May 1924. Young men from his graduating class were the pallbearers at his funeral.

The "roaring Twenties" ended. Automobiles were prevalent, women's skirts were shorter, and radio had become important in the life of most Andrews citizens. Both Andrews factories were doing well, but that little matter of the stock market crash in October 1929 would affect life in the 1930s, even in Andrews.

Chapter Three
1930-1939

NATIONAL

The 1930s offered some hard years for the nation, for Andrews, and for the businesses that were located here and the people who worked—or suddenly didn't work—here. It looks like at first Andrews was somewhat insulated from the events on Wall Street. A few people may have lost money in the stock market, but more specifically, the low prices farmers received for their crops at the time affected farmers and then small businesses. Construction began to lag, so Wasmuth-Endicott started losing orders and eventually laid off some employees. Banks were also under stress, and the State Bank of Andrews closed for a few days before and again during the "Banker's Holiday." President Roosevelt, as he took office, asked Congress to pass a lot of new bills, some of which were designed to help put people back to work, and some of which were charitable in nature. But until those laws began taking effect, it was up to Huntington County, and Andrews, to take care of their own people as best they could.

At first, churches and other organizations simply asked for donations, and the results were gratifying. In 1930 many families still felt like they were doing OK; they had outgrown or unwanted clothing to donate, and gardens were plentiful. But as time went by, more families crossed the line from "helping" to "needing help," and other answers were needed. The Red Cross was one organization that helped, and Andrews women assisted the Red Cross by sewing and knitting. Some of the churches had canning days, where donated poultry, fruits, and vegetables were canned and given to those in need. That project might have been more successful if the gardens and crops hadn't failed in the summer of 1932. All the churches had women who sewed, making quilts and blankets and all kinds of clothing, particularly for school-aged children who otherwise could not have attended classes. Churches and lodges continued having dinners and "markets," to raise money for their organization and sometimes also for a particular cause, but the associated prices dropped. In the 1920s a typical dinner at a church would cost 25 cents. In the 1930s, the meal would be 15 cents and perhaps not as plentiful as earlier.

Christmas baskets were distributed, based on the donations of local citizens, and anyone who could spare something probably did so. Even schoolchildren contributed to helping their classmates, by bringing in clothes, coats, shoes, and boots that they had outgrown but that another child could likely use. These donations, like the food for the Christmas baskets, were passed on to a charity relief committee, composed of representatives of each of the three churches and the president of the Women's Christian Temperance Union. The charity relief committee also put on a chicken dinner at the school in January 1933, which raised about $27. These proceeds were used to buy lunches for undernourished schoolchildren.

There are still people who can tell of the meals they ate "back in the day"; some of them would almost be considered child abuse now, such as lard sandwiches, soup beans with almost no meat for days or weeks in a row, and other hard-time meals. Some have said they couldn't go to school for a time because they lacked clothing or shoes.

Many teenagers in the 1930s had to drop out of school to take jobs, however poorly they may have been paid, to support their families. The Andrews High School class of 1934 had 25 graduates, but the class of 1936, which had gone through the worst of the Depression, included only 11 graduates. Employees sometimes continued to work without pay, or with only the promise of pay. Schoolteachers were a prime example: Their pay was months in arrears in 1934, and I found no article stating that they had received all of their pay. They did, however, receive a portion when the state gave emergency funds to the school districts.

Even the town library was a temporary casualty of the depression. During the winter of 1933, the library was closed because it could not buy fuel or electricity. When weather permitted, the library opened for about 20 minutes after school on Wednesdays so schoolchildren could get the books they needed for school. The library may have reopened for general use earlier, but the official announcement that it was open didn't come until June 1933. Perhaps it took that long to get the light bill paid.

Even before the state and national bank holidays, Huntington County was proactive in ensuring that banks would remain viable. In 1932, several banks in Huntington County, including the one in Andrews, announced restrictions on withdrawals for all funds that had been deposited more than two weeks earlier. Withdrawals of CDs and savings deposits made before January 18 were not permitted, and checking account withdrawals were limited to 1 percent of the funds in the account in any one week, but very small accounts, trust funds, and Christmas club balances were not affected. It's unclear how long these restrictions lasted, but perhaps it was not long enough to forestall further trouble. The State Bank of Andrews closed for a few days in late January 1933. The plan was to reopen, but there were new restrictions. Depositors were asked to give approval to a plan that would require approval from the bank itself before one could withdraw funds. This was considered a formality because of the proactive plans the bank had made in January. A letter to the editor from E. H. Stephan encouraged citizens to continue, or to begin, banking at the State Bank of Andrews, in order to make sure the bank stayed in the community. Even the *Huntington Herald Press*, in an editorial on February 3, 1933, stated, "To overlook the achievement of the citizens of the Andrews community in bringing about the reopening of the State Bank of Andrews after it had closed under the moratorium would be inexcusable. . . . Citizens of the Andrews community have always been known for their ability to carry on." The bank struggled, but it carried on. At the start of the decade, it had reported total assets of a little over $376,000, but by July 1932, the assets were reported to be worth $231,000. At the end of the decade, the total assets were still just below $233,000.

If you need further convincing that conditions in Andrews, and the county, were bad, consider this: Fewer basketball games were played between the schools in the 1933-34 basketball season. Typically the schools played 18-20 regular season games, but for this year, the number of games was 12 to 16. Other economy methods, such as reducing pay for officials, were also expected. When any sport, but especially basketball, is curtailed in Indiana, this is serious indeed.

TOWN GOVERNMENT AND INFRASTRUCTURE

Depression-era politics were no laughing matter, but at least some humor can be found in statements from an Andrews man, Tom Rockwell, who was running for the Republican nomination for congressman from the Fifth District. He was motivated to enter the race because he wanted to represent the "sub-flated," a term he apparently invented as a stronger word than "deflated," for those whose net worth was now below zero. Rockwell had been editing the *Andrews Clarion*, until it was forced to suspend publication. Before that, his book-publishing business in Chicago had failed, and his home there had been sold for taxes. Rockwell had graduated from Harvard College in 1914 with a degree in economics, and he thought he understood the plight of Americans. His campaign statement didn't mention what he could do to change the situation, and he failed to win the nomination, but he must have provided a chuckle or two along the way.

The town of Andrews was changing, too. With the November 1931 elections, all the Democrats were defeated and, for the first time in many years, Republicans were elected to every town office. E. M. Kitt was elected clerk-treasurer, and Charles Long, Roy Krontz, and Dorrance Cross were elected to the town council. Although I have not found a specific statement indicating that the town carried debt, a letter to the editor of the *Huntington Herald Press* from "A Resident of Andrews" suggested that a dog tax of $10 per dog would clear the town debt and also the debt on the schoolhouse. Ten dollars represented a lot of money in the Depression, and the suggestion was not acted on. The letter does, however, give us some insight into the state of town finances in March 1932.

Elections were held again in Andrews in 1933. This time, only two councilman positions were open, but Republicans Charles Long and L. W. Pratt were elected. Esser Kitt won the election for clerk treasurer by a wide margin, 172 votes to Ora Ross's 71 votes. By 1935 the Democrats were able to make a bit of a comeback, electing Democrats Bruce Glaze and Henry Yentes to council positions, as well as Esser Kitt, with John Gretzinger elected clerk-treasurer. In 1935 the state legislature passed a law that town elections would be held only every four years, instead of every two. We don't know whether or not the townspeople approved of this change; it was a done deal. In 1939 the town went straight Republican again, with John Gretzinger clerk-treasurer and Orval Adams, Esser Kitt, and Dorrance Cross as councilmen.

In 1935, more or less halfway through the Depression, we get a glimpse of town life through the publication of tax levies, including a town budget. The annual salary for the trustees was $120; for the clerk-treasurer, $100; for the marshal, $480; for the health officer, $25; for the town attorney, $40; for the firemen, $175. The largest budgeted amount was for heat, light, power, and water, $2,156.84. The amount of $3,897.85 was to be raised by the tax levy, which was pretty close to what had been collected in 1932 and 1934. Andrews ended 1935 with a balance of $775.18. It seems that Andrews was doing a good job of managing its budget, but we don't know what failed to be done during those years that should have been done.

Andrews was to be the site of one of the first three Red Cross highway aid stations in the county. As of yet, the station did not have a location, but it was to be offered as a service by the Red Cross, to aid motorists involved in automobile accidents. The Red Cross representatives would go to the scene of accidents to administer first aid. This might be the beginning of the first-responder status of fire stations. I didn't locate any specific follow-up stories to this, only occasional mentions that the Red Cross was at the scene of a specific crash.

A special election was held on September 30, 1938, so the town could vote on whether or not to buy the Andrews Water Company, Inc., and acquire its stock. The town actually owned the common stock, but the company as a corporation owned the preferred stock, and all of it needed to be in town hands so the town could apply for a grant from the Public Works Administration. The waterworks had been installed in 1919 and already was badly worn, inefficient, and costly to operate. Also there was no storage capacity, in case water was needed by the fire department and power was cut off. The town was seeking a grant of $25,000 to modernize the plant. Townspeople responded well, turning out in good numbers to vote for the proposal, 244 to 19. Although the grant received was only about 60 percent of the $25,000 requested, it would permit the purchase of new pumping equipment, some new wells, chlorination equipment, and probably a new storage facility. A new well was dug almost immediately, but the new storage facility and other work was actually postponed for about a year. In 1939 the town asked for bids for a water tank and construction of a well house. The bids were expected to come in at about $9,000 to $10,000 for the 75,000-gallon tank, and the low bid was $8,300. The well-house construction would cost an additional $19,494.

Town officials also were interested in a municipal power plant. They toured the plant in Warren and thought owning their own plant might be a better practice than purchasing power from the Northern Indiana Power Company, which was the arrangement as of 1933. The plan died a natural death. Perhaps in the Depression, purchasing the equipment necessary and hiring employees to run the plant were more than the town budget could stand. The utilities officials also approved the survey of Andrews for the purpose of installing natural gas mains for the town. Did "survey" mean a physical action, involving maps and plans, or did it mean asking the residents whether they were interested in becoming customers? Unfortunately, I found no follow-up articles about this, but it is believed that natural gas was not made available to the town at this time.

Utilities and infrastructure were already under periodic threat from weather conditions. In 1938 a snow and sleet storm cut telephone service to the town until linesmen from as far away as Noblesville came to help install new poles and lines where needed. Loon Creek was another problem. It flooded so badly that it cut a new channel to the Wabash River, across Wabash Railroad property and farmland owned by Frank Fults.

Finally, the Wabash Railroad upgraded its crossing signals for the Main Street (also referred to as the Charles Long road) crossing. The new signal was automatic, with four vertical beacons bearing the letters STOP and two horizontal red lights that flashed intermittently as a train approached. It doesn't sound like there was an actual bar that came down to block traffic from crossing. Did this mean a guard was no longer on duty at all times, to trip the signals? Were people on their own to cross the tracks on Market Street and on Snowden Street?

The interurban was changing, too. In 1933 the Andrews agency was abolished, meaning there was no one at the local depot to sell tickets or to handle goods that were being transported to other stations up and down the line. The situation soon worsened, however. In 1938 the interurban, known officially as the Indiana Service Corporation, ceased operation. Andrews citizens could no longer depend on this service to go to Huntington and Fort Wayne, or to Wabash and Peru. Buses took the place of the interurban cars, but of course they were not as convenient as the interurban had been. Andrews lost something when the interurban closed.

It took two years to get the Charles Long road improved. Part of the delay was due to the town limits not being clear. The county agreed to bear the cost of improving the road from the town limits to State Road 24, but they wanted to know where the town limits were. The town seemed to not know, so that negotiation took a bit of time. Then there were delays to determine where the right-of-way in the county actually was. Again, there were delays and negotiations. The county surveyor wasn't sure where to build the road, and even after it was finished and paved, a landowner came forward to say the road had been built partially on his land. He accepted $125 for the value that he had lost. The town paved its portion of the road, the county paved its portion, and two years later the state agreed to accept the road into the state highway system. The whole stretch of road was now State Road 105.

FACTORIES

Much of the economy of Andrews depended on the Wasmuth-Endicott company. The plant was doing well as the decade opened. Their 1930 sales conference had lasted four days, with the final celebration at the Elks club in Huntington. In 1931 the company decided to add another shift so they could have 24-hour-a-day operations. They had a lot of rush orders to get out by the end of the year and hoped that at least some of their bids that were now outstanding would be accepted, to place built-in cabinets in the kitchens of apartment buildings that were being constructed in the East. A year later, however, in what was termed a "friendly action," E. M. Wasmuth was appointed receiver for the Wasmuth-Endicott company. This was made necessary by "a restriction of credits" and was intended to protect stockholders and creditors alike. By May, a trustee, Peter Cortle of Fort Wayne, had been appointed by the district federal court. The plant was to continue to operate, except that it didn't. In July it was reported that the plant had been closed for a month, and there were no definite plans set for the plant's reopening. This was the end of the Wasmuth-Endicott company.

However, almost immediately, a new corporation was formed, called Kitchen Maid. Workers were expecting to be called back to work soon after the middle of July, although not all 75 employees would be called at once. The plant was reorganized, inventories were taken, and Kitchen Maid opened a display room in Andrews, where obsolete units could be purchased. Evidently the lines offered were being streamlined, or updated, or both. E. M. Wasmuth was the executive head of the company, A. F. Wasmuth was sales manager, C. E. Brady was credit manager, and R. E. Wasmuth was factory superintendent. It was still a family operation, and soon, D. A. Wasmuth quit his 30-year employment at First and Farmers State Bank of Roanoke to work as the sales manager of the central territory for the new company. He may have thought of this as a matter of self-preservation, because he had filed for bankruptcy listing debts of $200,000 and assets of $310. He had signed as a guarantor for all purchasers and owners of preferred capital stock of the former Wasmuth-Endicott company and other concerns of that company. He needed to make sure the new company would succeed.

Kitchen Maid developed new products and displayed them at the 1933-34 World's Fair in Chicago, It sounds very much like a modern kitchen, with built-in accessories and white enamel finish. These were shown in a model home at the fair, designed by architect John C. B. Moore.

In 1937 a union, affiliated with the CIO, wanted to represent the 137 or so workers at the plant. The general opinion, as expressed by Homer Ross, was that the men had been competent to work with the management up to that time, and they preferred to continue to represent themselves. The election was one-sided, with a vote of 105-32 against the CIO union.

Kitchen Maid workers produced more than just cabinets. A. D. Wasmuth advertised that he had several varieties of perennial flowers for sale at the Delphinium Gardens, located at the rear of the Kitchen Maid factory. He was an ardent gardener, and it may have been his work that later allowed for vegetable gardens and an orchard on that site.

Pauline Wilson advised me that the men were permitted to stay after work to use company machinery and equipment, with permission. She had a small table that her father, Glen Campbell, made in his spare time there, and she was justly proud of it. She mentioned that other people made musical instruments, or whatever small things their families might request. There is a tantalizing hint that Roy Eastes, who was later known as the town blacksmith, was one of those who made one or more musical instruments. I've seen a picture of a violin that had a label inside saying "Leroy H Eastes, Andrews, Indiana, 1937." In 1930 Roy H. Eastes was listed as a laborer at a cabinet factory in Andrews. I don't know when he left Kitchen Maid's employment, but perhaps he was there long enough to learn to make violins. By 1940 he was a blacksmith, but one wonders how many violins he made, and whether he played the violin.

The Gets company, which had started out so well in the 1920s, also suffered from the Depression. Nationally, auto production in 1928 had been about 3,000,000 vehicles. Five years later, auto production was about 1,300,000 units. Fewer spark plugs were needed for new vehicles, and although older vehicles stayed on the road longer, demand wasn't high enough to keep Gets employees busy. The company tried to make a correction by dropping out of the spark-plug business. In a November 17, 1932, article in the *Huntington Herald Press*, its product line is described as "driers for ladies' silk hose, radiator guards for tractors, fish knives which are put out under two trade names and signs for automobiles." Just about three weeks later, the company was forced into involuntary bankruptcy. They were still technically solvent, with assets of $10,000 and liabilities of $9,000, but they had a cash-flow problem and couldn't pay a $660 judgment against them. The plant was eventually sold to Bruce Glaze, who had invented the original spark plug and most of the machinery that was used at the Gets plant. He formed a new corporation, with himself, O. K. Gleason, and Eben Lesh as incorporators and himself, Gleason, Charles M. Long, Oren B. Foster, C. M. Denney, Ivan McDaniel, and Eben Lesh as directors. The plant reopened in 1933, with a reduced work force of only six or seven men.

Sometime in the 1920s (or possibly earlier), there was a Standard Oil bulk storage operation in Andrews. Emery Garretson was listed in the Polk Directory of 1926 as the agent. We know there was a bulk tank operation because Charles Long, town board president in 1930, received a certificate from Standard Oil, signed by none other than Charles Lindbergh, awarding recognition to the town of Andrews, Indiana, for making its name visible to aviators. The town name had been painted "on the roof of the bulk plant."

OTHER BUSINESSES

The factories were struggling, and the bank was not growing, but other businesses in Andrews continued to come and go, as they always had. The Markle funeral home moved from Huntington to Andrews in 1931 and established its office in the J. W. Markle furniture store. The store soon moved to the room below the IOOF Hall on Main Street, and the family moved to the Marker residence on Main Street. The family did not live long in this home, however, because Mr. Markle died suddenly of coronary thrombosis in 1937. By April 1938, his business had been purchased by Mr. and Mrs. Charles Zimmerman, of Fort

Wayne, and they soon became valued Andrews citizens. If the Markles didn't open the funeral home at the current Andrews location on North Main Street, the Zimmermans did. This was the old Congregational Church building, which was originally frame but at some point had been changed to a brick building.

Dr. G. B. Fults, dentist, and Dr. G. M. Lasalle, surgeon, moved to new offices in Andrews, although it appears that they both continued to live in Wabash and may not have practiced here long. Dr. R. S. Clymer had lived and practiced in Andrews since the late 1920s. He is shown in the 1930 census as living on McKeever Street. He was young and enthusiastic, and the town was lucky to have him for the years he was given.

It may have been in the early 1930s that Lawrence Wade observed, "I can recall Frushour's Garage up-town that had a big sign reading 'Good Gulf Saves' and then just up the street was the Holy Roller Church proudly announcing that 'Jesus Saves.' I often wondered which was correct." The "Holy Roller" reference would have been to the Pilgrim Holiness Church, newly built at the time.

Even in the Depression, there was some demand for restaurants. Wayne Sewell of Lagro opened a restaurant in the room formerly occupied by the Calvert Grocery. George Snyder bought the old Murray restaurant and moved it to the first door south of the Fults-Goodrich grocery, on Main Street. An old store and barn at Madison and Market streets, operated as a furniture store and undertaking establishment by B. E. Park, was torn down, and the lumber was salvaged by Herman and Wallace Favorite. In 1936 Miss Pauline Burkhart leased the Snyder restaurant, and she was assisted by her sisters Laveda and Thelma Burkhart. This business stayed in operation for quite some time, and some Andrews residents still remember the business and the "sweet ladies" who ran it.

The Fults and Goodrich store put a large bag of flour in its window at the end of 1933 and invited guesses as to the actual weight of the flour. The winner was based on a combination of accuracy and "serial number"; in case of a tie, the earliest entry would be chosen. Mrs. Pearl Willets won with a guess of 287¼ pound. She was 4 ounces off. It was mentioned in the January 4, 1934, *Andrews Clarion* that she entered without even seeing the bag. The prize wasn't stated, but runners-up won as much as 96 pounds of flour, so perhaps she won the entire bag.

Prohibition was repealed in 1933 on a national basis, and Indiana followed the nation, once again allowing alcohol to be legally sold and consumed. It wasn't until late 1935, however, that a newspaper advertisement appeared for a bar in Andrews. Even then, it was called "Busy Bee Parlor," not "saloon" or "bar." Five kinds of bottled beer and two beers on tap were advertised, along with live music (pianist and vocalist) three nights a week. The business was operated by Bonnie Richards, whose husband Byron worked at Kitchen Maid. It was located in back of the Blue Moon Cafe, in a much smaller building. Other men applied for liquor licenses, including John L. Hefner, but the results aren't printed in the paper.

Although Andrews was very involved in daily life and in the future, there were still fascinating facets of the past that we tend to forget. Roy Eastes was probably the last town blacksmith. In 1936 he moved his blacksmith shop to his new residence on Jefferson Street, three squares east of the drugstore. He continued as a blacksmith for many years, making a living and teaching young boys about life. In 1937 there are still pictures of horses and wagons on the streets of Andrews on a daily basis, too.

The blacksmith had his customers, and the automobile mechanics had theirs, and sometimes the same customers probably patronized both businesses, as old ways gave way to new. Roy Frushour moved his business to his new location, which we wouldn't be able to identify except for a comment in the "gossip" column that Mr. and Mrs. Roy Frushour had moved to the Morrison property on Market Street. The garage actually fronted on California Street and is still standing, though now privately owned. There were several gas stations in town, but I'm not sure which ones were open in the 1930s.

SCHOOL

The new school was occupied in January 1930. I've heard stories of the high school students, and possibly younger ones, forming a line from the old school to the new school and passing books from one person to another until the library had been moved. Possibly other school supplies and equipment were moved that way, too. It was an exciting time for Andrews. The new school, as stated in the *Huntington Herald Press* of January 3, 1930, "has been described as one of the finest and most efficient school plants in this section of the state." The gymnasium was officially dedicated during the first basketball game played there, against the Clear Creek Bulldogs. Up to that time, Andrews home games had been played in the "antiquated" opera house, where school and community meetings were also held.

School clubs were glad to have new facilities to showcase their functions and talents. The Andrews High School glee club put on a three-act "operetta," called *Tulip Time*. There were 32 students involved, but lead roles were played by Jack Endicott, Pauline Borders, Mildred Harvey, Ruth Fields, Clyde Wilson, Delana Garrison, Walter Collins, and Norman Wintrode. A few days later, the senior class presented their play, and some of the same people performed in it. This time the cast included Helen

61

Campbell, Willard Knight, Paul Bare, Mildred Harvey, Ward Leakey, Bernice Aldridge, Arthur Bare, Virginia Mitchell, William Small, Helen Brewer, Walter Collins, and Edith Botkin.

A new high school newspaper was started, *Up and at 'Em*. The name may have been changed before the first issue, because we do have one issue of a high school paper called *A.H.S. Reflector*. We aren't told when the *Andronian* quit publishing, or why. We are told that the new high school newspaper would be published biweekly and was intended to be a continuation of the newspaper published by the Boy Scouts during the summer. In 1932 the school newspaper was called *The Andrews Signal*. The first issue featured the typical school news, a little bit of gossip, and advertising from Wasmuth Lumber & Supply Co., Tip Top Garage, H. A. Calvert (groceries), Wm. Shinkel (shoes and boots), Andrews Elevator, Murray's Cafe, Breeding's Barber Shop, Claude Wilson (general trucking), and Earl A. Lyons (real estate and insurance). There are a dozen more questions I'd like to have answered about these newspapers, and about the presence or absence of a newspaper for adults, but some of our town history has slipped through our fingertips.

The township trustee, A. O. Garretson, retired, and in his honor the Andrews schoolteachers, past and present, gave him a farewell party that included a social time and an oyster supper. This was in January 1931, before the Depression had changed the town's eating habits. Garretson had seen the township through some big challenges, including getting the new school built, and he probably deserved both retirement and an oyster supper.

Four young men's singing talents brought a touch of fame to Andrews. The Andronian Four, composed of Paul Bare, Norman Wintrode, Sidney Cooper, and Walter Collins, not only performed at local and county events, but also performed live on the big radio station of the time,

WOWO, and on station WGL. They were accompanied by Mrs. Irene Roser at the piano. These were 15-minute programs. At least once, it was announced that the program would consist of "requests." It's not clear whether the requests were made in advance, or if someone would call in and ask for a particular song, as is sometimes still done on radio stations that play recorded music. Songs that might have been requested were "Makin' Whoopee," made famous by Bing Crosby; "In the Jailhouse Now," by Jimmie Rodgers; and "Swanee," by Al Johnson. The young men also sang at the Indiana State Fair, but soon enough they went their separate ways as life called them. In 1932 Sidney Cooper and Norman Wintrode, who were part of the Andronians, formed a new group. The Aereo Four also included Charles Adams and Orville Urschel, but it appears they were not as successful as the Andronians.

School during the 1930s included more than classes. There were sports teams, the newspaper (rather sporadically), a glee club, a band, drama clubs, sometimes an orchestra, senior plays, junior-senior receptions, class parties, Christmas events, programs by the younger children, field trips, and more. In 1933 the high school part of a Patron's Day program consisted of tumbling routines and relays and races. It's not clear whether everyone participated, or mainly those who were athletically inclined. Of course, the culmination of each school year was the high school graduation ceremony, sometimes held at the opera house, sometimes at the school, and sometimes at the Methodist church. The number of graduates varied during the 1930s, from 8 to 25, but an average year probably had about 14 graduates. The graduating class of 1936, for instance, had started with 35 students, and during the first year in the new building had 56 students. They graduated as a class of 11; Margaret Knee, Kenneth Fitch, and Ben Garretson were the only original members of the class.

Grades were considered so important that, as part of the 1934 "Patron's Day," which was actually an evening event, the grades of all highschoolers were printed and posted in the classrooms, to be viewed by anyone who cared to do so. School, despite all the fun activities, was still serious business.

"School" also involved all the citizens of Andrews. A call went out in September 1931 to "farmers, citizens, and all persons interested in the welfare of the school," to bring equipment on Saturday, September 25, to landscape the school building and level the baseball diamond. There were no school funds available for such a purpose, but the work needed to be done. Fifty men, seven teams of horses, two trucks, and a tractor were put to good use.

Some years, there was a tremendous turnover in teaching staff. For the 1931-32 school year, only one teacher had returned, Velma Thomas of Lagro. New teachers who were mentioned by name either had several years of teaching experience, or a college degree, or possibly both. It may be that with the Depression starting to take hold, it was easier to find qualified staff members who had taken the education classes that were now regarded as necessary. It also may be that these facts conceal a story that is lost to us.

I was surprised to find that the junior class of the high school ordered class rings in 1934. First, I didn't realize the tradition went back that far. Second, 1934 would not seem to have been an easy year to find the money for class rings. I wonder how many of the class actually were able to purchase the rings.

A sad side note to the occupation of the new building is that the old school, the third one built on the site of what is now the town park, was put up for sale to the highest bidder. The building had been condemned, so it was being sold for what would most likely be salvage material. Roy Krontz was the winning bidder, at a sale price of $125.

Henry Miller of Andrews assisted in the demolition, and he received a broken arm for his efforts when removing the boiler from the building.

The school faculty for the 1936-37 school year was still small. The principal was Carl R. Stephens, and high school teachers were Edward T. Cleaver, Don Butt, Miss Helen Pugh, and Mrs. Ersel Leakey, with a music and art instructor yet to be selected. The grade school teachers were Clyde Thompson, Mrs. Doris Denton, Miss Virginia Mitchell, Miss Gertrude Peting, and Miss Mary Ulrey. We are even told the "hack" (school bus) drivers' names: Chester Poe, James Tommason, and Guy Prilliman. Samuel Gerard was janitor. It was a small staff for such a big job.

It may have been in the 1936-37 school year that the tradition of the junior class selling candy and ice cream as a fund-raiser began. At least, this is the first year it is mentioned in the available newspapers. As many will remember, fund-raising became a big part of student (and family!) life, in order to raise funds for a class trip, a senior gift, or whatever the class decided needed to be done. Somehow, fund-raising went on even during the Depression.

The parent-teacher organization was an on-again, off-again, group. In 1936 it was on again, with Glynn Rudig as president, Mrs. Thomas Rockwell as vice president, and Mrs. Edgar Keefer as secretary-treasurer. Mrs. John Markle was chairman of the program committee.

The Sunshine Society was a "new" club for the high school, and installation was by officers of the Huntington High School chapter. Thirty-five members from the Andrews school were inducted into the organization, including Phyllis Cross, Wilma Robb, Thada Caster, Rose Mary Stephan, Esther Garrison, Waneta Bunker, Mary Frybarger, Alberta Bailey, Mary Bradburn, Vivian Burkart, Betty Lou Boone, Annice Ellison, Marjorie Reemer,

Kathryn Smith, Nondas Theobald, Phyllis Warfel, Marcella Welch, Geneva Dille, Elizabeth King, Mary Jane Abernathy, Arliss Boyer, Maxine Meyer, Mary M. Rudig, Evelyn Van Meter, Mary Forrest, Margaret Wasmuth, Mary McDaniel, Dorothy Denton, Annabel Robb, June Flora, Devota Scott, Janice Roberts, Rosemary Keefer, Jean Roberts, and Ella Garrison. Mrs. Leakey was the faculty adviser.

The school at the end of 1939 had prepared its students for life in a small town and, for some, for life in the big city, wherever life might take them. But it had also, unknowingly, been preparing students for war. Soon enough, many of the graduates and pupils of the Andrews school would be leaving for places they may not even have studied in geography class. They had, however, been taught patriotism and their duty to their country, and they would answer the call, when it came.

CHURCHES

The churches continued with their activities, holding revivals, union services, Sunday schools, worship services, meetings for men and meetings for women, and sometimes summer programs for children, in addition to taking care of their members. There were social events, too, such as picnics and wiener roasts, class parties, and ice cream socials. But work, both spiritual and physical, was the purpose of the church. In 1931, 15 men from the Methodist church shucked corn for Ed Watson, who had been ill for several weeks. They spent most of the day at his farm, shucking 250 bushels of corn. The shuckers (and probably the watchers) included John Strickler, Wesley Wolverton, Julius Rudig, George Randolph, John Markle, Frank Ray, Raymond Schmalzried, Rev. J. W. Borders, Will Sharp, George Stephan, and William Shinkel.

One interesting question always is, "Why were events held away from the church building?" For instance, the Ladies Aid Society of the Church of the Brethren served a "penny supper" at the hotel building in 1931. Was their building not available, for some reason, or did they hope the downtown location would bring foot traffic, or was there another reason? It does show us that the hotel was still in use, at least occasionally.

The Methodist church celebrated its 75th anniversary in 1935, with almost a full week of special services and programs. The outstanding event may have been a pageant written and directed by Mr. and Mrs. Edgar Keefer, depicting the 75 years the church had been in existence. It looks like many members of the church had a part in the pageant, with each person portraying those pioneers, and later members, who helped build the church. Mrs. Earl Lyons and son Max, and Ruth and Gege Knight were honored as being descendants of Mr. and Mrs. John Morris, who were charter members of the church.

Perhaps the Methodist church was just as happy when, in 1936, they were able to pay off the mortgage on their building. In those hopeful 1920s, they had borrowed money for building repairs and the purchase and installation of a pipe organ, and in the 1930s the mortgage had become a real burden to them.

Some events continue to remind us that there are facts of Andrews life in the 1930s that we don't really understand. Although there had been a new furnace installed at the Christian Church earlier, it must have been a wood-burning furnace, because in 1932 several men spent the day cutting 15 cords of wood that A. C. Hahn had donated to the church. The men involved were Charles Hahn, Charles Brewer, Rev. J. J. Bare, Howard Caster, Frank Brown, S. E. Ellison, Will Sharp, Chester Heslet, Will Haley, Claude Wilson, Earl Bolton, George Hoch, Ed Chronister, Edwin Small, William

Small, Eugene Moore, Walter Collins, Paul Bare, and Eldon Stouder. If this wood wasn't for the church building, it may have been for the parsonage, or it may have been donated so the church would have wood to supply to the needy.

I found only one brief reference to the Pilgrim Holiness Church in the 1930s. It's not known whether they were meeting regularly. They weren't mentioned as participating in any of the church union services, and officers' names were not printed in the newspapers I read. It is entirely possible that they did meet and worship together as a small congregation and that for whatever reason, their events weren't reported in the paper. It's also possible that the church was on an unintended hiatus during this time.

LODGES AND CLUBS

Clubs and lodges were probably more essential to town life than ever in the 1930s. Both types of groups, along with the churches, worked together to take care of townspeople who needed a little extra help, but they each had their own goals to work toward, too. The Andrews Library Club, for instance, still had a debt to pay off for their building, which required more fund-raising efforts. Many of these were fun events for the fund-raisers and those who contributed by attending whatever event was held. Plays were one of the favored methods of raising funds, so they must have been successful. One such play, called *Here Comes Arabella*, was presented in the opera house in early 1930. This was a three-act play, with additional entertainment before and after the play and between acts. Mrs. Lavern Wright, Sidney Cooper, Walt Collins, Paul Bauer, Bob Warfel, Mary Ellen Endicott, Thelma Wilson, Pauline Border, Thelma Foust, Ethel Schmalzried, Nina Bodkin, Elizabeth Bare, and Edgar Keefer all had parts in the play.

Here Comes Arabella must have been something of a success, but the club still owed money on the mortgage, so another play was presented in October 1930. This one was performed at the high school auditorium. There were more dinners, more plays, a donkey basket ball game, and talent and hometown movie shows held throughout the years.

The Library Club joined with the Andrews band to sponsor several homecomings during this period. Some years the plans were more elaborate than others, but they always included food and fun, such as the businessmen playing wheelbarrow polo for the crowd's amusement. Some years there were contests in which chickens were thrown from the roof of the hotel; the person who caught the chicken would receive his or her catch as the prize. In 1931 there was a slow-driving contest for vehicles in high gear. (Honest, I couldn't make this stuff up!)

We are fortunate to have a copy of the printed program for the 1936 show, "Jolly Jokers Minstrel," which was a benefit for the Library Club but involved mostly men in the actual performance. The program itself was an eight-page booklet, much of it advertising. Among Andrews advertisers were the State Bank of Andrews; Kitchen Maid; Fults & Goodrich; Wasmuth Lumber & Supply Co.; L. E. Knee garage; Andrews Elevator; Notter's Garage; Russel's Cafe; Calvert's groceries; J. W. Markle (wall paper, furniture, fishing tackle, funeral director); Ivan McDaniel (electrical contractor, plumbing and spouting); Schaefer's Drug Store; Burkhart's Cafe; Edgar Keefer Flower Gardens; J. R. Small (coal); Spencer's Home Bakery; Frushour Garage; H. R. Rupel, agent for Standard Oil Company; and Mrs. H. R. Rupel, New-Way Dry Cleaners.

The musical director for the show was Mrs. Thomas R. Rockwell, and the show manager was E. H. Cooper. The orchestra was composed of Miss Joy Altoan, J. Endicott, William Calvert, and C. Cole. J. D. Miller was the interlocutor, and end-men were Roy Frushour, Art Stouder, Ed Nichols, and Louis Goebel. Chorus members (many of these also performed separately or in duets or quartets) were Laban Finton, E. Garrison, Walter Collins, Edgar Keefer, Nelson Latta, Hildra Rupel, Eugene Jellison, Eugene Moore, Glynn Rudig, Ivan McDaniel, Paul Warschko, William Haley, Johnny Riggars, Ed Chronister, Joe Bannister, Sidney Cooper, Forest Bare, Richard Ross, Herbert Yenter, Bert Flemming, Gilbert Yentes, Andy Mueller, Adolph Riggars, and Raymond Fields. While we might regret the choice of the minstrel theme, it was a different time with different social mores, and this program does show that the whole community worked together to put on a good show. It was a one-night performance on Wednesday, April 15, 1936, at the high school auditorium.

Fund-raising for the library building wasn't the club's only purpose. The ladies were also responsible for planting trees along the major highways of town (presumably Main Street and McKeever Street) as well as at other locations. Some of those trees are still providing shade and beauty to our town, so that was certainly a job well done! Each year new officers of the club were elected. They frequently included Mrs. O. K. Gleason, Mrs. Carl Endicott, and Mrs. G. V. Nichols, among others. Club members still often gave the programs, although outside speakers and musicians were also featured. At a meeting in 1935, entertainment was by the McDaniel string ensemble, composed of Mr. and Mrs. Ivan McDaniel, Mrs. H. R. Rupel, Miss Avis Ellison, and Miss Lucile Prilliman. Music was still a part of Andrews.

Eventually the mortgage was paid off, and funds raised afterward were used to support the library or to purchase books. By 1939 the club was no longer able to run the library, since many members had grown older or moved out of town, so, after much discussion and the encouragement of E. P. Cubberly, the club sold the building to the Public Library board for $1. The club continued to meet for a time and continued to raise money for new books, but they were no longer totally responsible for the building they had so lovingly built in the roaring twenties and maintained throughout the Depression years.

Other lodges and clubs continued as well. Because many of their meetings and events were not publicized, we have no blow-by-blow descriptions of them. Most years, lists of newly elected or installed officers were printed in the newspapers, and sometimes there are write-ups of an Andrews lodge attending another lodge's meeting, or of another lodge coming to Andrews for a joint meeting. We can say that the Masonic Lodge and the IOOF were still active, as were the Eastern Star and the Rebekahs. The Native Daughters, associated with the Knights of Pythias, held an annual dinner in 1931, and at least 61 families attended, some from as far away as Sioux City, Iowa, and Detroit, Michigan. It looks like all of these people had Andrews connections, if they weren't current residents. By 1937, 42 families were listed as in attendance, so either the Depression intervened, or lodge membership was decreasing, or both. There was no mention of the Knights of Pythias for several years, and in 1938 a new lodge was formed. State officers gave a charter to the lodge, which had 25 charter members. There were also smaller organizations associated with some of the lodges, composed of people who had served as the leader of the lodge for a year, or sometimes more. If you were a lodge member, you were probably busy. The IOOF still owned Riverside Cemetery, and in 1933 Charles Brewer was appointed caretaker in place of George Stephan, who had held that position for three years.

The Women's Christian Temperance Union stayed active during the first half of the decade, as they continued to support Prohibition. After Prohibition ended, they sought to educate the public, especially young people, about the problems associated with alcohol. Nationally and on a statewide basis, the WCTU was a lobbying organization as well as an educational organization, but it's hard to point out exactly what Andrews did to support these aims.

Some clubs, of course, were more successful than others, and some existed for only a short time. For instance, there was a group of young people at Andrews who formed a drama club called the "Play Shot." High school students were not permitted to join, but youth was not otherwise a barrier, so it may be that some who belonged and performed were of school age but no longer attending school. This club may have given one play before disbanding.

The Dallas Township Conservation Club, which was organized about 1934, seems to have been composed mainly of Andrews men. The first officers were Dorrance Cross, L. C. Schaefer, and John Markle, and the first project the club planned to tackle was to build a fish pond for the raising of fingerlings.

Children and youth were not left out as far as clubs go. There were active 4-H clubs throughout the decade, although membership seems to have varied. Many members lived on farms, but many were from Andrews. Some farm children didn't participate in 4-H because it was hard for them to attend the meetings that were held in town. Some town children had relatives or friends in the township and could complete their animal projects there. The 4-H clubs usually formed in winter months and continued through the county and state fairs.

The Boy Scouts had been active during the 1920s, but the organization was always dependent on the availability of adult leaders. In 1937 a new troop was begun under the leadership of Rev. Kenneth Ball of the Christian Church. He was young and enthusiastic and soon had the boys taking a

14-mile hike to qualify for their first class badges. Unfortunately, he stayed in town only a few years, but while he was here the Boy Scouts seem to have thrived.

The new club in town was the Lions Club. It was first chartered in January 1939, with Arnold P. Spencer serving as president; G. M. Prilliman, Huel E. Goodrich, and Richard E. Shaw as vice presidents; I. M. Wiley as secretary-treasurer; Stanford Young as Lion tamer; J. Arthur Fults as tail twister; and Homer Calvert, Lucian C. Schaefer, Harry R. Wasmuth, and Chauncey R. Theobald as directors. Other charter members were Bert Anson, Dr. S. S. Frybarger, Ralph Notter, Sam H. Wasmuth, and Rev. R. Lowell Wilson. Their first big event, or at least their first publicized event, was a Halloween parade down Main Street. All costumed persons were welcome to join in, and prizes were given for the best costumes. A special feature was the offer of free sandwiches to all who came, or at least the first 2,500 people, for that is how many sandwiches they planned to prepare. Sixty persons (wives included) were at the next meeting of the club, so the club was growing.

The Andrews band was still making music. They presented regular concerts during the 1930 and 1931 summers, at least once sharing the billing with an eight-round boxing exhibition. The night of the boxing event, 500 people attended. As is often the case when one must rely on sketchy newspaper accounts, it's difficult to determine which references to "Andrews bands" mean the community band, and which mean the school band. In 1934 the Andrews Community band was specifically mentioned as having been reorganized, and the director was T. D. Weesner, supervisor of instrumental music in the Huntington schools. Students from Huntington High School would be performing with the Andrews band for an outdoor concert at "the public square" on August 22. That's the last mention of the band I found for the 1930s.

CRIMES

A newspaper in Andrews called *The Andrews Clarion* was published for a short time starting about the first of December 1933. In volume one, number 5, published January 4, 1934, a front-page article noted that William Tidrick had completed his 13th year as town marshal and had just been reappointed for another two years by the town council. He had lived in Andrews since 1887 and was first selected town marshal in 1920. During his first year in office, there had been 52 criminal cases, and during his second year 32 criminal cases. In the five years leading up to 1934, there had been cases of public intoxication, bootlegging, chicken thievery, and reckless driving. However, during 1933, Tidrick had made only one arrest, that of an out-of-town driver, for speeding. He felt that few towns could claim such a group of law-abiding citizens. However, there were several stories that came from the 1930s.

When we think of the 1930s and crime, certain nationally known criminals come to mind, such as Al Capone, John Dillinger, and Bonnie and Clyde. Andrews had its own share of criminals, not nationally known, not connected to organized crime, and not always related to Prohibition. Probably economic pressures contributed to some of the crimes, some may have been committed for "the thrill of it," and some probably arose from domestic disputes. Whatever the reason, Andrews and Huntington County law enforcement officials were kept busy during the decade. Men were caught in Prohibition-related charges. One of them was Jacob White of Andrews, who was arrested and charged with possession of intoxicating liquor in July 1931. Thirteen gallons of "home brew" were confiscated, and the newspaper reported there were four cars parked at his home at the time of the raid, perhaps insinuating that the home may have been a speakeasy. However, he was sentenced to 30 days in jail and a $100 fine, with the jail time to be suspended when the fine was paid. To make it even easier on White, he was given 90 days in which to pay the fine. Richard Miller, however, was not given such a light sentence. He pled guilty to charges of possession of intoxicating liquor and was sentenced to 30 days at the state penal farm, plus a fine. He could not pay the fine; but instead of giving him 90 days to pay it, the judge ordered that he spend additional time in prison, getting credit for $1 a day until the fine of $100 was paid. It may have been a different judge, or a different court, or there may have been other reasons for the different penalties.

Economic pressures caused John Gillmore to become a chicken thief, and a pretty good one, at that. The sacks he carried the chickens in had holes in them, neatly hemmed, so the chickens could be carried with their heads out of the sacks, to get air. He was charged with stealing six chickens. In his comments to the sheriff, he said that he was hungry and wanted to trade the chickens for food. He stated that he had several times asked the township trustee for funds and had been denied. Gillmore was 66 years old and deaf, and the judge showed some leniency when he sentenced him to 30 days at the state farm, plus fines and costs of $30.

A more serious crime was committed at the Wabash Railroad construction camp near Andrews on August 31, 1930. Two men, Robert Barron and William Slayton, were arrested. Barron was charged with robbery and Slayton was charged with conspiracy to commit a felony. The victim was Robert Wyatt, who was robbed at knife-point and then slashed across the back when released.

Crime didn't pay. Neither did being a good citizen, it seems. Archie Knee, who had a gas station in town, was awakened at 4:00 a.m. on January 2, 1934, by five men who told him they would buy a tankful of gas if he would help

75

them out by taking gas to their vehicle, which had run out of gas. Knee obligingly took five gallons to the vehicle, and the men, as promised, returned to the station to fill their tank. Then their script changed, and instead of paying Knee, they forced him at gunpoint into the car, drove him back north across the Wabash River, and forced him out of the vehicle and onto his knees, where he was robbed of the small amount of money he carried with him. They then drove off and left him to walk back to his home. He was so rattled he didn't get a license number and could give no description of the men, other than that they were driving a 1932 Chevy.

Just as Lessel Long, 20 years earlier, had faced accusations of embezzlement, another of Andrews's most prominent citizens, Carl Endicott, faced charges of fraud in 1934. Endicott had left the State Bank of Andrews to become part of Gets Manufacturing before going to Citizens State Bank in Huntington to found the trust department, in 1927. By 1934 the bank had closed, and five bankers, including Endicott, were accused of embezzlement in administering funds, based on the report of a state auditor. Of the five men, Endicott appears to have been in the most trouble. There were five charges against him, some relating to personal use of bank funds and some relating to bonds he had purchased from a cousin at face value for the bank, bonds that, allegedly, he knew were worthless. Attorneys for the bank fired back, saying the bankers had used $400,000 of their own funds to try to keep the bank running. Obviously, the auditor had not understood all the workings of the bank. Eventually, one indictment was quashed. A first grand jury had found no cause for any indictments, a second had issued the indictments, and a third, which had to be convened because there were no women in the jury pool for the second grand jury term, found insufficient evidence to issue indictments against Endicott or the other bankers involved in the case. They cited poor management and poor bookkeeping, but the bank had already failed by this time (1936), so the case was moot. Or was it? There was still a civil case pending. The state department of financial institutions on behalf of the closed Citizens State Bank sued a bonding company to recover funds supposedly mishandled by Endicott. I have not been able to find a record of the result of that action.

The David Sellers family had lived in or near Andrews since at least 1880. They had at least three sons, two of whom caused grief to their parents. In 1935, 50-year-old Orth Sellers was living with his parents. He had been a prison guard at the Pendleton reformatory and at a Stillwater, Minnesota, prison but was no longer employed. He was intoxicated on the night of November 12, 1935, and his brother Don got him home and into an upstairs bedroom. Don locked the door to the stairs, and that apparently enraged Orth. Orth started firing shots from two pistols he had in his possession, which meant law enforcement had to be called. Orth shot at the officers' feet; eventually tear gas was used to good effect, and Orth came downstairs and surrendered. In this day and age, he would have been imprisoned and eventually sentenced to long years in prison, but in 1935 the punishment, rendered by a Huntington city court judge, was six months at the state farm and a $180 fine, which would mean he could be at the farm for more than a year if the fine wasn't paid. Needless to say, the older Sellers couple was quite shaken by the ordeal, although early in the crisis they had been moved to safety.

Later, Don Sellers became famous or notorious for his abuse of alcohol. He was arrested frequently, given many "second chances," and at one point was arrested within 24 hours of being released from the state farm after serving a six-month term for public intoxication.

77

Life quieted down for a while in Andrews after that. There were the usual school break-ins, some just involving the school office and some a total ransacking of the building. Motives appeared to be pure vandalism, or looking for money, or even looking for sectional basketball tickets. Someone stole a boat from Fred Hull and planned to travel down to New Orleans with it but was stopped at Belden.

More professional thieves burglarized the Wasmuth Lumber Company. They prepared for the event by purchasing naphtha soap at a local grocery, to use in plugging holes in the safe, silencing the drill and preventing fingerprints, and they robbed the Ed Kelly blacksmith shop for tools used to enter the building and work on the safe. The safe was broken into, and it appeared that about $200 was missing, plus there was considerable damage to the personal property in the office. The newspaper article referred to a "dog and pony show" on the other side of town, which apparently meant there was some kind of diversion that captured the attention of any town citizens who were up in the middle of the night. It was also believed that the explosives had been set off when a Wabash train came over the tracks, as the lumber company was located next to the tracks. Fortunately, valuable papers were eventually found near the junction of highways 105 and 16. They didn't replace the cash that was stolen, but the Lumber Company was saved some effort that would have been needed to replace the papers.

Lawrence Bitzer, a service station attendant just outside of Andrews, was another crime victim. He was robbed in September 1926, at gunpoint. Three men were involved, two of them taking $35 in cash, a money changer, and some other small items, while the third man was the driver of the car. These men were arrested and confessed to other robberies in Berne, Anderson, Alexandria, and Greentown and an attempted holdup in Marion.

A basketball game in Andrews led to a criminal arrest. Everett E. Campbell and Harold Howes got carried away in the heat of the contest and were charged first with inciting a riot and later with assault and battery against the game referee. The men entered guilty pleas and were fined, but the Indiana High School Athletic Association held their own investigation.

Ed Kelly, the town marshal, was shot in the line of duty on December 19, 1937. Fortunately, his injuries were not life-threatening, and it appears that the incident was handled well. Arthur Ferris had a grudge against the marshal related to a previous interaction, when Kelly had gone to the residence on a domestic disturbance call. In what appeared to be an intoxicated condition, Ferris decided to pay a visit to the Kelly residence, and he took a borrowed shotgun with him. The discussion became heated and Ferris raised the gun. Ed Kelly and an unidentified son tussled with him and the gun went off. Kelly was wounded in the leg, but he and his son were able to subdue Ferris and hold him until the sheriff arrived. By December 24, Ferris pled guilty to a charge of assault with intent to commit a felony and was sentenced to 1 to 10 years in prison. It was noted that Ferris was a peaceable and industrious man, except when he was intoxicated. He was a veteran of World War I, where he served for about a year in the US Navy.

The printers used a lot of ink in telling, and retelling, the story of the death of Henry Cross. Cross, Ray Shenefield, and Mrs. Frances Lewis were out for the evening on August 25, 1939. Part of the evening apparently involved alcohol, and part involved competition of two men for the attentions of one woman. The stories of what happened changed with the developments, but the end result was that Henry Cross, thought to be "only" drunk when he was

79

jailed, worsened and died at the hospital the next day. Shenefield and Mrs. Lewis were also jailed for intoxication. As the facts developed, it seems that although there had been some kind of automobile accident, the cause of Cross's death was a large skull fracture behind his left ear. Shenefield was accused of striking a blow there, according to Mrs. Lewis, with a bottle of some kind. Shenefield was then charged with voluntary manslaughter by a grand jury called to investigate the facts surrounding Cross's death. The trial lasted three days, and the jury had a hard time reaching a verdict. They deliberated over a period of 24 hours and were deadlocked, six to six. The judge released them, but there was to be a second trial for Shenefield.

There were fires in Andrews, too, although not as many or as serious as in some decades. The Wesley Wolverton home on North Market Street was destroyed by fire on April 8, 1932. The 10-room home of Mr. and Mrs. Roy Clemmons on North Jackson Street was pretty much burned to the ground on June 21, 1932. The home and garage owned by Thad Hart and occupied by Mr. and Mrs. Frank Aldridge, located just a half-mile east of Andrews, was a total loss after another fire. The fire that was probably talked about most in downtown Andrews was the one at a metal-covered frame building on Main Street in Andrews. It is described as being across the street from Harry R. Wasmuth's store and next to the post office, so it must have been just next to the railroad tracks, on the south side of Main Street. Wasmuth used the building as a warehouse. There was a wind that afternoon, but the fire department did a good job of keeping the fire from spreading.

OTHER NEWS AND HAPPENINGS

Due to patriotism, ambition, or a desire to help his family, or possibly all three, Floyd L. Botkin, who graduated in the

Andrews High School class of 1931, enlisted in the US Army in April 1933. He served during World War II (in 1940, he was stationed in Hawaii as a sergeant, so he may or may not have been there when the Japanese attacked on December 7, 1941) and the Korean War. He retired in 1953 as a chief warrant officer, so he had advanced far up the ranks. After his retirement, he worked for eight years as a "staff assistant" with Sandia Corporation, which operated under the Western Electric umbrella but had much to do with national security. Botkin died in 1964 at the young age of 51. He is an unrecognized hero from Andrews.

During most of the decade, memorial services, held in the middle of June, continued. There are records of such services up through at least 1937, but it may be that the crowds got smaller and smaller. In 1931 committees were needed to handle the parking and to build a stand for the speakers at Riverside Cemetery, but later the crowd was small enough that the Christian Church was on standby. The services would be held there in case of rain. Originally the memorial services had been planned by members of the GAR. In the early 1930s, they were planned by the churches and the lodges together. It seems that perhaps there was no service in 1936, because in 1937 the service was planned by the lodges alone, with the comment that it was expected to be an annual event thereafter. No longer were 2,500 people willing to come to Andrews to honor their families and especially their war dead.

The post office personnel went through some rough times in the 1930s, but in 1936 they had a picnic in celebration of the marriage of Assistant Postmaster and Mrs. J. D. Miller. Attending were Postmaster and Mrs. John Markle and family; route carrier Glynn Rudig, Mrs. Rudig, and family; Edgar Keefer and Mrs. Keefer and Ned; and assistants Frank Brown and wife, Archie Knee and wife, A. E. Mattern, and Mrs. Edward Chronister and spouse. The happy couple received gifts from the picnic attenders, and a good time was had by all.

The Clark Twins, identified in the newspaper as being from Huntington, were making headlines by the end of the decade. This family, who lived on Maple Grove Road before moving to Andrews, had four sets of twins, the most at the annual twins convention held in 1939 in Fort Wayne. The twins were Ross and Robert, Donald and Dale, James and Joseph, and Margaret and Mildred. Much more will be told of their story in chapter 8..

There was a fad of sorts in the late 1920s and 1930s, of young men and women going to another county or state to marry and then returning home as if nothing had happened. Sometimes the motivation for living apart was economic, sometimes it had to do with education, sometimes one or both parties were reluctant for the parents to know, and sometimes the reasons will remain unknown to us. Treva Hefner and Samuel Ellison, both of Andrews but neither a teenager, went to Urbana, Illinois, and were married at the home of the groom's sister on February 22, 1931. It wasn't until early in June that the event was announced at a bridge party. The bride's mother was presented a prize, which included a card announcing the marriage. If it wasn't known to the bride's mother ahead of time, what a shock it would have been to learn about her daughter's marriage at a public event! Samuel Ellison, age 41, was the postmaster of Andrews at the time. His first wife had died in 1926. Treva, at 29 years old, was assistant cashier at the bank and was living with her mother. Surely it was no secret that the two were courting. The announcement of these secret weddings at a party months or occasionally even more than a year later was not uncommon. It certainly gave the town women something to talk about!

As we try to track the history of the hotel, a cooking school was held there in June 1931. Alma Harshbarger, of the Northern Indiana Power Company, was the instructor, and there were afternoon and evening classes. Presumably the kitchen was still in functioning condition then.

Of course, weather during the 1930s must have been a topic of those who occupied the liar's bench in town. It was sometimes too hot, sometimes too cold, sometimes too wet, and sometimes too dry. A drought in 1932-33 severely impacted crops in the area, at just the time when good crops were needed. Railroad crews that year were ordered to watch the fields as they passed, because several grass fires had been started by sparks from passing trains. The whole county suffered under a dust storm in March 1935. It was just a small taste of what the Great Plains endured for two years, but may have given residents a bit more empathy for those suffering elsewhere.

Occasionally, people from Andrews were mentioned in the newspaper for activities either unusual or outstanding. The *Herald Press* pictured Ruth Ann and Meredith Hanselman, and David and Billy Wasmuth, as newspaper carriers for the town in 1935. Floyd Andrew and Kenneth Benson of Andrews seem to have set a record for ice-skating from Andrews to Huntington on US 24. They made the trip in one hour and 15 minutes and then returned to Andrews by the same route. Further afield, Frank Stephan, formerly of Andrews, was nominated as the GOP candidate for governor of the state of Idaho. He had already been the attorney general for that state and had founded a successful law firm in Twin Falls, Idaho. He was a 1904 graduate of Andrews High School. Probably he was most famous for prosecuting "Lady Bluebeard," a woman who was found guilty of murdering one husband and was suspected in the death of several others. It was a sensational case that made the front page of the *New York Times*.

PASSINGS

Of course, individual families still had reason to visit Riverside Cemetery, regardless of whether there was an official Decoration Day program. The list of obituaries for the decade is long, but it seems good to at least mention those who had been the builders of Andrews. Raymond O. Bixby died February 25, 1930. He had been a bookkeeper at the local bank when Carl Endicott was cashier, and was later promoted to cashier himself. He'd served there for about 20 years, in addition to being a part owner of Spencer's bakery and a frequent participant in town events. He was still relatively young, just 41 years old, when he died.

George Barcus died of injuries when a ladder fell on him while helping a neighbor pick pears, October 31, 1931. He was listed as retired at the time of his death, but he had a remarkable history. He may or may not have been an Andrews resident when he first came to Gets Manufacturing, but he lived in Andrews by 1920 and was an important part of the success that Gets had. He was still a director of the company when he died. He had helped develop some of the machinery and equipment used by the company, had filed patents to improve the spark plug they manufactured, and had run several successful businesses in Wabash before coming to Andrews. He seems to have been as much engineer as businessman, and as much businessman as engineer.

Andrews must have been greatly saddened by the death of four of the five Helvie brothers in a car accident in New York state on April 24, 1932. Reverend Otto Helvie was going to preach his first sermon at his new church assignment, and as was tradition, three of his brothers were going to be there for his first service. They were evidently not familiar with the area, and their vehicle was struck by a freight train. The four brothers were killed and another occupant of the car, apparently not related, was seriously injured. Otto Helvie was buried in New York, since his wife was from that area, but the three brothers, Charles, Zachariah, and Lewis, were returned to Andrews for burial. James Helvie, the remaining brother who was an Andrews resident, made the final arrangements. All three men were veterans of World War I, and Charles was married to the former Georgia Forst. Reuben and Lettie Helvie, the parents, had lived in Andrews for at least 10 years, as they were on the 1920 census here. At the time of the accident, Lettie was a widow and had just moved to New York to be with her sons.

Emmanuel H. Stephan, who had lived in Andrews since about 1900, died April 17, 1934. He had owned a hardware store in Andrews for 25 years, before purchasing and running a grocery store.

H. G. (Bert) Bowles died in 1934, just a few years after the death of his father, John. John was a Civil War veteran known forever after as the Civil War fifer. Bert, his son, was a paperhanger like his father, but he had the misfortune to take a bad fall from a ladder and suffered a broken neck.

Charles Fults lived south of Andrews, but when he died April 16, 1935, it had a big impact on Andrews. Fults at the time of his death was president of the State Bank of Andrews, and his short illness left little time for the bank, the family, or the town to prepare.

James Murray, restaurant owner in Andrews, died March 30, 1934. Mrs. Murray, the former Malinda Pauline Rudig, kept the restaurant going but may have overworked, as she suffered a stroke and then died on February 24, 1936. Murray's restaurant had been a part of Andrews for many years, and it would be missed.

William Cole, who operated a drugstore in Andrews for many years, died on February 17, 1936. It's not clear whether he was still operating the drugstore at the time of his death.

R. H. Forst lived in Andrews for only a few years, but his death marked the end of an era. He was the last surviving member of the Andrews GAR Post, and died at age 88. Now there was no one left in Andrews to tell the Civil War stories.

Although he was not a resident of Andrews, the death of Pastor Lawrence R. Goodmiller was an occasion of grief for much of Andrews. He was the pastor of the Church of the Brethren here at the time of his death August 23, 1936, and had served the church a total of eight years. Pastor Goodmiller had been preaching since he was 19 and died at age 37.

Traffic accidents took the lives of Jacob Wintrode, who at one time had owned and run a lunch counter in Andrews, and of Mrs. Bertha Beedy, who stepped from a bus and in front of a car. Charles Bricker died when he fell from a truck loaded with hay. He was a trucker by occupation, so perhaps he was checking the load at the time. This occurred at the "John Markle farm on North Market Street," stated the article on November 11, 1937, in the *Huntington Herald Press*.

Less than two years later, John Markle was dead, too. He had lived in Andrews for about 10 years and owned a furniture store, as well as being the town undertaker and the town postmaster. He was only 34 years old, and died of a heart attack. Markle had been active in town life, and it was a shock to the town to lose this man.

Finally, there is the story of Mrs. Nora Ferris. She was the foster mother of Arthur Ferris, who shot Marshal Ed Kelly. Her despondency over that incident, and her own ill health, reportedly caused her to climb into a cistern and drown herself. She somehow managed to pull a table over the cistern and then pull a cement cover over the cistern itself, to make it more difficult to find her body. It was a sad ending for a woman who had been a member of the Methodist church and two lodges.

The 1930s had been hard for the town, but as the decade ended, things were looking up. Most men were employed, and nationally, at least, both the town and the country were working back to prosperity. It looked like the 1940s would bring good things—unless of course, one was reading the newspaper or listening to the radio news or watching newsreels. Europe was already engaged in what would become a fight to the death. Even in Andrews, people were shuddering, and preparing.

Chapter Four
World War II and Andrews

The 1940s were not the worst of times, unless you were a serviceman or -woman, or related to one; and they weren't the best of times, unless you were still in school and your parents kept you away from the worst of the news. For all those who fell somewhere in the middle, the first half of the 1940s were difficult years, but there was a sense of purpose, a sense of strong family ties for most, and a sense of patriotism. Andrews felt all those emotions, and more. It is hard for those who didn't live through those years to imagine the fear, the hope, and then the elation as the war drew to a close. It's also hard to remember all the sacrifices made by the American people, including every single person in Andrews, due to nationwide rationing. We have trouble imagining a time when one could not buy a new pair of shoes, or an automobile tire, or meat, or sugar, or any of dozens of other things, simply because the government said the servicemen needed those items more. It's hard to imagine children being asked to gather milkweed pods and bring them to school, because the air corps needed them, or women being asked to roll bandages week after week to treat wounded soldiers. All one had to do was say "For the war effort" and purses and wallets were opened, for one Red Cross drive after another. Even in Andrews, the 1940s were marked by all of these situations, and more.

Germany had invaded Poland in 1939, and then Great Britain entered what became World War II. The citizens of America squirmed, but they also breathed a sigh of relief that it was "over there, not here." It took the German invasion of France in 1940 to move Congress to the first beginnings of action. In September 1940, the first draft was called for. Men between ages 18 and 45 had to register for the draft on or soon after October 16. In Andrews, they registered at the town library. In my mind's eye, I can see men from all walks of life lining up, those just out of school and perhaps not yet fully employed, and factory workers who were married and had almost-grown children, as well as farmers and merchants. Perhaps some of the oldest to register were grandfathers, and surely the oldest remembered the World War I draft. I wonder how long the lines to register were, especially at lunchtime and quitting time at the factories. Most of the men would have been thinking, "This is just a precaution. They won't really draft me," and a few of those men were correct. Many, however, had just taken the first step in a journey that would likely take them halfway around the world, and a few, but too many, would not come home again. It must have added an extra layer of meaning to the Thanksgiving and Christmas celebrations of 1940.

As men prepared to answer the call they hoped wouldn't be coming, other citizens prepared to do their part by giving to the first of many Red Cross drives or helping administer the drives. There had been membership campaigns annually, of course, but this one asked for pledges over and above the membership dues. Among early contributors in Andrews were the Factory Employees Association Welfare club, the Andrews school, Kitchen Maid, the State Bank of Andrews, and John Hefner. The county goal for 1940 was $2,000. By 1942 there was a special collection for the "Huntington County Red Cross

War Relief Fund," and donations were generous. There is a list of contributors in the March 12, 1942, issue of the *Huntington Herald Press*, and it seems to include every person in Dallas Township. The amounts donated ranged from 20 cents to 50 dollars. Mrs. J. Arthur Fults was township chairman for the drive, and other workers were Mary McDaniel, Ivan McDaniel, Jane Kline, J. R. Small, Carl Brumbaugh, Charles Fitch, Mrs. F. E. Fults, Mary Butt, Bernice Zimmerman, Mrs. Alta Roberts, Clarence Roberts, Winifred Notter, Wilson King, Mrs. Anna King, C. A. Willets, Mrs. C. A. Willets, Earl Owens, Ralph Notter, and Mrs. Dean Bickel. Another drive in 1943 had a much larger "quota," $16,200. Andrews again responded, but this time part of the money came from a benefit basketball game played at the high school. Even in wartime, Andrews loved its sports.

While the Red Cross and other charities were collecting, there was also a constant sale of "war bonds," through which people could contribute directly to the war effort, with the promise of receiving their principal plus interest back when the war was won. Andrews did well in this effort, too, because the Andrews State Bank put a notice in the lobby, stating that war bond sales there had been close to the average of $43,338 for banks of its size in 11 central and southwestern states. This was in August 1942, and war bond sales continued throughout the war.

Soon enough, the war effort hit not only men, and not only the pocketbook, but also the stomachs of Andrews people. Rationing began to take effect in 1942, starting with sugar. The initial amount allotted to each person was a half-pound of sugar per week, but it was lowered if a household already had sugar on hand, and that amount had to be declared when one signed up for the ration book. Businesses, such as bakeries and restaurants, were cut to about 70 percent of the sugar they would normally use, so heading to Spencer's for pie might not be a solution. One half-pound of sugar a week might sound like enough to us today, but in 1942 most people did their own cooking most of the time, "from scratch." For those who liked cake and coffee every day, it was likely a challenge. As the war went on, other items, right down to nylons and fats, were rationed. It would seem that surely enough food was directed toward the servicepeople that the rations here could be increased, but many ships carrying precious sugar were sunk in both the Atlantic and Pacific oceans. Those who had served in the war, when they returned afterward, were surprised to learn how much the folks back home had sacrificed, since many soldiers and sailors still suffered from poor diets and not enough calories, during much of the fighting. There were also "meatless Wednesdays" and "wheatless Fridays" to comply with, so it took a bit of juggling to make sure families still had healthful meals. Some of the recipes from those days are ones we wouldn't want to serve.

Gas rationing began in late 1942, as well as mileage rationing. It must have been a rare occasion to have enough gas, tires that were safe enough, and mileage available, to be able to take a trip to see family 50 miles away. One certainly didn't drive to Huntington to pick up a few groceries, but of course, there were several grocery stores in Andrews, so the need for an "emergency run" was probably rare.

By 1944 there were so many ration books and stamps and so many regulations regarding them, it seems it would have taken an accountant to keep track of them. Stamps were identified by letter, then by number. Some stamps needed to be torn from the ration books by the retailer. Tire inspections were held every two, three, four, or six months, depending on the letter of the book. All ration books for those who entered the service as well as for those who had died had to be turned in. It was a most complicated system, but people somehow got the hang of it.

Retailers also had problems learning the system, although they had received more education about it than the general consumer. B. A. Park, doing business as the Park Grocery, was given a 15-day suspension order in 1944, during which he could not sell any rationed items, because he had failed to register as a dealer. He had apparently opened a new store, thus not receiving the original training that others had received, and said he had "spoiled" the registration form. When given a second chance, he said he didn't know how to fill out the form because he didn't know the volume of rationed food sold in his first month of business. It may well have been more than his competitors, following the rules, had sold. He wasn't the only Andrews merchant to receive a suspension.

Those citizens who stayed home had to get used to more than just rationing, the shortage of men, and news from overseas. There were also neighborhood organizations formed, part Civil Defense, part victory garden, and part morale "booster" (or not). In July 1942, Homer Bitzer was made chairman of the Dallas Township organization, assisted by Ferrel Flora, Mrs. Albert Moore, Robert Reust, Wilbur Mundy, Mrs. Sophia Diefenbaugh, John L. Bickel, Mrs. Paul Warschko, Lester Stephan, William Rudig, Mrs. Elizabeth Purcell, Harmon Stensel, Carl Brumbaugh, Mrs. Marguerite Snyder, Dale Leakey, Sam Ellison, Mrs. Geneva Robb, Bill Campbell, Delbert King, Mrs. Nellie Rudig, and Floyd Andrew. It seems that these volunteers helped monitor blackout drills; encouraged participation in scrap drives, war bond sales, planting of home gardens, and preserving the food; reinforced government propaganda; and perhaps reported anyone who did not appear to be participating wholeheartedly in the war effort. One article mentioned "the eradication of propaganda (from the other side) by not listening to or repeating rumors and gossip." Dallas Township had many families of German descent, some of whom had been here for 115 years when the war began. I haven't yet heard of any Andrews families who thought they were being harassed or scrutinized, but it certainly happened elsewhere.

During the war, there was a large tomato crop grown and harvested in the Warren area. By September 1942, the crop was ready to be harvested but there were not enough workers in the fields. Andrews sent women volunteers to go to Plum Tree to help sort, peel, and pack tomatoes. It's not clear whether or not the women were paid, but it was essential that the job get done, because much of the harvest was designated for United States servicepeople.

Another job the women did was to make bandages. They started out using the Knights of Pythias Lodge building for the task but later moved to the Andrews library. The women met on Tuesday and Wednesday evenings to cut and roll surgical dressings and bandages needed overseas, throughout most of the war. It may have been tedious at times, but for those who had loved ones in harm's way, the realization that their soldier or sailor might need bandages was all the motivation the women needed. One report from September 1944 says 11,675 surgical dressings were made during the month of August, and there was still an urgent need for more workers, so these ladies weren't slowing down a bit. A newly formed Boy Scout troop helped out, too, by keeping the premises clean and "spruced up" at the Lodge building. They also committed to keeping the lawn mowed there. This scout troop included John Ellet, Jerry Brown, Tommy Hefner, Richard and James Fields, Harold Long, Richard Klotz, Edwin Goodrich, and Roger Leakey.

"Give till it hurts" might have been the slogan for buying US War Bonds. Employees were "encouraged" to devote 10 percent of each and every paycheck to the purchase of war bonds. The workers at Kitchen Maid responded. They were the first company in the county and the second in the state with 100 percent of employees having at least 10 percent of their paycheck deducted to buy war bonds. They were honored with a special ceremony and the presentation of a "Minute Man" flag, recalling "the shot heard round the world" at Concord, and a comparison was made to the production of war supplies by Andrews workers. Kitchen Maid at this time was still making kitchen and bathroom cabinets, which were being installed in officers' housing at military bases across the country.

Victory gardens were planted not only at home, but also, at least in Andrews, at work. Kitchen Maid apparently allowed the use of some of their land, and 23 employees each planted a garden strip 15 feet wide by 300 feet long. This was an impromptu contest to see which gardener was able to harvest the most produce, and it was encouraged by Walter Rusk, the County Extension agent. The gardeners were Ed Reemer, Glen Campbell, M. J. Luker, Brice Ware, Ward Denman, Roy Huston, A. F. Wasmuth, John Howell, Leonard Beeks, Jack Barnhisel, Fred Boone, Maurice Sandlin, J. W. O'Harrow, Burl Millman, James King, C. H. Martin, Fred Smith, Ray Fields, (?) B. Zimmerman, Hugh Marshall, Claude Glass, C. A. Willets, and Ernest Toerpel. Apparently none of the women employees had time to spare for such a contest. The article doesn't note whether the vegetables were to be donated to the Red Cross or another charity, or whether they were for home consumption, or some combination thereof.

As the war continued, a new organization, the "Mothers of World War II" was formed in Andrews in July 1943. It was part of the county, state, and national organization formed to "provide consistent aid to the war effort, and make plans for the protection of the men and women returning from the battlefronts to civilian life at the close of the war." Local officers in the new organization were Mrs. Clarence Stallings, Mrs. Earl Lyons, Mrs. Arthur Wasmuth, Mrs. Sam Wintrode, Mrs. Everett Bigelow, and Mrs. James Small. Later, this organization morphed into the "Victory Circle" and included wives and sisters of servicemen as well as mothers, with the same objectives. These groups packed Christmas boxes for shipment overseas. They soon began conducting fund-raisers such as bake sales to support the work they had started.

Schoolchildren of Andrews were also affected by the war. Perhaps their fathers or uncles had gone to war. Perhaps they had fewer clothes and wore shoes longer than was good for their feet. Certainly, if Mom had gone to work for the war effort, and perhaps if she hadn't, there were more chores to do, including working in the victory garden and helping to separate things to be saved for the scrap drives. They also ate fewer varieties of food, and perhaps could not eat as much as they'd like. In addition, schoolchildren had their own projects. As school began in 1944, they were asked to collect milkweed pods to be used in life preservers, as a substitute for kapok. The children and youth must have enjoyed this project. I've been told about it by several of those who participated, and they felt they were making a real contribution to the war effort and possibly helping to save the lives of their own family members. Milkweed grew along country roads, the railroad track, and probably fencerows in the country, so there was plenty of area to be covered. The pods were dried in mesh onion bags. By the time the collection was over, the young people of Dallas Township school had collected 84 bags of milkweed pods, which would make about 50 life preservers. This was a statewide project that resulted in about 200,000 bags or 120,000 life preservers. It was a tremendous success.

As the war slowly was won, plans were made to move into the future. On May 1, 1945, it was announced that all four churches and the War Mothers would participate in V-E Services at the Christian Church, within 24 hours of the date notification was received. The official V-E (Victory in Europe) celebration was held on May 8, 1945. Many mothers felt a great sense of relief along with a nagging sense of foreboding, because the war was not yet over. The war in the Pacific would continue for three more months.

Citizens of Andrews, especially the women, had much to cope with during World War II. The hardest challenge of all would have been watching loved ones go to war, not knowing if, when, or how they would return. Many women had to add "fear" to the long list of changes in their lives. A monument at the Andrews Public Library, dedicated less than a year after the end of the war, honors the men and women from Dallas Township who served in the Armed Forces during World War II. Seven of the names have stars after them, indicating that those men were killed in the line of duty. There were others who had been prisoners of war, either of the Germans or the Japanese. Many "boys" came back men, having seen more than they wanted to, but also having traveled to places they never thought they'd see, and having learned things they'd never thought they would learn. Andrews provided men who became airplane pilots and navigators, machinist mates, foot soldiers, medics, cooks, and just about any other specialty that Uncle Sam needed. And some gave all.

Those brave men who did not return are Herman E. Everhart, Spencer Forrest, Clarence Iry, Charles Martin Jr., James Russell, Robert L. Stallings, and Herbert E. Yentes.

Clarence Iry was the first casualty of the war. Perhaps not many people in Andrews remembered him, for he had graduated from Andrews High School in 1908, one of only four graduates that year. He also graduated from Purdue

University and then went to the Mexican border and into Mexico with a "Purdue battalion," helping chase Pancho Villa. He then enlisted in the Army and was commissioned a second lieutenant in the Engineers. He went to Europe as one of the first Americans in World War I and was one of the last Americans to come home, having served almost five years overseas. He was wounded and hospitalized, and he suffered what we now know as post-traumatic stress disorder for the rest of his life. For the next 20 years he served in the Engineering Corps, doing flood control work much of the time. He was a lieutenant colonel stationed at Fort Belvoir near Washington, DC. On December 12, 1941, just days after Pearl Harbor, he ended his own life. He was 50 years old and left a widow and two young sons. We'll never know what caused his death, but he had served his country well and his name is on the Dallas Township monument, with a star indicating that he died in the war.

Second Lieutenant J. M. Russell died in the line of duty on December 22, 1942, in a plane crash 80 miles northeast of San Francisco. He graduated from Andrews High School in 1934 and in 1940 lived with his parents in Warren Township, Huntington County. He worked at Kitchen Maid at that time, and had not gone on to college. Five days after the attack on Pearl Harbor, on December 12, 1941, he enlisted in the Army Air Force, ready to do his duty to his country. He quickly rose in the ranks and was commissioned a navigator in July 1942. His crew had been assigned to ferrying missions, and he was on an operational flight when the plane crashed. Four other men were killed with him. This was the first war death to touch the heart and soul of Andrews, but more would come.

Private Herbert Yentes drowned in a private lake in Florida in June 1944. He was a graduate of the class of 1934 at Andrews and then had gone to college at Ball State. He was a coach at Pennville, Indiana, for four years before being accepted into the Army Air Corps on July 26, 1943. After receiving his training, he was assigned to a post in Florida as an instructor in celestial navigation, perhaps an acknowledgment of physical issues that had kept the Navy from accepting him earlier.

Spencer Forrest, whose parents lived on River Road outside of Andrews, was the first Andrews area citizen to die overseas. He attended the Andrews schools but didn't graduate. Listed as a day laborer in the 1940 census, he did mostly carpentry and painting. Forrest had entered the service as a draftee on June 20, 1942, and had received training in five different states. His death came in France on July 13, 1944, just a little over a month after the D-Day invasion. His parents received a letter he'd written on July 10, but we don't know how long he had been in France. He had been promoted to Technician fifth grade.

Charles J. Martin, son of Charles and Betty Martin, was just 19 when he was killed in action in Germany on January 30, 1945. He was a Private First Class and had worked at Kitchen Maid before entering the army on March 2, 1943. He saw action in Holland and Belgium before entering Germany. His body was returned for burial in March 1949, a sad reminder that the war wasn't over when the war ended.

Another of Andrews' finest, Lieutenant Herman E. Everhart, was killed in action March 21 "in the European theater of war." He entered the service on March 6, 1942, became a pilot, and was killed on his 62nd bombing mission. He was a 1936 graduate of Andrews High School.

First Lieutenant Robert L. Stallings was piloting a P51 Mustang fighter, on his way back to England from an aborted mission to Hamburg, Germany, when his plane ditched in the North Sea and his life was lost. He had enlisted in the Army Air Corps on August 20, 1941. In the 1940 census, he was a farm laborer who had finished two years of college. He was the son of C. R. and Bertha Stallings.

These men were from Andrews, and the town grieved for their deaths. Other families grieved, but perhaps were more alone in their sorrows. For instance, Jesse R. Farthing, who was the son of Mrs. Gus Harvey of Andrews, died on December 26, 1942, in British Guiana, a victim of a drowning. He was a member of the US Army serving on the northern coast of South America, perhaps receiving training of some sort. His body was returned to his mother in March 1948. Other families knew the sorrow of losing nephews, brothers, or cousins in the war.

Of course, there were many men from Andrews who were injured, too, and at least one who was a German prisoner of war. There were training accidents, such as the one that injured Grover Lee Bullinger, who broke a leg during parachute training. John Lyons had a "slug" removed from a leg, probably somewhere in the Pacific (this was a guess on the parents' part, as this was classified information). Herbert D. Wintrode was wounded in North Africa. Everett Kellam was seriously wounded in France. Robert Ferrell was wounded in action while serving in the South Pacific. Otis Springer was wounded in France on September 4, 1944, and again on October 15. Louis Haley was wounded in Germany. Gordon Schaefer was wounded in Germany on November 19, 1944. James L. Smith received an arm wound and was hospitalized somewhere in France, where he enjoyed Christmas dinner with all the trimmings. Russell Leakey was wounded in action in Belgium on January 15, 1945. Allen Wasmuth received a flesh wound in his leg in Germany, serious enough to require hospitalization, and his brother David received an arm injury during an airplane crash "in the Asiatic." Later David was seriously wounded, again in the Asiatic theater of operations. Wilbur Ellet received wounds while fighting near Luzon, in the Philippine Islands. Robert L. Stephan received a head wound March 1, 1945, while leading a tank attack in Germany. I'm sure I've missed listing many others, and I haven't mentioned those who were hospitalized due to illness, mostly illnesses those that folks at home were never exposed to. I hope that this listing at least gives an idea of the sacrifices of these men, of the places they served and the work they did. Andrews can be proud of its human contribution to the war.

It would be a mistake to think that only men served in the war. Rosemary Keefer served as an army nurse, and Wilma and Annabel Robb enlisted in the WAVES. These women all graduated from the Andrews school, and they all served their community and their country well.

Yes, even in Andrews, as in every hamlet, town, and city in America, our men and women stepped forward and did their duty. For those who remained at home, life continued.

Chapter Five
1940-1949

TOWN GOVERNMENT AND INFRASTRUCTURE

War or no war, government in Andrews continued to be interesting. In January 1940 the town board consisted of Orval Adams, president, Esser Kitt, and Dorrance Cross. Byron Scott was town marshal, succeeding Ed Kelly. John Wintrode, acting postmaster since the sudden death of John Markle, was endorsed for permanent appointment by the Democratic precinct committeemen of Andrews and surrounding areas. J. D. Miller and Norman D. Stouder also applied for the position, but the choice of Wintrode was unanimous. The choice needed to be approved by government officials in Washington, however.

Andrews had a recreation center, operated by the WPA, stated the January 28, 1940, issue of the *Huntington Herald Press*. To start with, the offerings would be games and crafts, and later music instruction was expected to be added. Henry Miller and Charles Glaze were in charge of the operation. This is the only reference I found to the center, and no one seems to remember it, so I don't know how long it operated. It may have faded away as the war began, but in April 1945, the idea of a youth center was recycled. This time, the youth would have a say in it. The *Herald Press* article says only that a place had been provided and was being decorated. Adult committees and supervisors had been chosen, but the students had not yet chosen their representatives,. There was to be a recreation room, and outdoor events were also planned. Again in 1949, a program for youths was being discussed. The impetus seems to have been the perception that Andrews was experiencing what some would call juvenile delinquency and others might call high jinks. It was determined that offering activities for the youth, from skating parties to other social events and even community projects, was one answer to the problem. Each civic group in Andrews sent either a president or a vice president to a planning meeting, and churches as well as the school were also represented. Those involved in the planning were Rev. Don Blake, Ivan McDaniel, Claude Garretson, Arnold Spencer, Arthur Everhart, Mrs. Edna Bitzer, Mrs. Carl Goebel, Irwin Wiley, O. W. Beitelshees, Mrs. Nina Cleaver, Rev. George Manley, Ratio Wilson, J. D. Miller, Ed Reemer, Mrs. Earl Krile, Fred Shellenbarger, Howard Jeffrey, Frank Heitz, Mrs. Mary Harshbarger, Adrian Little, and Eugene Moore.

One problem that local government always has is collecting back taxes. The Depression, of course, had probably worsened that problem. About 50 names are listed in the January 22, 1940, issue of the *Herald Press*. Doubtless some are absentee landlords. Some owed very small amounts, as little as $4.79, but Getz Manufacturing owed $1,272.09. Hopefully this situation was rectified and more money came into the county and town bank accounts. The town budget for 1941 was $7,300.84, with about 143 taxable polls, or households, and the budget for the township was about $29,000, with 219 taxable polls. Most of the township budget was school-related. Teacher salaries were budgeted at a total of $13,940, so no one was getting rich teaching school.

Something may have happened to the fire department during the Depression years, because it appears the department was starting from scratch when a fire association was formed in November 1940. Perhaps it was merely expanding, but the purchase of new equipment might indicate a rebirth of some sort. The town purchased a pumper and a "chemical truck," Lawrence Garretson stated. This appears to be the first time that fire protection was made available to those outside of town limits. They were to pay a fee set by the governing board. The fire department would respond to calls from nonmembers, as long as the trucks were not already in use, and the charge would be $50. A working copy of the contract indicates that a committee composed of the township trustee, the fire chief, residents of Andrews and of the township, and one or more town council members would have general oversight, but the fire chief was in charge at all fire calls.

Roy Krontz was named justice of the peace for two years, beginning in January 1940, to complete the unexpired term of the late Squire L. A. Strevey. Krontz resigned in March 1942, and Orville Adams was appointed. Incidentally, each of these men was referred to as "Squire" during his term of office.

Again traffic violations were a concern, said a statement by Town Marshal Byron Scott and deputy Chet Poe. Reckless driving, rounding corners too fast, taking off too fast, speeding, driving without lights or proper muffler, and parking on the wrong side of the street were all noted. Also, stoplights were to be observed and bicycles were to stay off the sidewalks. (Bicycles had been a problem for at least 50 years. Some things never change.) When asked, Meredith Hanselman remembered that there was once a stoplight at the corner of Main and Jefferson streets. In 1945, Chester Poe, now marshal, issued a warning to "fire fans" about following fire trucks too closely and speeding to fires. Only members of the fire department were permitted to follow the trucks, using their own vehicles as needed. There had been three narrow escapes involving vehicles speeding after the fire trucks.

Andrews had a new post office in May 1941. It was on Main Street, across from the frame one-story building that had long been home to the post office. The new building was brick, 48 by 23 feet, with 327 individual boxes for Andrews residents. Guy Prilaman, Frank C. Brown, Charles Andrews, Russell Leakey, Klinger and Day, and Burton and Kennedy had constructed the building, with all building supplies coming from the Wasmuth Lumber Company. John Wintrode was the postmaster and Edgar Keefer and Glynn Rudig were the mail carriers. However, the war interfered with John Wintrode's appointment when he entered the Army. His wife, Helen Farhnow Wintrode, was appointed postmaster or postmistress in his place, and she served until John came back from the war.

In May 1941, the library announced that it would be open every afternoon and evening Monday through Saturday, with Miss Betty Boone in charge. These may have been summer hours. The Andrews library board, appointed by Otto H. Krieg of the circuit court, included Mrs. Estella Wolverton, Mrs. Mary Schaefer, and Mrs. Harry Wasmuth. In January 1944 the library received an anonymous gift of 25 books, all of them publications of the Yale University Press. The state library and other libraries in Indiana received similar donations, and apparently the donor remained anonymous. Shortly after this initial gift, Andrews was one of 40 small libraries in Indiana to receive $25 from a bequest by a former Chicago bookseller, Clement V. Ritter. It was decided to buy basic research books with the bequest.

Town elections were held in 1943, but the Democrats didn't name a slate of candidates. Therefore, Walter Collins,

Esser Kitt, and Guy Prilaman would be the trustees, and Arthur Wasmuth would be clerk-treasurer. The Democrats did not make the same mistake in the 1947 election. For positions as town trustees, Myron Jennings, Democrat, defeated Ben Garretson; Edward Reemer, Democrat, defeated Eugene Moore; and Republican Lloyd Heck narrowly defeated Democrat Wilbur Akers. Democrat George Kellam defeated Clyde Wilson in the election for clerk-treasurer.

Although it would be many years before the town's sewage situation was addressed, Moses Shepler was made an example of the problem. He was charged with maintaining a nuisance, because he had ignored demands by both county and state health department officials to clean up a cesspool he maintained on his property.

When the time came for state elections, occasionally a candidate came to Andrews. Richard T. James, running for lieutenant governor, was the main speaker for a rally in October 1944, with the Erie band providing music. A. V. Burch of Evansville, state auditor, appeared at a rally for the Republicans in October 1946. As musical entertainment, an all-girl accordion band, also from Evansville, performed,

In November 1948 things were happening in Andrews partly as a result of collaboration between the town officials and the Lions Club. The town put up new street signs, and the Lions Club installed lights at the new ball diamond, near the school. The Lions Club was interested in helping boost the idea of a sewage system, to improve the overall health of the town. Private disposal methods were not working well, but the expense of a new system seemed overwhelming.

I. M. Wiley, who was in his third (nonconsecutive) term as Dallas Township trustee, resigned his post in February 1949 due to ill health. Ivan McDaniel was appointed in his place. McDaniel was the "M" in the M.C.B. Company, engaged in manufacturing pumps of various kinds. He was also a school "hack" driver and was president of the Andrews Parent Teacher Association.

FACTORIES

After the war, business and life got back to some sort of normal. Kitchen Maid, which had operated all through the war making cabinets for the government, now had a chance to develop new lines of cabinets. One of the new lines, called "Flo-line styling," was designed to harmonize with "modern" appliances. Gould Manor, in Huntington, used these in all of their apartments. The company advertised repeatedly for new employees, including, in 1946, common laborers, machine operators, cabinet builders, finish sanders, trimmers, inspectors, and storeroom attendants. They advertised various benefits, including five 10-hour work days per week; morning and afternoon rest periods; time and a half for overtime; group life, accident, and sickness hospitalization insurance; and even "transportation by city bus line from and to your residence."

In January 1947, Kitchen Maid held an Open House at the plant, and about 400 people attended. During the program, E. M. Wasmuth announced that the company was giving Andrews High School a trophy that would be inscribed each year with the name of the outstanding athlete for the year. Also announced was a $200 college scholarship that would be granted each year to an Andrews High School graduate. Long-term employees were recognized: Frank Willets had started with the company in 1902; Laurence Millman, 1904; C. A. Willets, 1906: Bert Forst, 1909; Leonard Beeks, 1910; Roy Smith, 1911; Oliver Wade, 1914; Evan Bigelow, 1914; Ed Reemer, 1916; Glen Campbell, 1917; Henry Yentes, 1918; and Noah Botkin, 1919. An earlier newspaper article had mentioned a Kitchen Maid recognition of Leonard Beeks's 75th birthday in 1946, so these men didn't believe in early retirement.

An article in the October 15, 1948, *Huntington Herald Press* listed the officers of the business as E. M. Wasmuth, chairman of the board of directors; A. F. Wasmuth, president; R. E. Wasmuth, vice president; H. K. Ware, secretary; J. W. O'Harrow Sr., vice president in charge of sales; and C. E. Brady, treasurer.

E. M. Wasmuth was busy outside of the company, too. He was appointed Huntington County chairman of the national Committee for Economic Development, which was part of a state and national organization that intended to "get every industry in Huntington county to start its own post-war planning for markets, product development, and other factors which will create and sustain continued high levels of employment after the war." The Chamber of Commerce promised its support, but this was still a big job, even for Wasmuth.

Little was heard of Glaze Manufacturing during this time period. It's believed that during the war their primary product was "some kind of military knife." A brief mention in the October 8, 1948, *Huntington Herald Press* stated that the company had been in operation a number of years. They had been producing war materials during the war, but since the war they were manufacturing wristwatch expansion bands, women's bracelets, and other jewelry. It was a small organization compared to the bustle of the earlier years.

OTHER BUSINESSES

Other businesses in Andrews were smaller, and it's hard to tell how successful they might have been from a monetary viewpoint. However, if they kept a family eating, and if the businessmen and -women were contributing to the life of the town, they achieved some degree of success. Some businesses seem to have been respected or respectable, such as the bank and the funeral home, and others were perhaps not as respected but still supported, such as the saloons and bars. They all played a part in the makeup of the town.

The State Bank of Andrews started the decade with total assets of roughly $337,000. Their total liabilities, meaning time and demand deposits, came to about $197,000. Charles Stouder, F. E. Fults, Samuel McKeever, and A. E. Mattern were directors. In 1942 Glynn Rudig, F. E. Fults, and Charles Stouder were directors. In June of that year, Clarence Huffman, who had been cashier of the bank, resigned to take over farming operations that had been the responsibility of his son, who had gone to war. J. D. Debuchananne was named bank cashier. He was new to the Andrews area but had a personal friendship with John Sees, Huntington attorney, and on Sees's recommendation was immediately elected a director of the bank. He had already purchased the interests of several nonresident shareholders in the bank. However it happened, the bank suddenly started growing by leaps and bounds. In June 1942 the total assets had increased to $479,000, with $439,000 in deposits, and in October 1943 the assets were $687,000 with $645,000 on deposit. The board of directors changed, too. At the October 1943 statement, the directors were J. D. Debuchananne, S. E. Ellison, Treva Ellison, and F. E. Fults. By July 1945 the assets had increased to $795,000, with deposits of $747,000. At that time, the board of directors included B. L. Debuchananne, J. D. Debuchananne, S. E. Ellison, Treva Ellison, and Arthur Sapp.

But the bank again changed hands in January 1946; the new owners were K. W. Bellrose of Denver, Colorado, and Claude L. Stout of Idaho Springs, Colorado. In addition to Bellrose and Stout, directors would include Martha Bellrose and Mrs. Stout, and Mrs. Elizabeth Gleason, director and cashier. J. D. Debuchananne had moved to Warsaw to become president of the Citizens State Bank at Milford, where S. E. Ellison had also gone. Mr. Bellrose temporarily moved into a newly constructed apartment on the second floor of the bank building. Both Mr. Bellrose and Stout had been bank examiners in Colorado, so perhaps the town felt comfortable knowing that men with banking knowledge were taking over the bank. If so, their trust was misplaced.

On September 13, 1946, the *Huntington Herald Press* announced that the bank had closed as of Thursday, September 12. The bank would stay open for 60 days to allow depositors to withdraw their deposits, and it was expected that depositors would receive every penny in their accounts. The only reason given for the closure was, "From a permanent investment standpoint present analysis does not indicate future profitable operation of the bank." Perhaps Andrews was left wondering whether due diligence had been done during the previous two bank sales. Perhaps they wondered if the bank could be put up for sale and maintained as a going operation until such time as a sale was final. Perhaps they wondered why the last sale was made, to Colorado investors. It was a sad day for Andrews, I'm sure.

Early in 1940, Forest Bare took over the filling station on Main Street formerly operated by Boyd Hollowell. John Hefner applied for renewal of his liquor permit, for beer sales only. He is listed in the 1941 Polk County directory as the owner of a restaurant, but I've not determined what the name of the business was. The Pohler sandwich shop, located in the building that housed the old opera house, hosted a "chop suey luncheon" as a birthday celebration for Maxine Laymon. Guests were all employees of the office at Kitchen Maid. The sandwich shop, also known as the ice cream shop, was operated by Julius Pohler.

John Gretzinger, who had a dry goods business in Andrews for many years, determined to go out of business in November 1940 and held an auction over the course of three days to dispose of his merchandise, showcases, and sales counters. He had lived in Andrews all his life, had served as clerk-treasurer of the town, had operated this store since a young man, and was probably ready to retire. Fults and Goodrich purchased two rooms in the Taylor building, which meant the Burkhart cafe would have to move. Pauline Burkhart purchased the Krieg room formerly occupied by Pohler Double Dip and moved her restaurant there. At the end of 1941, the Andrews Elevator was purchased by Mel Collier, who had a feed mill in Huntington.

Dr. Roger Ware came to practice medicine in Andrews in 1939, more or less replacing Dr. Clymer. However, he was drafted into the Army in June 1942, and that left Andrews without a physician. Dr. Frybarger had left town in late 1941. Andrews may have been without a physician for about five years, but in April 1946 Dr. Trevelyn W. Omstead came to Andrews. The Lions Club, town trustees, and prominent citizens worked together to bring him to town. Dr. Omstead had graduated from the IU School of Medicine in 1925 and had practiced medicine for 15 years in New York before entering the Army, where he achieved the rank of major. His first office in Andrews was on North Main Street, but many recall a later office on Washington Street.

Hollowell Brothers (Ollie and Boyd) advertised as buyers of hogs, sheep, and cattle. They gave an Andrews phone number (10F14) but it is likely that this business operated out of the home of one or both of them.

Sometimes we only know of businesses because of advertisements that they placed in the *Huntington Herald Press* at county and sectional tourney time, supporting the

110

Andrews Cardinals. In February 1943, five Andrews businesses advertised. Tuckers Restaurant, with no other location given than Andrews, is one. Garretson's Service and Bitzer Standard Station were on two corners of the US 24 and State Road 105 intersection. Fults and Goodrich advertised "General Merchandise," and Schaefer Drug Store also had an advertisement. In 1945 there were changes and deletions to the advertisers. Wasmuth Lumber and Supply, Garretson's Service, the Blue Moon Cafe, S. & S. Garage, Bitzer Standard Station, Fults and Goodrich, Spencer's Home Bakery, Hollowell's Snack Shop, Schaefer Drug Store, and Park Grocery all advertised. "S. & S Garage" was a newcomer, and so far I've uncovered nothing more about them. Were they the same people who advertised as "George and Bill's Garage" in 1946, or were they at least at the same location?

There was a lengthy communication in the April 7, 1944, *Huntington Herald Press*, in which the Union Telephone Company (which included Lagro as well as Andrews) instructed all its customers to begin calling by number and not by name, due to shortages caused by wartime conditions. It appears that one still called the operator, but giving the operator John Doe's number instead of his name made it easier for the operator to make the connection needed. The notice also asked for patrons to be "patient, considerate, and cooperative."

The securities commissioner of the state received the authority in 1943 to hold hearings to remove defunct and nonoperative corporations from the state books. Usually the entity had just quit operating and failed to notify the state. The first round printed in the *Herald Press* included Andrews Cabinet Company, E. R. Colbert; Andrews Equity Exchange company, Adam Schenkel; Andrews Gas & Oil Company, F. E. Fults; and Andrews Home Promotion company, R. O, Bixby. The men named were likely either the president or the secretary of the corporation at the time of last communication with the state.

The Blue Moon Cafe had been open in Andrews for some time, but it announced on December 19, 1944, that it was open under new management. W. H. Gaskill was the "Proprietor." Gaskill must have received a liquor license, because in March 1945 he advertised the grand opening of the "Blue Moon Cafe and Tavern." Fried chicken was available for two hours as part of the celebration. Fried chicken must have been a powerful attraction, because Ralph's Place advertised ½ fried chicken for $1 on Wednesday, October 3, 1945, and the Blue Moon countered three days later with a steak supper served until 2:00 a.m. By 1947 the Blue Moon Cafe (no mention of "tavern") was operated by E. H. Keefer. Ralph's Place frequently offered live entertainment. At various times in the late 1940s, one could hear "Meta at the Solovox," "Evelyn Bragg's Boogie-Woogie," or Eddie Baker and his accordion.

The Solovox was a keyboard attachment to a piano, and when played it added an organ-like sound to the music. It sounds like a cross between an organ and a keyboard. It was all the rage for a time in the late 1940s, in both Andrews and Huntington.

Roy Frushour had a garage business for quite some time, but he was also the "Frushour" of "Frushour's Sales and Service." He began dealing in appliances and in 1946 was advertising an interesting appliance. It was a combination home freezer-refrigerator, with nine cubic feet of food freezer and one and one-half cubic feet of refrigerator. It also included nine inches of insulation. Later he was a Philco dealer, advertising "Philco Table and Console Combinations, Philco, Coolerator, and Deep Freeze Home Freezers, Gas Ranges, Premier Sweepers and Washers, Gas, Oil and Electric Water Heaters, with Terms If Desired." At the end 1949, he held an auction to close his business, as he had decided to go to Florida. He had earned that opportunity.

The 1946 school yearbook, *Cardinal Echoes*, gives a pretty fair depiction of businesses in Andrews that were prosperous or supportive enough to place an advertisement in the yearbook. Kitchen Maid had a full-page ad, of course. Other Andrews advertisers were Mel Collier of the Andrews Elevator; Roy Frushour, advertising appliances; Gene Wilson, "Your City Service Dealer"; Park Home Store; Schenkel's Sanitary Dairy (I believe this was a Huntington business, but they also listed an Andrews phone number); Zimmerman Mortuary (also advertised ambulance day and night); Earl E. Ellet (plumbing, heating, electric wiring); Fults and Goodrich Grocery; Garretson's Service Station; the State Bank of Andrews; Wasmuth Lumber and Supply Company; George and Bill's Garage; Schaefer's Drug Store; North End Grocery (Ethel Stevens); Bitzer's Standard Station (L. J. Bitzer); Crull Pump; Home Bakery of Andrews; J. R. Small Company (coal and coke); Ralph's Place (short orders and sandwiches); Snyder's Cities Service Station; Dr. R. J. Coss, Dentist; Russell Leakey (plumbing, heating, and electric contractor); Edgar Keefer Greenhouses; Ollie's Snack Shop; Burkhart's Cafe; James Russell (not sure of his business; he may have been a school booster only); Andrews Beauty Shop; Breeding's Barber Shop; and Frank Brown, a manufacturer of concrete.

The Texaco station on Main Street changed hands in 1947, or at least the management changed. Severin Hoffman thanked readers for their past patronage and said the station was open for business under new management. A 1947 ad now listed it as "Burkart's Texaco Service." Soon the Max and Dick Cities Service Station, at the north end of Andrews, was under new management, with all new and modern equipment. Brothers Dick and Max Close were the proprietors. Garretson's Service Station, at the junction of

US 24 and State Road 105, closed, because they lost their lease. Sometimes the business scene must have seemed like a revolving door, or does it only look like that from a distance?

A new company was formed in Andrews in January 1947, the "Antioch Machine and Tool Company," with principal offices in Andrews. The incorporators were Maurice F. Smith, Mark C. Riseborough, and Joseph H. Lesh. Joining them as directors were Harry Jacoby and Samuel Wasmuth. The company expected to own and operate a machine shop or shops "and transact any other kind of business." (MCB Manufacturing Company was formed about the same time, and will be mentioned further in chapter 6.)

Clyde Wilson, who was listed as cashier of the bank in 1941, owned the Andrews Feed Store by 1947. This was the building on Main Street that later became the town building, where the fire station, the police station, and a meeting room shared close quarters. Also in the same 1947 "We're rooting for you Cardinals" group of advertisements is one for "Frank's Grocery," which sold groceries, meats, produce, and notions.

Sometimes businesses failed due to lack of capital, sometimes due to changes in the economy, and sometimes due to partners' difficulties in getting along. Charles C. Wintrode and H. G. Williams formed a partnership in November 1945, known as the Acme Rafter Company. Sixteen months later, Wintrode sued to have the partnership dissolved. He felt that he had invested more than Williams had, and asked for an accounting of the books, which Williams kept. This is the only reference I found to this particular company, and it's a reminder that there may have been other businesses in Andrews of which we know nothing. If they didn't advertise, and they complied with all the laws regarding taxes and record-keeping, a business could come and go, leaving no trace to be found 50 to 100 years later.

A business that received little publicity but that had been in business since the 1920s was the Keefer greenhouse. Not everyone remembers that the greenhouse also had a three-acre apple orchard located just next to the school. The *Fort Wayne News Sentinel*, on January 4, 1947, published a short article highlighting the "deal" the Keefers worked out with the schoolchildren. They kept a bushel of apples at the disposal of schoolchildren, who were allowed to take two apples a day. The Keefers agreed to continue this tradition with the understanding that there would be no "raiding" of the apple orchard, where they grew 10 or 11 different varieties.

John Chronister was almost always to be found at his shop, as had been the case for 50 years when the *Huntington Herald Press* interviewed him May 26, 1949. He had a harness and shoe repair shop in Andrews for 50 years, so had come to town just before the end of the 19th century, and he also ran a sporting-goods store that featured fishing tackle. At the time of the interview, Chronister was 83 years young, and going strong.

One last business changed hands in the late 1940s. Charles. Zimmerman, the funeral home director, died suddenly. The family kept the business going until it was sold to the Metz family.

SCHOOL

School life continued to be busy, during the war and after. There were 13 graduates in 1940, several of whom have been mentioned already in connection with the war. John Lewis Bickel, Ross Thomas Clark, Lucinda Mae Cook, Foster M. Cross, Geneva Opal Dille, Louis Edward Haley, J. Forrest Luker, George Harold Robison, George William

Stallings, Rose Mary Stephan, Phyllis June Warfel, Margaret Ann Wasmuth, and Marcella Marie Welch graduated with one eye on the war already waging in Europe, and the other on a normal future. For some, the future would be much different than they thought, and for many, it was a future delayed. In the meantime, there were a senior play and a junior-senior reception to enjoy.

More landscaping was done at the school in 1940. High school students provided most of the labor, but several parents were involved in hauling black dirt to be used in the planting of trees. Three trees were planted on the first workday, and about 50 more were expected to be planted as soon as they arrived.

Teachers for the 1940-41 school year were Carl Stephens, principal; Dean Snider, coach; Donald Galey, band; and Don Butt, Fern Jackson, Josephine Miller, Helen Pugh, Richard Shaw, Clyde Thompson, Ruth A. Ellerman, Pauline Schmalzried, Doris Benton, and Lucile Lewis. However, the opening of school was delayed for two weeks (as well as church meetings and all public gatherings) due to a case of infantile paralysis. The general public had requested the delay.

One fun and educational event that may or may not have been a tradition and may or may not have been repeated, was a train trip to Detroit taken by 52 Andrews students and seven teachers. During the course of the day, they visited Ford's River Rouge Plant; Edison's Institute; Greenfield Village; Belle Isle; Windsor, Canada; and the WJR radio broadcasting station. Probably the students slept on their way home! Another event that seems to have been a tradition but was not previously mentioned in the newspapers was an "annual fall frolic," held by the seniors in November 1940. Games and dancing furnished the entertainment, although there is no mention of the music provided.

116

Eiffel Plasterer, who had some fame in Huntington County and beyond, presented his "Bubbles Concerto" at the school under the sponsorship of the Andrews Parent-Teacher organization. This may have been a fund-raiser.

Members of the cast for the junior class play, presented on April 4, 1941, were David Wasmuth, Betty Lee Fults, Ruth Ellen Ellison, Eugene Smith, Ned Keefer, Keith Burkhart, Ruth Knight, Mabel King, Annetta Pinkerton, Lawrence Leakey, and Meredith Hanselman.

The 1941 class of high school graduates numbered 19, including, again, several who would serve in the armed forces during the next years. June Flora, Mary Forst, Esther Garrison, Richard Hefner, Clarence McDaniel, Harry Manson, Martha Mundy, Annabel Robb, James Roberts, Janice Roberts, Mary Margaret Rudig, Raymond Satchwill, Richard Schenkel, Devota Scott, Rex Smuts, Thelma Way, Elizabeth Wilkinson, James Wintrode, and H. Glenn Kennedy made up the last peacetime class at Andrews. The 1942 class graduated 17 students, and in 1943, there were 19 graduates. By now, the students knew that many of them would soon be going to war.

For the 1943-44 school year, there were many changes in faculty. Lloyd Austill was now the principal, with Mrs. Lloyd Austill, Ruth Mohler, Beulah Cline, June McCreary, Dean Snider, and Donald Galey teaching the upper grades and Elaine Fisher, Kathryn Wade, Doris Walton, Mary Lyons, and Luella Lewis teaching the lower grades. Each of these teachers had classes including two grades, so it appears that the students may have been divided somewhat by ability. Of course, there could have been other reasons also, such as enrollment in each grade, but it is certainly different from what one would find in the schools today.

The April 1944 school play was actually put on by the junior and senior English students. The play was *My Wife's Family*, and the cast included Roger Leakey, Betty Reemer,

John Goebel, Mae Stephan, Joan Flora, Gale Eller, Mary Haley, Joan Slagle, William Wasmuth, Helen Stensil, and Fred Warfel.

An intriguing experiment was conducted in the 1944-45 school year in Huntington County, and Andrews Hhigh School was the first to participate. Schools established a student traffic and safety court, with three teachers and six students, all elected by the student body, in charge. Members of the court were briefly trained by the county prosecutor and the county clerk as to how to proceed with the legal technicalities. Reading between the lines, students who exhibited bad driving, or who actually broke traffic laws, could be taken before the school court rather than the usual traffic court in Huntington. It's not clear whether the student court had the authority to dismiss charges, or to impose a penalty other than what was required by law. It did, however, give students who served in the program a chance to learn about the court and how it worked. The program was sponsored by the Exchange Club; its degree of success and duration is not known.

The 1945 senior class play was *The Mummy and the Mumps*. Bill Wasmuth, John Goebel, Roger Leakey, Joe Clark, Herbert Satchwill, Joan Slagle, Bill Snyder, Doris Scott, Mary Haley, and Wilma Dean Snyder made up the cast. There were 13 graduates in 1945.

It had been a five-year tradition for the Andrews High School band to combine with Clear Creek and Warren township bands for opening night at the 4-H Fair in Huntington. The August 1945 joint performance was possibly the last, as Donald Galey, the Andrews band director who had spearheaded this tradition, was leaving to take a position as principal elsewhere. Band members from Andrews were Elizabeth Warschko, Suzanne Miltonberger, Enid Rudig, Pat Hetter, Joan Russel, Barbara Snyder, Esther Van Meter, Miriam Smith, Edwin Goodrich, Norman Krile,

Jay Kitt, Norma Bricker, Mary Yentes, Alice Forst, Frederick Warfel, Charles Miltonberger, Richard Klotz, Mark Anson, and Joe Brumbaugh.

The 14 graduates of the class of 1946 had a different kind of world ahead of them. Men had less chance of entering the armed forces, unless they wanted to sign up. Women didn't necessarily go directly to the work world, or to postgraduate training. They could, if they chose, marry young and plan on being a homemaker, although those plans didn't necessarily work out. Choices were open to everyone that had not been so obvious the previous year.

The school faculty for the start of the 1946-47 school year changed significantly. Whether or not this was part of the postwar changes, we can only wonder. The principal was O. C. Beitelshees, with Laverne Hollowell, Helen Hunter, James Hughes (new coach), a vacancy yet to be filled, and, in the lower grades, Elaine Fisher, Cathlyn Wade, Bernice Fulton, Gertrude Peting Goebels, Doris Walton, and Mary Lyons.

Perhaps the handwriting was on the wall as early as 1947 regarding school reorganization or consolidation. The state passed a law granting permissive "county consolidation," and a hearing was set by the county board of education and the county school superintendent. A public hearing was held to consider the question, "Shall the provisions of Chapter 231 of the acts of 1947 concerning the creation of a county school corporation and county board of education be made effective in Huntington County?" It was to be discussed at a public meeting that included the township trustees of all twelve townships and the county school superintendent, with input from the public. The board would listen to the discussion and take the matter "under advisement" for several months, the *Huntington Herald Press* reported on March 23, 1947.

The Andrews Lions, always willing and eager to help the town solve its challenges, heard a proposal by J. Frank Stouder to have four school districts in the county, with high schools at Warren, Roanoke, Andrews, and Huntington Township. He advocated for this plan in some form for several years, but 1947 seems to be the first time it was presented publicly. The Andrews Parent Teacher Association heard Dr. T. W. Omstead present a program regarding what a well-rounded curriculum should include, and at the same meeting, it was voted to ask the county board of education to delay a final vote on their plan, "pending further discussion." In retrospect, it appears that this war had already been lost. The county was already well on its way to making a one-high-school decision for the county, and the best that Andrews, and the other small towns, could do was to fight with delaying tactics.

Nevertheless, school life continued. The seniors in 1947 presented their play, *Galloping Ghosts*, on April 11, with baccalaureate on April 20 and commencement on April 24. It must have been a busy month for these student-graduates!

The faculty for the 1947-48 school year changed yet again. O. W. Beitelshees was the principal and also taught social science studies, Maurice F. Durfee was the band instructor, Mary Helen Fast taught English and physical education, Rex Hunter taught commerce and science, and Ersell Leakey taught mathematics and Latin.

The school building was only about 18 years old, but already problems were developing. The school had to be closed for a day in November 1947 because of several leaks in the furnace flues. The heating system proved a challenge for the maintenance men all through the history of that building, I'm told.

The cast of the 1948 senior class play included Glenna Campbell, Jean Ann Percell, Enid Rudig, Anna Garrison,

Mark Anson, Norman Beeks, JoAnn Russell, and David Boone. They presented *Here Goes the Groom*, which was a "royalty play," according to the *Herald Press* of March 31. The cast was small, probably because it was in competition with the Andrews Chorus play. It appears that most if not all of the seniors were in one play or another, and a few were in both. Additional seniors that year were Joanna Bare, Max Botkin, Patricia Heater, Evelyn Miller, Irene Millican, Patricia Poehler, Orville Rupel, Charles Snyder, and Norma Bricker. I would imagine there might have been a bit of grousing among the students, because this is the first year I can find when the class did not graduate until May. It's true that the date was May 1, but most classes had graduated in late April, so this may have been an indication that more school days were being added to the calendar.

The saga of the frame addition to the school building began in 1948. Dallas Township put in a successful bid for two surplus buildings at a sale conducted by the war-assets administration. The sale was at Baer Field, but it's believed the buildings may actually have come from Camp Atterbury in southern Indiana. The successful bid for the two buildings was $67, and they were valued at $1,340. The catch? The buildings had to be dismantled, moved, and re-erected. Fortunately, the Andrews Lions Club agreed to do this. Eventually, the addition would house a school cafeteria, a music room, and some small offices, but it took some time to actually get the addition dismantled, moved, and then erected and adapted for use.

The 1949 senior play was presented in November 1948 rather than the traditional month of April. The play, directed by Mrs. Ruth Stookey, was *It's Papa Who Pays*. The list of actors included Richard Fields, Charles Garrison, Rosemarie Goodrich, Miriam Smith, Dick Quinn, Barbara Douglas, Phillip Keefer, Doris Smuts, Bonnie Scott, Drake Omstead, and Jim Haley.

Maurice Durfee was the band director at Andrews, and he also played in the North Manchester Civic and Manchester College Symphony Orchestra. He was able to use his influence to persuade the group to come to Andrews to put on a benefit concert, with the proceeds going to help purchase uniforms for the Andrews High School band. This was a 55-member orchestra, so was a step above what the town was used to hearing from the school band, and it appears that the concert was well attended and well received. Mr. Durfee was given the honor of conducting the last song, "Stars and Stripes Forever," and I can hear the crowd now. They must have loved that!

Mr. Durfee must have been well liked by his students. The *Huntington Herald Press* published a letter to the editor on March 30, 1949 as follows:

We as band members would like to express our thoughts of Andrews High School.

First, Mr. Durfee is the best band director we have had and if he resigns our band will go back to wreck and ruin.

Second, we would like to use one school bus on Monday to go to Bippus to practice for a contest. When we got ready to go they said we couldn't use the bus. What is a school bus for if it isn't for the school kids.

Some of the band members were going to walk to Bippus. Do you suppose we'll have to walk to Hartford City?

Our band has done more and gone further than ever before since Mr. Durfee has been our director.

We band members think pretty much of him.

The town is always wishing to get something started.
Well, if they would let us use the bus maybe we
could.

From the Band Members of Andrews High School.

Reading between the lines, one can assume that use of
the school buses was not permitted for extracurricular
activities. We know there were earlier examples (debate
club going to Wabash, for instance) when it had been
permitted, so one wonders what caused the change in
protocol, and how long it lasted.

April 1949 was a busy month for the students. Besides
baccalaureate and commencement, there were an all-school
program, a reception for the members of the basketball
team, the junior-senior reception, a junior class play, a
senior variety show, and a Good Friday observance at the
Methodist Church, planned for the school and the
community. The junior-senior reception was held at the
Hotel LaFontaine in Huntington. This is the first mention I
found of it in several years, but I don't know whether the
tradition had been dropped and then picked up again, or
whether it had actually continued all along and just didn't
get mentioned in the newspaper.

Graduates for the last year of the decade were Barbara
Douglas, Richard Fields, Loretta Fisher, Charles Garrison,
Dorothea Garrison, Rosemarie Goodrich, James Haley, Joan
Haley, Phillip Keefer, Jannetta Kelly, Norma Krile Kitt,
Drake Omstead, Richard Quinn, Bonnie Scott, Miriam
Smith, and Doris Smuts.

Other big school news of 1949 included the first
tentative steps toward merging the Dallas and Polk
Township School Districts. Petitions calling for an election
to vote on the matter were circulated, and public meetings
were held in both Andrews and Monument City to discuss
the proposal. Although it appears that the law was clear that

the election needed to be held within 60 days, the county commissioners overruled that and postponed the election until the spring of 1950, citing the cost of holding a separate election versus the cost of adding a question to the ballot of an already scheduled election.

After the school term was concluded, use of the school building continued. The PTA sponsored a "home talent variety show" to raise money for the school building fund. Among the performers were Marjorie Bitzer, Bob Spencer, Mary Lyons, J. D. Miller, Carrie Goebel, James Hughes, and Claude Garrison, with others who presented special musical numbers.

The Dallas Township Home Economics club was doing their part for the school, too. In August 1949, they announced that the outdoor ovens were ready for use at the school, and tables had been installed. There was a hierarchy as to who was to get priority in holding events there, as well as rules for behavior at the site and for cleaning up afterward. We might call the "ovens" outdoor fireplaces, and it's not known how many there were. Apparently the school site was being used somewhat as a town park, also, since there was no park at this time in Andrews. The ovens and tables were in operation for only a very few years, and few people now remember them.

Despite a polio scare, schools opened on time in 1949. The school enrollment must have been increasing, because the seventh-grade class had a wiener roast at the school, and 40 students were in attendance. That class, the class of 1955, later graduated 25 students, so there was a high attrition (dropout?) rate. This may reflect a rise and fall in factory jobs in Andrews, early marriage, or any number of other factors, but it's intriguing. What happened to those other 15 students?

The comments of the band students about how much they liked Mr. Durfee may have fallen on deaf ears, because by 1949 a new band director was in place. His "debut" seems to have been the Christmas program put on by the whole school, when the band performed several numbers. The rest of the program consisted of a Christmas pageant, depicting the Nativity. There were parts for 39 people, and the rest of the school was part of one or another of the choirs. In addition to the high school choir, the girls' glee club and girls' chorus also presented numbers, but it seems that there were no boys' groups, at least not during this school year.

CHURCHES

Of course Andrews still received the benefits of having active churches, lodges, civic groups, and youth groups, each of which added to town life. The four churches were the Methodist Episcopal, the Christian, the "United Brethren" (probably an error for "Brethren Church"), and the Pilgrim Holiness.

The Pilgrim Holiness congregation first met in a building that looked more like a storefront, on the southwest corner of Madison and Main streets. The congregation dedicated their parsonage in 1948 and their new church in 1949. These were both located on Madison Street, between Main and Snowden streets, and both were recently demolished. The Andrews church was erected from materials from the dismantled Pilgrim Holiness Church at LaFontaine. The Andrews church added a full basement, a vestibule, and a belfry, and the main auditorium was 60 by 45 feet in size. Members and friends of the church donated most of the labor for the construction project.

One church in Andrews receives only a single brief mention during the 1940s. On February 1, 1948, Richard J. Meredith, a representative of Watch Tower, gave a public address at "Kingdom Hall," at the corner Jefferson and Snowden. This may have been the former Knights of the Pythias building. I've not been able to locate anything additional about this group, and it's believed that if they were ever a "going" church, they did not stay in Andrews for long.

Each church had their own programs and services, but they also cooperated in many ways. For instance, the Methodist Church, the Christian Church, and businessmen of the community presented three showings of the motion picture *Golgotha*. This was an entertaining movie but also told the story of Christ's Passion. A French film featuring a cast of 6,000, it was the first "talking" moving picture that depicted Jesus. Admission was charged, but discount tickets were available from the merchants in town. Another joint project, sponsored by all four churches, began in 1949: bus service to all the Sunday schools, for a payment of five cents. This meant that children and older people, as well as those adults for whom transportation was a challenge, now had little excuse for missing services. The churches also offered annual vacation Bible schools on a joint basis. In 1949 the average attendance was about 145 for the two-week school, with 25 to 28 teachers and three pastors assisting.

Children of each church usually presented at least one play or program annually. In 1946 the participants at the Christian Church were Frank C. Huston, Laura Ellen Sharp, Carolyn McBride, Diann Moore, Shirley Small, Billy Jones, Susan Clements, Leon Smith, Linda Garrison, Deanna McBride, Jon Kellam, Patty Dickson, Hollis Millman, Jane Woodward, Bobby Kellam, Colleen Reemer, Peggy Smuts, Barbara Beeks, Sharon Sandlin, Frances Jones, Pauline Garrison, Shelbylynn Millman, Carolyn Fields, Lois Dickson, Janet Bare, Marcia Reemer, Richard Klotz, Kathy Kellam, Bobby Kellam, Bobby Reemer, Marilyn Woodward, Bonnie Beeks, Jerry Kellam, Ann Kellam, Norma Cocklin,

Donna Smuts, Zane Pegg, Earl Pegg, Donald Beeks, Shirley Garrison, Joan Garrison, Linda Pressler, Faith Smith, Carol Small, and Lura Williams.

The program put on by the Pilgrim Holiness Church in 1947 included pieces by Sharon Glass, Mary Pegg, Wilma Miller, John Penn, Shirley Glass, Ruth Ellen Pegg, Edith Ruth Everroad, James Pegg, George Hodson, Frances Glass, Charles Penn, David Pearson, Billy Joe Smith, Charlotte Glass, Charles Penn, Charles Pearson, Janice Hamman, Raymond Quakenbush, Sharon Pearson, Evangeline Hamman, Shirley Owen, Jean Everroad, Peggy Everroad, Rosemary Quakenbush, Norma Owen, and Erma Pearson.

The 1949 Church of the Brethren Christmas program included as participants Terry Plasterer, Teddy Chapman, Sandra Dinius, Tommy Plasterer, Angela Garrison, Linda Oswalt, Sam Quinn, Sally Huston, Johnny Wayne Chapman, Larry Quinn, Virginia Chapman, Garry Tuggle, May Quinn, Jay Dee Rittenhouse, Sharon Dinius, Walter Tuggle, Mary Lee Sands, Anna Mae Crull, Tom McDavid, Donna Tuggle, Carol Young, Patty Sands, Carolyn Bigelow, Sandra McDaniel, Tom McDaniel, and Henry Crull.

LODGES AND CLUBS

Lodges typically kept their good works secret, so we don't know what they accomplished for the town. Their members were active in town affairs whether or not they accomplished anything that they could point to as "their project." A chorus named "The Gleaners," from the Andrews Chapter of the Eastern Star, sang several selections at the Indiana Grand Chapter session in April 1949. The chorus included Mrs. Lindel Buckles, Mrs. Mary Clements, Mrs. Lena Bailey, Mrs. Docia Predmore, Mrs. Elizabeth Moore, Mrs. Lucille Fulton, and Mrs. Floris Keefer. The Rebekahs had a district meeting in LaFontaine about the same time. The Past Matrons Club still met regularly as well, but this may have been more of a social occasion. The Masonic Lodge and the IOOF were active, also.

Whether or not the war had any bearing on the formation of a new club, the Thea (probably meant to be "Theta") Rho Girls Club was started, sponsored by the IOOF and Rebekah lodges. The club was instituted at Andrews and, at least at first, was meant to include girls from Huntington and Wabash counties. Two years later, the Iris Theta Rho club of Andrews had a mother-daughter banquet to celebrate the second anniversary of the club's formation. Girls present were Nancy Oswalt, Bettie Millican, Irene Millican, Wilma Wright, Mary Theobald, Doris Tuggle, Kathryn Lease, Estella Kelly, Jannetta Kelly, Norma Krile, Gloria Krile, and a visitor, Joanna Bare.

The Andrews chapter No. 189, Order of the Eastern Star, celebrated their golden anniversary in November 1946. They had been operating as a lodge since 1896. There were about 150 people present for the celebration, including representatives from other lodges in Fort Wayne, Markle, Warren, Columbia City, Roanoke, Lagro, Bluffton, Huntington, and South Whitley. At the close of the decade, in 1949, the members included Mrs. Lena Bailey, Mrs. Lindel Buckles, Mrs. Pauline Wilson, Mrs. Nina Cleaver, Mrs. Mary Clements, Mrs. Kay Omstead, Mrs. Adia Schoolman, Mrs. Merle Paul, Mrs. Elenor Notter, and Loretta Everhart.

A list of the past masters of Antioch Lodge Number 410, F. & A.M was published as part of a retrospective article in the August 23, 1948, issue of the *Herald Press*. Names on the list of those who served at various times from 1916 to 1948, included David Alpaugh, Howard Warfel, Charles Keefer, Bruce Glaze, Robert Weber, Harry Wasmuth, Lewis Pratt, James Haley, Arnold Spencer, Samuel Ellison, Dorrence Cross, Edward Cleaver, Clayton Wagner, Samuel Wasmuth,

Andrew Krumanaker, Chauncey Theobald, Huel Goodrich, Edgar Keefer, and Russel Leakey.

For the youth, there were Boy Scout and Girl Scout troops and 4-H clubs, all designed to teach as well as provide entertainment. The 4-H clubs displayed their projects, including their animals, at the 4-H Fair in Huntington. I was surprised to learn that many of the "farm kids" didn't participate in 4-H. They lived too far away from the meeting place (frequently the school or the library), and the only means of transportation was often with Dad, but he would have been at work when the meetings occurred. The same is likely true for Boy Scout and Girl Scout troops. There was a bit of a cultural divide between town and country, it seems. The troops had camporees and activities designed to help them earn badges to recognize successful completion of a series of assigned tasks or projects. Boys and girls alike enjoyed earning these badges.

The Dallas Township Home Ec Club was still meeting regularly, as was the Library Club. An article in the January 23, 1948, issue of the *Huntington Herald Press* listed 37 members of the Home Ec Club in attendance at one of the meetings, so it's no wonder that this group was able to get ovens and tables installed at the school.

And finally, there was the Lions Club. It was chartered in 1939, its members of course not realizing that the war was coming. In 1940 the club sponsored a soapbox derby in conjunction with a carnival in July. The derby was held on "Theobald Hill" on State Road 105, a half-mile south of Andrews, and was open to boys ages 12-15.

The Lions Club also sponsored a Halloween contest, with several prizes for adults as well as children. By now, this was considered an "annual affair," and over 1,000 people attended the event and enjoyed free sandwiches. Then, there is a silence of about five years regarding the Lions Club. We don't know whether it continued in existence or whether it couldn't continue as members went off to war and those left behind had other duties in the war effort. Current members of the club say the charter dates to 1945, so probably the club folded and then reorganized. The first event we learn of from the newspaper was again a Halloween party in October 1946. This year, the merchants contributed prizes for various categories. Some sound hilarious, but others make us shake our heads, as prizes were to be awarded for "best Negro mammy" in the adult section and "best Negro mammy child" in the children's class. I didn't find a report of the prize winners for that year.

The Lions Club sponsored a valentine dance in 1947, held at the town hall, and they also were in charge of a three-day carnival and street fair September 4-6 in Andrews. Little information is given about the carnival rides, but there were three days of contests, mostly for children and youth. These were the typical pie-eating, greased-pole type contests we all have read about, and maybe even watched or participated in. There was also a beauty contest and a band concert. Mary Lou Fisher and Mary Edith McDaniel were beauty prize winners.

In March 1948 the club was busy preparing for a fish fry to be held at the school building. There would be a special program with a talk by E. E. "Abe" Andrews, who was a former newspaper editor and a radio commentator on outdoor life. Money raised by the dinner would go toward purchasing floodlights for the baseball diamond. Those lights at the ball diamond must have been expensive, because in June 1948 the Lions Club promised a "stupendous, side splitting, singing and dancing production of 'The Big Baby Revue'" at the high school. It featured all local performers, including Arnold Spencer, Mr. Fults, Ben Garretson, Rev. Donald Blake, Frank Bomersback, Gene Wilson, and Basil Metz. Each man portrayed a female character known to town members, such as Gypsy Rose Lee, Mae West, and Sally Rand. We can only imagine! Admission was 60 cents for adults and 30 cents for children.

The Lions Club took on a large project when they agreed to bring the surplus Army buildings the township had purchased back to Andrews from Baer Field . It took time to get everything organized, and in the meanwhile, during that time, thieves were stealing material from inside the buildings. The move was finally made in August 1948, with the intent to build a shop, a music room, and a home economics room with the buildings. The walls and roofs had to be sawn into lengths that could be transported on a truck operated by Lawrence Geiger. Erection of the building would be completed when the foundations were installed and steam lines were placed to hook up to radiators that were purchased as part of the buildings. I'm not sure that this refers to the same buildings, but the Lions held a fund-raiser with profits to go toward the "community building at the Andrews school" in December 1948. It was called a "Skru-ball game" and was played with three-wheel bicycles, each holding two persons. Apparently one person pedaled and the other rode on a platform and presumably made and blocked shots, passed the ball, and in general acted as the "player."

The final big event of the decade for the Lions Club was the Andrews Halloween party. There was a contest for most popular girl, with the outcome that Janis Tullis was crowned "Queen of Andrews." Other participants were Bonnie Beeks, Joan Bare, Barbara Burkhart, Carol Niblick, and Betty Satchwill. This was apparently the first, but not the last, Halloween party providing refreshments of cider and doughnuts. (Someone probably got tired from making over 1,000 sandwiches for this event!)

CRIMES

The stack of newspapers about crimes and criminals during the 1940s is quite large compared to those for the previous decades. Some crimes were connected with alcohol, and many of the incidents involved automobiles, in one form or another. Don Sellers continued his string of arrests on drunkenness charges in Huntington County, reaching at least a dozen such charges. It seems that he was well-liked, and he generally received light sentences of no more than six months at a time. He was even brought back from the state farm at Putnamville so that he could attend funeral services for his brother, Orph. The sheriff brought him to Huntington and took him back to the state farm, and he was required to be in the jail overnight. But in 1942, there was yet another arrest after Sellers had walked away from a job supervised by the sheriff. I'm not sure whether he was on a work crew from the jail or whether the sheriff was trying to give him a break by giving him a job. Either way, he ended up back at the state farm, with a six-month sentence plus fines and costs that would likely extend his sentence. He was sentenced in August 1942, served his time, and was arrested again in April 1943.

Frank Huston was the victim of some sort of crime in January 1940. Apparently his wife was drugged and then a dresser drawer was opened and about $35 taken from the hiding spot. Mrs. Huston said a man had given her a glass of "colored" water and that seemed to be the last thing she really remembered. (Mrs. Huston was already ill at the time.) This event became more mysterious when most of the money was returned to the Hustons by being shoved through a partly opened window. Speculation was that the guilty party thought that because part of the money was returned, if he or she was caught the charges would be more lenient since the total amount stolen was now less than $10.

Three Huntington County men were arrested in September 1941 on charges of possessing a slot machine. The Andrews man was Ernest Toerpel, operator of John Hefner's tavern in Andrews. State officers had operated the machine and won a prize, and then the arrest was made, along with confiscation of the machine. The machine was ordered destroyed, and the money within was turned over to the court. Toerpel was fined a total of about $60, including costs.

Wayne Chapman was one of three men who were jailed at the Andrews jail for several hours on July 29, 1942. They each needed to raise about $14 in fines and costs before being released. The two younger men were from Lagro, where Chapman, a former Andrews resident, also now lived. A fourth man, the driver of the car, was in more serious trouble, for driving away from the scene where he had been stopped, driving while intoxicated and driving without a license. Chapman might have been let off easier had he not threatened to "put the marshal in his place" when he was pulled from the car.

An episode involving public intoxication and assault and battery by a Huntington resident occurred at the home of Mrs. Helena Kuchel (Kuschel?) in May 1943. Afterward, Marshal Chester Poe announced that visitors from Huntington and other places were welcome in Andrews so long as they conducted themselves well, but that he would be quick to arrest anyone for any further disturbances of this type.

Paul Warschko had the misfortune to have his car stolen from his farm, but the car was eventually recovered in Oklahoma. The four thieves managed to make it that far because gas ration tickets were found in the car. Warschko planned to go to Oklahoma to recover the vehicle.

However, this was wartime (1944) and his gas tickets were gone. I wonder where he found more, in order to get the vehicle home. The youths were named in the article, but I'm not sure they were area residents.

Donald Malone, an Andrews resident, was in trouble with the law not once, but twice. First he was arrested in Fayette County, Indiana, on charges of defrauding a Connersville man of several hundred dollars in some sort of "termite racket." He was released on bond there and came to Huntington County, where he somehow persuaded Wilson King, formerly of Andrews but now of Markle, to loan him $200. Malone in turn gave King a bad check for $300 and the title to his automobile. When the Kings came to Andrews to get the title, Mrs. Malone was at work, so a young woman who was working for the couple forged Mrs. Malone's signature. That earned her a trip to the county jail. It took a few minutes for the authorities to locate Malone, because he had used a dresser to reach a trapdoor leading to the attic. He was found in a corner of the attic, apparently reluctant to be caught again. He was in more trouble than he'd bargained for. He received four months at the state farm for the charges in Connersville, which were tried first. Huntington County authorities were tying to decide whether to have him brought back to face the Huntington County charges.

Chester Poe had a run-in with Morris Sandlin at a restaurant in Andrews in May 1945. The marshal had put Sandlin and Mrs. Sandlin in their car and told them to "go home." Sandlin stated that he would, but that he was coming back with a gun, and that is just what he did. He entered the Blue Moon Cafe with a fully loaded .41 caliber revolver, and other patrons of the establishment weren't comfortable with his behavior. He was "entertained" while someone slipped away to call the sheriff. It took the sheriff and several other men to disarm and subdue Sandlin, He was charged only with disorderly conduct. It is interesting that the newspaper saw fit to say of Sandlin that he was a "former resident of Kentucky."

There were other incidents in the taverns, usually resulting in disorderly conduct or public drunkenness charges, but there were incidents in other parts of Andrews, too. For instance, a man from Wabash who was estranged from his wife came to Andrews, where his wife worked. There were two other persons in the vehicle from Wabash, but their involvement isn't clear. What is clear is that the wife, having spoken to her husband, turned away, apparently to go back to her job. He then grabbed her by the head, and when the sheriff arrived, he was bumping the head of his wife against the automobile. For this, the man was charged with assault and battery and had to pay $10 in fines, plus costs. Laws and cultural mores have changed since 1946.

Bruce Millican was reported to be an Andrews resident when he was charged with entering a home in Huntington to commit a felony. The charges could have been worse, since his landlady found clothes and furs, belonging to a recently burglarized couple, in a suitcase belonging to Millican. He was apparently trying to raise money to pay back support to his former wife, who lived in the Akron, Ohio, area. Millican was born in Wabash County, but his family had moved to Akron when he was a boy. It's not clear why he had returned to Andrews to live. At any rate, the charge here resulted in a 1-to-10-year sentence at the Pendleton Reformatory, and the former Mrs. Millican could expect no further child support.

Sometimes boys will be boys, but in the wrong place at the wrong time doing wrong things. Three young men, Paul Evans, Morris Wade, and an unnamed juvenile, broke into the school on at least two occasions. On one (or more) of those occasions, one of them rode a motor scooter all over the newly refinished gym floor, ruining the finish and leaving a gouge in the floor. The young men paid for the damage and then were fined $5 plus $13 in costs, each. Justice of the Peace F. A. Kelley told them he could take their money away faster than they could make it, and told them to stay away from school property. Evans failed to learn his lesson from this experience, and shortly after the school incident, he quit his job at Kitchen Maid in Andrews. Perhaps he still had access to truck keys, or he knew where they were located, because he stole one of the Kitchen Maid trucks and ended up in jail in Lima, Ohio, after being stopped for a traffic violation. He had also been questioned in Fort Wayne for "loitering" but was released there. It should be noted that Morris Wade did learn his lesson and put that unfortunate incident behind him. He served in the US Air Force and retired as a Master Sergeant.

The school wasn't the only building in Andrews that was a target of break-ins. The railroad station also was a frequent target. It was hit again in 1948, when the messenger box containing about $100 and railroad papers were stolen. A few days later, the messenger box was found in the Wabash River. The money was missing, but some of the railroad's records were saved. When that burglary was solved, the juveniles involved also confessed to a burglary at the Fults and Goodrich grocery three months earlier, and to a recent theft of two steers from a farm south of Andrews.

It may have been other juveniles who were responsible for stealing bulbs (lights, or ornaments?) from the Andrews Christmas tree, which had been erected on the Andrews library grounds. Juveniles were also responsible for a theft at the Andrews drugstore, and possibly at the Andrews elevator and several service stations. The newspaper account is confusing, also mentioning the Bippus elevator, so perhaps the Andrews elevator was not robbed, or perhaps the Bippus elevator was not robbed.

It almost sounds like there was a gang operating, for many of these crimes have connections that lead to others. A robbery at the Close filling station at Andrews was admitted to by Kenneth Tuggle. About the same time, a car was stolen in Wabash by a juvenile and was later seen in Andrews and then abandoned at the same Stouder farm that was believed to have been used for the cattle thefts and for opening the safe from the railroad station.

Men old enough to know better, including Harold Helvie of Andrews, were charged with damaging or destroying 23 headstones at the Andrews cemetery, a case of malicious vandalism. Some of the stones were damaged beyond repair when they were pushed over, and some of the stones were so heavy that a "derrick" would be required to lift them back into place. Reportedly, the men took lead that was located between the stones and the bases, and they admitted to having been intoxicated at the time of their actions. Sadly, this was not the last time the cemetery was vandalized.

Andrews didn't have all the latest conveniences for firefighting. In December 1948, smoke was smoldering in corncobs being stored upstairs at the Fults and Goodrich grocery. The smoke was intense, and Andrews had no smoke mask of any kind, so the Huntington fire department, which did have such equipment, came to put out the fire.

One of the largest fires that Andrews firemen responded to during the 1940s was actually in Lagro. The Lagro grain elevator caught fire, and it must have been pretty spectacular. Both the Andrews and the Wabash fire departments were called for help, but there was an inadequate water supply (two private wells), so the departments wisely used their limited resources to protect nearby buildings, such as homes, the Celotex buildings, and the Duffey stockyards. Some of the homes had paint that blistered, but apparently none suffered serious damage. The elevator lost 6,000 bushels of wheat and oats in addition to the building itself.

Other fires during the decade were smaller in size, although just as devastating to the owners of the properties involved. Fires that were reported in the *Herald Press* included those at the Howard Bruss farm (the house was vacant) and at the residences of Mr. and Mrs. James Garrison and of Mr. and Mrs. Harry Garrison. The most newsworthy fire was at the Charles Stouder farm on June 13, 1942. Barn fires are often spectacular, but in this case, the fire department faced an additional challenge because the fire truck wouldn't start. Roy Frushour, a member of the department, hitched the truck to the end of his tow car and pulled it to the Stouder farm. The fire truck finally started as it was pulled onto the lane that led back to the fire, but it was too late to save the barn. The other buildings, however, were saved. This fire was started by a lightning bolt, and continuing winds made it difficult to fight.

OTHER TOWN NEWS AND HAPPENINGS

Andrews still participated in most if not all of the announced fund drives for various causes. The Red Cross quota in 1949 was $275. The chairman for this drive was Rev. George Manley, who was joined by workers Mrs. Garnett Keel, Mrs. Bessie Eastes, Mrs. Ruth Smith, Mrs. Forrest Gray, Mrs. Kate McDaniel, Mrs. Roy Hanselman, Mrs. Lloyd Heck, Basil Metz, and Mrs. Arlena Winkler.

Most people in Andrews lived lives of quiet goodness, following rhythms of the seasons and of life that their ancestors had lived for generations prior. Through the generosity of Nancy Casey Lewis, I have a typed transcript of a diary that Elva Fults Knee kept from January 1947 until

November 1948. It makes us realize, again, what we are missing in not having a good newspaper record of the events of the town. For instance, she reports that on March 30, during Sunday school, the Christian Church caught on fire. It must have been quickly contained, as she doesn't mention it again. Spring was late arriving that year; by April 30 there were no oats planted, and no garden out. The trees in the woods were showing just a faint tinge of green, and peach blossoms (buds) were just showing faintly pink. There was snow on the ground on May 8 that year. June was cool, too, but by July 2 corn was finally peeking through the ground, and then the next weather comments are about how hot it was. By August, everything was drying up.

In March 1948, a small tornado hit town. Some trees on Main Street were destroyed, and the Krile, Andrews, and Ross barns were blown away. At the Knee farm, "We have barn windows out, shingles off, and toilet blown over. Phone out and no power for motors but weak lights. Water everywhere. Every south window in the house had water coming in. Leaked in living room ceiling." Mrs. Knee also talked about church and family life and about "Aid" meetings and quiltings that she attended, and she mentioned several marriages, births, and deaths.

Probably there were many servicemen who married women they met while in the service, and Harold Miller of Andrews was one of those servicemen. Miller had been in the Marines during World War II and had served 8 or 10 months of that time in American Samoa. He met his bride, Juliana Toilolo, there, and they continued to correspond during and after the war, although it appears that they did not meet again until she, along with her older brother and her young daughter Jessie, arrived in Huntington. The couple soon married and went to live with his parents, Earl and Lydia Miller. Harold was a factory worker. He had worked at Kitchen Maid before entering the service and perhaps had gone back to work there. The *Herald Press* article reported that the new Mrs. Miller spoke excellent English and had good business and housekeeping skills. The Toilolo family ruled about one-fourth of the island of Samoa at the time, but Mrs. Miller had always wanted to come to the United States.

Alvin Eugene Smith, who graduated from Andrews High School in 1942 and was known as Gene, returned from serving in the Army during World War II and then graduated from Huntington College with a Bachelor of Science degree. His first job was as athletic director of the Lagro high school, but he then taught government and economics in the Niles, Michigan, high schools for about 30 years.

Closer to home, Henry (Perk) Miller achieved local, if fleeting, fame when he landed a "Mississippi catfish" weighing 20 and a half pounds and measuring 34 inches long. Bud Miller and Ted Rittenhouse helped land the fish.

The newly married couple of William A. Oatess, a retired farmer, and Katherine O. Mote already had years of experience to assist them in adjusting to married life. Mr. Oatess had been married three times previously and Mrs. Mote four times. All the previous marriages had ended with the death of the spouses.

Floodwaters in 1943 caused more than the usual rampaging of Loon Creek. A group of children were wading in the floodwaters near the bridge on State Road 105 when a five-year-old boy, the son of Mrs. Ira Schlemmer of Main Street, lost his footing and was in danger of being swept away. Robert Smuts, who was older and stronger, was able to grab the boy and bring him back to safety. Meanwhile, Wabash Railroad crews were called in to protect the bridge over Loon Creek, which was in danger of being flooded.

Homer Ross must have been something of a "character," judging from his letters to the editor in the *Herald Press.*

Homer was a foreman at Kitchen Maid when he began his letter-writing "career." Frequently he commented on the virtues of life in Andrews. For instance, in his March 30, 1947, letter, he noted: "We have four churches, the K.M. Corp., the Gets Mfg. Co., two good general stores, two coal yards, an elevator, a lumber yard and three saloons. We don't need the saloons though as we have a good supply of fine water. But some folks don't like water so we have three saloons." He mentions that there was a creek that ran through town, with three bridges to span it. Two were safe for pedestrians and there was one good bridge. In another letter he says, "In the early days it [Andrews] was undecided as to which way to expand. It started north and ran into the Wabash river—then east until it ran into Walter Rudig's gravel pit. After these setbacks it went west several blocks, got tired, and just stopped." Often he would stir up controversy, sometimes receiving letters at his home that were signed "Anonymous." Not everyone realized that he was actually a town booster and dearly loved his town. I wish I had known him and been able to enjoy some of his stories and comments firsthand!

PASSINGS

Life in Andrews, as elsewhere, also meant saying goodbye as town leaders, businessmen, and loved ones left this earth. During the 1940s, there were several notable deaths. The former marshal of Andrews, John William Tidrick, died on April 9, 1940. He was also a carpenter.

Dr. Russell Clymer, who had been a physician in Andrews for ten years, suffered injuries that proved fatal when his automobile collided with another, northwest of North Webster. Ned Keefer, who was with him at the time, was less seriously hurt in the July 10, 1940, incident. The loss of Dr. Clymer, who was only 38 years old, was a blow to the town.

Lewis A. Strevey died at age 84, in December 1940. He had been the justice of the peace for Dallas Township for many years and also operated a junk business.

George Stephan spent most of his life outside of Andrews, but when he died in 1941, he was probably one of the few living graduates of "Antioch Seminary," the high school in Antioch/Andrews in the 1870s. He taught school in Huntington County for 18 years, was a Polk Township trustee and treasurer of Huntington County, and was active in his church and in civic organizations. Andrews could point to him with pride and say "He started here . . . ."

John Hemmick, who had owned a barbershop in Andrews at one time, passed away at age 73, in August 1941.

Ezra H. Carson had lived most of his life in Andrews, from 1885 until 1934, when he moved to the Masonic Home in Franklin, Indiana. He had worked for the Wabash Railroad as a brakeman and then a conductor, and later was a general laborer in Andrews. He was active in town life as marshal and town trustee at various times, and the town remembered him.

Earl Props, who was in the garage business with Ralph Notter in Andrews after World War I, died on May 2, 1942. He was the owner of a garage on US 24 just west of Huntington at the time of his death, but Andrews remembered him, too.

George Nichols, who had operated a hardware business in Andrews for many years, passed away on October 26, 1942.

Daniel Wasmuth was not a resident of Andrews but was a salesman for Kitchen Maid corporation and thus would have been known to Andrews residents when he passed away on January 18, 1942, Two of his brothers, A. D.

Wasmuth and Harry Wasmuth, lived in Andrews, and so the town would have grieved with them.

Charles Long was just 59 when he died of pneumonia on February 23, 1942. He had lived in Andrews for about 20 years. Long had been employed at Wasmuth-Endicott and at Gets Manufacturing, and then worked with Dorrance Cross in a woodworking factory, before ending his work life at Orton Crane in Huntington just a few months before his death. He had served on the Andrews town board as a Republican and was active in other civic groups. His death was a loss to the town.

A tragic death occurred on August 5, 1943. Eighteen-month-old Robert Leroy Chapman, whose family lived on West McKeever Street, somehow managed to open a screen door and leave his home. His little legs took him to Loon Creek, which had flooded its banks. The boy was exploring and was caught up in the current of the stream. His body was found about an hour after the search began, by Allen Wasmuth. A human bridge was formed to bring the child to safety, but resuscitation efforts were not successful. He was the son of Mrs. and Mrs. Wayne Chapman. Infant and childhood deaths were not as common as they had been, and this was a particularly sad manner of death.

Another man from earlier Andrews days. Walter Cogswell, passed away in January 1944. Walter Cogswell had operated a drugstore, purchased from W. D. Cole, for about 10 years from 1910 to 1920. Doubtless many of the older folks remembered him well.

Dr. L. W. (Lewis Wetzel) Pratt's life didn't make the newspapers on a regular basis. He was one of the quiet builders and citizens of Andrews. Pratt was a veterinary surgeon at Andrews for 35 years, so most residents would have known him, and certainly the farmers around Andrews knew him. He was a member of the Methodist Church and the Andrews lodge of the Free and Accepted

Masons, but seems not to have taken a lot of leadership positions. Perhaps his practice kept him too busy to do much more than show up for various events. When he died January 13, 1944, he left behind a widow, a son, three daughters, and a grandson. He was just finishing up a professional call at a farm when he suffered a sudden and fatal heart attack. His funeral featured 18 flower-bearers, which is some measure of the esteem in which he was held.

Ed Taylor passed away in 1945. He had been a fixture in Andrews for many years, his most recent occupation being stock buyer. When Andrews had stockyards about where the Preferred/Essex/Dana etc. factory is now, he was the owner and operator. He also owned business buildings, was a bank director, and farmed.

Arthur Long also died in 1945. He lived in Andrews his entire life and was an employee at Kitchen Maid for many years. His death was notable because he was the last surviving child of Lessel Long, who was a large part of the early history of Antioch and Andrews.

In March 1946, Otto K. (O. K.) Gleason died. He also had been a great influence in Andrews. He published the *Andrews Signal* from 1903 to 1918 and was an officer in the Gets Spark Plug factory and the Glaze Manufacturing Company. He, along with both his first wife and his second wife, was quite active in community affairs for many years. He was a member of the Christian Church and the Masonic Lodge.

Another pillar of the community, Frank Fults, died on May 31, 1946. He was a director of the Andrews State Bank for many years and cofounder of the Andrews Telephone Company. He was president of the Farm Loan Association of Huntington County for many years also. He had owned a hardware store and then a grocery store in Andrews, and had farmed for many years as well.

Former merchant Charles Hegel died just a few weeks later, on July 1. Mr. Hegel had operated the Equity Exchange and owned a garage, had been employed at Kitchen Maid, and also sold insurance.

A particularly sad death occurred on May 17, 1947, when Jack W. Tullis, just 14 years old, died from a bullet wound to the head. He had been scuffling with two younger brothers, and surely they were not aware that the rifle, which was not usually kept in the bedroom of the younger boys, was loaded. (It had been placed there while another room was being repapered). It was a horrible tragedy for the family, for the community, and surely for the surviving brothers. Jack was a freshman at Andrews High School, senior patrol leader of Boy Scout Troop 120, and Den Chief for Cub Scout Den 3, so he was a young man of promise.

Perhaps that death also sadly impacted Chester Poe, marshal of Andrews, who died suddenly on May 21, 1947. He had a massive heart attack while on his way downtown. He had lived in Andrews for 23 years and had been the marshal for several years. Before that, he had been a truck driver.

Just a few days later, on May 25, Homer Stevens died. He was the owner-proprietor of the North End grocery store on Main Street. After his death, his widow, Ethel, operated the store for many more years, and she is still remembered with fondness.

Although it had been about 25 years since Dr. Albert Chenowith lived and practiced in Andrews, his life while in Andrews had been notable, especially during the Spanish flu epidemic of 1918-19. He had practiced medicine in Huntington until 1942, and there were probably some from Andrews for whom he was always "their doctor." He died October 6, 1947, at age 70, having lived in Huntington County almost all his life.

Everyone in Andrews would have been shocked to learn of the death of Charles Zimmerman on November 26, 1947, in an auto accident. Mr. Zimmerman owned and operated the funeral home in Andrews for about 10 years. He was just 56 years old and was a great asset to the town, participating in church and civic organizations. As was the custom for funeral-home owners, he also operated an ambulance service for the town. He was a veteran of World War I and had been sheriff in Steuben County, Indiana, for two terms. He left a widow, but no children.

Some residents of Andrews perhaps remembered Ida Mae Tuttle, nee Pattison. She died on February 16, 1948, in Portales, New Mexico. She was a member of the Pattison family that operated the old Andrews Hotel (the one on Jackson Street) when the railroad shops were in Andrews.

Death also came to another well-known business man, William Shinkel. He had operated a shoe store and harness shop for 38 years in Andrews and was a member of the Methodist Church when he died on May 29, 1948, at age 85.

Accidental deaths are always hard on the family, but they can also be particularly hard on the town, especially if the accident occurs right in the middle of town. Frank S. Plasterer, 58 years old, was driving his car when it was stuck by a Wabash train at the Main Street crossing in Andrews on August 18, 1948. He died five days later. He was a cabinetmaker at Kitchen Maid and attended the Andrews Church of the Brethren.

Olive Glaze died September 17, 1948. This may be the first time we have seen her name in the newspaper, and it appears that it was reported incorrectly. In the newspaper account, she is called "Allie May" Glaze, but her name was Olive. We know her better through newspaper articles referring to her as Mrs. Bruce Glaze. She had lived in Andrews since shortly after her marriage to Bruce Glaze in 1905. She was buried in the same cemetery in Van Wert,

Ohio, as her first husband, who had died in 1902. In Andrews, she was active in the Library Club and other organizations.

Clyde Reemer was only 35 years old when he died in a traffic accident just three miles south of Andrews. He was on his way to work at the Farnsworth Radio and Television plant in Marion when his vehicle and one owned by the Andrews Elevator collided. Clyde lived near his parents, Mr. and Mrs. William Reemer, on the north end of Andrews. He had graduated with the Andrews High School class of 1931.

Simon S. Beauchamp was 89 years old when he died September 26, 1949, in Sioux City, Iowa. He had lived in Andrews about 80 of his 89 years, having spent a few years in Montana and then the last years of his life in Iowa. He operated a grocery and shoe store in Andrews and had been the manager for Cloverleaf Creamery. Later he sold real estate and insurance from an office on Main Street, about where the Bethesda Freewill Baptist Church is now.

Another "old-timer," John Gretzinger, died October 28, 1948. He operated a dry goods store in Andrews for many years and had served as clerk-treasurer for the town as well. He was a member of the Methodist Church, the Masonic lodge, and the Order of the Eastern Star.

E. M. Wasmuth had no Andrews roots, but he certainly influenced Andrews for many years. He was involved in the Wasmuth-Endicott Company almost since its beginnings and was the past president of Kitchen Maid corporation and chairman of the board at the time of his death on January 3, 1949. He was credited with moving the company forward with the vision of building cabinet units of standardized sizes so they could be easily installed in the kitchens of the day. He had been an important part of the Wasmuth business enterprises, which included businesses in Huntington and Roanoke as well as in Andrews. Family members who also played a great part in the life of Andrews were two brothers, A. W. Wasmuth and H. R. Wasmuth, and a sister, Mrs. Carl Endicott. Andrews residents, especially Kitchen Maid workers, surely had a lot of stories to tell about this man.

Later that same year, on October 15, 1949, Carl Endicott died in North Manchester. He was a part of Andrews for many years, having come to town in 1903 to become cashier of the Andrews State bank. He was also involved with the Wasmuth-Endicott company, later Kitchen Maid, and he was the "E" in the original Gets Spark Plug Company. Later he set up the trust department of Citizens State Bank in Huntington. He was known throughout the nation and Canada as a past president of Kiwanis International.

Just 14 months after the death of Frank Plasterer at the railroad tracks in Andrews, Laura Wolverton, 73 years old and the wife of Wesley Wolverton, was killed when she was struck by a train at the Market Street crossing in Andrews, on November 10, 1949. She was with a friend and apparently intended to go to a grocery store "uptown," but tried to beat the train. Unfortunately, the train won. Her home was just two houses north of the tracks. The couple had lived in Andrews for 25 years. I didn't find anything that suggested that the railroad perhaps needed to install better warning systems for these crossings.

Another longtime Andrews resident, Lewis Reiff, died December 12, 1949. He is reported to have been a telephone lineman. His wife, Hazel, lived many more years, and there was one daughter, Edith.

These were some of the prominent people who died during the 1940s. They also were people who paid their taxes, built their town, served in various churches and civic organizations, raised their families (although a surprising number of the people I looked at for this chapter were childless), supported the school and the sports teams, and worked. Respect is due them.

Photos

Andrews Pilgrim Holiness and then Andrews
Wesleyan church, since demolished.

First Christian Church Sunday School, not dated

On Main Street in Andrews, building on left was a feed supply store

Main Street in Andrews, Burkart Cafe; fire station-town-township offices (built 1911)

First Christian Church Men's Sunday school class, not dated.

First Christian Church, Women's Sunday school class, 1928

Hearse in front of Deal Funeral Home, which was previously the Markle, Metz, and Zimmerman funeral home, respectively. Hearse was owned by Robert Deal.

Eighth grade class at Andrews school, October 1931

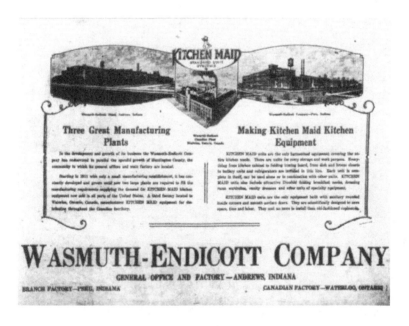

Wasmuth-Endicott Company advertisement, prior to 1933. Note the three locations.

Chapter Six
1950-1959

NATIONAL

America in the 1950s was a confusing mixture, looking back on it. It was the "Golden Age of Television," and of American Bandstand and cowboy westerns. There were soda shops, and those who were lucky enough to be teenagers then had a few years of relative prosperity, of freedom from the worries of war, and of being able to celebrate our nation. It was a good time—unless, that is, we remember just how many of our young men and women were called into the military during the 1950s. Men and women from Andrews served all over the world, many for the second time, having also served in World War II. The "police action" in Korea, the tensions between East and West Germany, and the Cold War in general meant that if someone was drafted in the 1950s, they would have no idea where they would serve. Our men and women did themselves and the town proud, no matter where they were stationed.

The people I'll mention here are almost certainly not the only ones who served from Andrews. These are the ones I found mentioned at least once in the Huntington newspaper. I'm sure I missed some, and I'm sure there were others who preferred that their names not be in the paper, for whatever reason. Others came to Andrews after they were released from the military and only then became

"Andrews people." Still, this listing will give a decent idea of how, even in Andrews, young people served their country, and their town.

The county's draft quota in October 1950 included two men, "Rct" (possibly a typo for Pvt) James R. Beeks and Pvt. Robert VanMeter Jr. Within six months of reentering the service, Beeks was on the front lines in Korea, and he noted in a letter to friends that it was still rather frigid, in May 1951. Lt. Ned Keefer was assigned to Fort Sill, Oklahoma, in November 1950. He was discharged about March 1, 1952, and returned to Andrews to work in the family greenhouse. Pfc. Robert Hamman served in Korea from August 1951 to April 1952 and rotated home with his unit. It operated for some time at the 38th parallel, which divided North and South Korea.

Sergeant Lawrence Smith, son of Mr. and Mrs. William F. Smith, was transferred from Great Falls, Montana, to McClellan AFB in Sacramento, California. He had been in the service for eight years, having spent 20 months in the Mediterranean theater during World War II. Also serving in the US Air Force was Pfc. Morris Wade. In June 1951, he had graduated from mechanics school at Sheppard AFB in Texas and was awaiting reassignment. That assignment turned out to be Yokohama, Japan, where he was part of the Third Rescue Squadron. The Japan assignment was short, because in October he was in Korea, having been appointed to the character guidance board of the 37th Air Rescue squadron there. He expected to be in Korea for a total of three years. I'm not sure whether this goes in the Air Force reports or not, but Corporal Lawrence Stallings was due to report to Hickam Air Field in Hawaii, where he was assigned for the completion of a three-year tour of duty. Airman Second Class David Pearson, son of Mr. and Mrs. Ed Pearson, was assigned to Torrejon AFB, Madrid, Spain, while his brother Charles, A3C, was assigned to Aviano Air

Base in Italy. Both of the Pearson men had been stationed stateside before their overseas assignments.

Walter Satchwill entered the Army as a "selectee" on September 8, 1950. He rose to the rank of sergeant, serving in Japan and Korea. He was a member of a reconnaissance unit, living for six months in the bunkers on the hills in central Korea. He was the first "selectee" of the Korean police action to return home, being officially released on July 7, 1952. His two-year service requirement was reduced by 3 months because of the 20 months he spent overseas. Daniel Wintrode, son of Mr. and Mrs. Robert Wintrode of Andrews, was a private stationed in Korea in the neighborhood of "Old Baldy." This was the scene of ongoing battles with the Chinese from June 1952 well into 1953, but it's not clear whether Pvt. Wintrode was there for the actual battles, as the newspaper giving his mailing address was dated May 18, 1953. He had entered the Army on October 31, 1952. He was later promoted to corporal and was part of a division baseball team that played against other division teams in Korea. He probably never imagined, while playing sports in Andrews, that baseball practice would take him so far. Cpl. Bob Whitesell was in Korea, too. Well, actually, he made the "Men in Service" column in the *Huntington Herald Press* because, in January 1954, he received a seven-day rest and recreation leave to Kobe, Japan, staying at "one of Japan's best resort hotels." On normal days, he was a cook with the 40th Infantry division's 40th Reconnaissance company.

Other Andrews soldiers served elsewhere. Warrant Officer Verland Wintrode rotated home from Germany in May 1953, after serving there for three and a half years. He had been in the service for 10 years. Lee Haines, son of Mrs. Mary Haines, was briefly home from Germany before returning for three more years. Private Ralph C. Hunnicutt served in the Panama Canal Zone. Cpl. Jesse Finton enlisted in the Army in 1948 and had served in Korea. After five years in the Army, he was "Soldier of the Month" at the US Army station at LaGrange, Illinois. He planned to make a career of the Army.

Pvt. Donald D. Beeks had an APO address of San Francisco and was with the 14th Infantry in Korea. The fighting was over, but the need for troops was still present. Arden Hanselman didn't make it quite all the way to Korea, it appears. As a private, he served with the 29th Combat unit at Okinawa starting in November 1954. Army Cpl. James Fields went to Germany with the First Infantry division, where he was a correspondence clerk. He entered the Army in August 1953 and went to Germany in March 1954. Pfc. Larry Hollowell, who served with the Army in Germany, managed to take a 3,000-mile tour of southern Europe with three Army friends while he was overseas. James R. Small, Army Specialist Second Class, was a mess sergeant in Germany, assigned to the 511th Infantry Regiment. James Proffitt was promoted to private first class while serving in Germany with the 587th engineering company.

Clyde Glass was another Andrews man of whom Andrews can be proud. He entered the Army in early 1955, after having graduated from Andrews High School, Presbyterian College in Clinton, South Carolina, and Valparaiso Technical Institute, earning both a bachelor of science and a radio engineering degree. He was an electronic laboratory technician and then an audio recording specialist. When he was discharged from the Army as a specialist third class, he went to work at the Hanford Atomic Products Operation in Richland, Washington. He can also tell some interesting stories about his hitchhiking days, as he traveled back and forth to school and work.

Andrews had sailors as well as soldiers. William A. Schneider was hospitalman third class on the USS *Haven*, one of the Navy's floating hospitals. His ship cared for the wounded at Korea, operating at the port of Inchon "whenever the port is in United States hands," said the *Herald Press* of April 26, 1951. Donald Montel was in Andrews and spending time with his mother, Mrs. Elizabeth Montel. He had been in the Navy for nine and a half years, so since 1942, serving most of his time in the Pacific area. It's not clear whether he ever lived in Andrews. Airman Larry D. McDaniel, son of Mr. and Mrs. W. A. McDaniel was stationed on the USS *Block Island* with Air AntiSubmarine Squadron 30. He served a tour of duty in the Mediterranean after drilling with British squadrons in waters near Northern Ireland and Scotland.

The Marines also attracted some Andrews men. Gene Rupel was a sergeant in the Marines, and in June 1951 was serving with the "marine air wing near Korea." He had been in the Okinawa campaign during World War II and was discharged in 1946, then called back to duty in August 1950 and discharged in September 1951. He was a radio relay repairman and had been attending Texas Christian University. George Stallings, who had made newspaper headlines due to his action in World War II, was recalled to duty in the Marine Corps. He was a fighter pilot, and by May 1952, fighter pilots were in short supply. He had a refresher course at Glenview Naval Air Station and then was sent to Cherry Point, North Carolina, for further training. Stallings had to take a leave of absence from his job as mathematics teacher and basketball coach at Lincoln School in Huntington to answer the call of duty. He served until November 1, 1953, and was promoted to captain before his release. He had again been doing a dangerous job, serving with the ground-control intercept squadrons. Marine Pfc. Rudy Decker arrived at Inchon, Korea, to join the first

Marine division in May 1954. Edgar Kitt, a sergeant in the Marine Corps, was stationed at Yokohama, Japan, in 1956 and 1957. He was a member of the First Special Communications platoon, and one of his duties was to sing in the Kami boys barbershop quartet.

DeWayne Keefer, son of Mr. and Mrs. Clarence Keefer, seems to have been one of the first men from Andrews who was wounded in the Korean conflict. He was a Seaman Apprentice on the USS *Paricutin*, an ammunition ship, and was hit in the side by shrapnel when a gun near him was hit.

These are the names I've gleaned from the newspaper. I don't know how many of these men were drafted and how many enlisted. I don't know if there were women from Andrews who served during the 1950s. (Rosemary Keefer was a career nurse, entering during World War II, but I didn't see mention of her during this time period). There may have been other servicemembers who were injured in Korea. However, these brief mentions will give some idea that young men from Andrews served their country, and served well, during the 1950s. And while they served, life in Andrews went on.

As the conflicts from Korea to the Cold War raged on, Indiana and even Andrews were not immune to the effects. Indiana State Civil Defense pushed a plan for all students to be issued metal ID tags that could be worn under the students' clothing. They didn't come right out and say why the students would ever need to be identified, but a mention that the metal used in the tags was the same as in military dog tags and that they would not melt at 2,500 degrees Fahrenheit may have given some parents pause. The cost per tag was 25 cents and the county wanted to make sure that every child in Huntington County had one.

Even small children helped in the effort to defeat the North Korean enemy. Lonna Harvey, at age three in 1952, took a jug filled with 2,250 "Roosevelt dimes" to the bank and bought US savings bonds with them. The jug weighed 14 pounds, so perhaps she had some help carrying it. The three $100 bonds that she purchased were the start of her college savings fund. This was far-sighted, since she wouldn't graduate from high school until 1967.

TOWN GOVERNMENT AND INFRASTRUCTURE

Andrews at the start of the 1950s had a population of 1,083, which was up from 954 in 1940, according to figures provided by the US Census director. Perhaps the increase was partly due to the increased employment at Kitchen Maid, and the early years of Huntington Manufacturing. Perhaps it was a rebound from the Depression years, when people may have lived on farms so they could at least raise food for their family. Prospects for the town looked good. The Andrews budget was slowly increasing. In August 1952 the total taxes expected to be collected were $9,167.89, of which $1,212.53 would be for the library fund. Net taxable property for the town was valued at $942,610.

Discussions about the proposed sewer system and sewage plant continued through the mid 1950s. A meeting at the school on March 30, 1953, included a presentation from consulting engineers and representatives of the state board of health. This may have been a question-and-answer session; it was intended to educate the town about the need for the system. The meeting may not have gone as expected, though, because the town council decided to delay a referendum vote in order to provide voters with additional information. One sticking point seemed to be the bond of about $303,000 that would be necessary. Each water user would be mailed or delivered a pamphlet answering some of the questions that the board felt had not been adequately addressed at the earlier meeting. Either the referendum was never held, or it failed, because sewers were not installed at this time. Cost seems to have been the biggest issue, but there was also concern over whether or not it would be mandatory for property owners to hook up to the sewer lines.

However, Andrews had other projects going on. Bond bids were opened by the town on October 1, 1954, to allow the town to purchase the feed building owned by Arnold Spencer and previously owned by Claude Wilson. It was a block building on Main Street, north of Jefferson Street, and when converted to town use, it would include the fire station, the jail, public restrooms, and space to store equipment. The bonds would mature at different times, with the last being due in 1970. The amount to be raised by the bond issuance was $21,973, which included the purchase of the land and the building, as well as the renovations. The town budget for 1956 included $1,528 for the payment of interest on the bonds and retirement of bonds. An open house was held on November 29, 1955, when the building needed only a few final finishing touches. The two-story building that the town and the township had constructed in 1909 was presumably left empty when the town offices moved.

Whether the bond issue and the discussion over the proposed sewer system had anything to do with it or not, Andrews was going to have a new town board after the election of November 1955. Ed Reemer, Ed Buckles, and Max Jennings were not running, or perhaps were not chosen by their town conventions. The Republican slate would be Harry Goebel, Clyde Wilson, and Morris Sandlin, with Mrs. Fred Bammerlin as clerk. The Democrats chose Bill Snyder, Ned Keefer, and H. Burl Millman, with Edwin Goodrich as clerk. The Republican slate won, except that somehow the clerk-treasurer elected was Mrs. Stella Coss.

During the late 1950s, Andrews, as well as Dallas Township, gradually gave up some of its rights to the county, agreeing to have the County Planning Commission take charge of zoning issues within town and township limits. This simplified matters for the town but also meant they had little say in how the town developed.

Ed Kelley, who had been the town marshal for several years, retired in July 1958, and the town lost no time in appointing a new marshal, Louis (probably Lewis) Bigelow. Bigelow, age 34, was a lifelong resident of Andrews. He had been working for the Erie Railroad and was also a two-year veteran of World War II. Just a few months later, in January 1959, Arlo Gephart is mentioned in a *Herald Press* article as being the town marshal. He was warning people to keep their dogs tied up, which was a recurring problem in Andrews.

Four years after Andrews voted straight Republican in the 1955 town election, they voted straight Democrat in the 1959 election. William Snyder, Fred Warfel, and Burl Millman would lead the town, with Mrs. Barbara Boone as clerk-treasurer.

Occasionally, candidates for state and even national political offices came to Andrews. In October 1954, James R. Walsh, Democratic candidate for US Representative, was here, speaking about what the Republican congressman, John Beamer, had voted for and against, especially as it concerned farmers. A men's quartet of Lester Stephan, John Bickel, Dean Bickel, and Louis Goebel sang, but the most appreciated entertainment seems to have been a "Ladies Kitchen Band" made up of Mrs. Charles Fix, Mrs. Frank Rudig, Mrs. Ralph Dillon, Mrs. Elmer Stephan, Mrs. Marvin Purcell, Mrs. Charles Harvey, Mrs. John Snyder, Mrs. Hale Harvey, Miss Myrneth Satterthwaite, Mrs. Lester Stephan, and Mrs. Carl Goebel.

Congressman Beamer also appeared in Andrews, but it was two years later, and time to stand again for reelection. His speech appears to have been one of "name-dropping," talking mostly about the men in power in Washington and attacking Democrats. Still, by today's standards, it was probably a pretty tame speech. Beamer had defeated Walsh in the 1950 election and was still serving.

In 1958 J. Edward Roush was the Democratic candidate for the same Fifth District Congressional seat, and he, too, came to Andrews for a rally. His campaign was successful, and he returned to Andrews at least one more time, in 1967, as Congressman Roush.

The fire department posed in front of what appears to be a Kitchen Maid building on April 6, 1953. The occasion was the upcoming retirement of the 1909 vintage pumper. It had originally been horse-drawn, but was mounted on a 1928 truck chassis when it was finally retired. The department now had a modern pumper, which was dedicated to Dallas Township fires only. Members of the fire department at the time were Gene Wilson, chief; Mel Dinius, assistant; Henry Miller Jr.; Leland Flickinger; Roy Huston; Gene More; Earl Ellet; and Roy Frushour.

Just because Andrews had telephone service, it didn't mean Andrews had good telephone service. Indiana Bell purchased the Union Telephone Company (among others) when the owner passed away, and Andrews and Lagro were on the list of small communities who would have their service upgraded. The sale was not actually completed until September 1955. Hand-cranked phones would be a thing of the past, and party lines would be limited to a maximum of six per line. Previously some party lines (not sure if this applied to Andrews or not) had up to 17 families on one line. Danny Smith remembers that his family's "ring" was three longs, two shorts. By the end of 1956, Bell Telephone expected to construct a new building that would provide a dial telephone service, which would make it possible to call Huntington or Lagro without a long-distance charge. Andrews numbers would have the prefix ST. Clyde Wilson, president of the Andrews town board, was given the honor of making the first official dialed call from Andrews.

Nowhere in the newspaper articles is it mentioned that telephone operators would lose their jobs because of these changes. However, when it happened, it was a sad day for Andrews. Just one story will illustrate why.

Cheri Keefer Auman graciously shared this story from her childhood: "I was at the babysitter's when I hit my head. The babysitter fainted from all the blood. So I pulled a chair up to the phone. Had to crank it and the operator came on. I told her I was bleeding and wanted my mommy. She said 'What is your Mom's name?' I said 'Mommy.' She said 'What does she do?' 'Makes pretty flowers.' Operator said 'Just a minute honey,' and my Mom came on the phone. (She was the town's florist.) The babysitter was waking up and I was bending over her, dripping blood on her. She fainted again. Mom came and took me to the hospital, where I got stitches." The telephone operators, on top of everything else, were 911-like dispatchers, it seems.

The bridge on State Road 105 over the Wabash River was badly damaged in January 1959 by ice jams that, when they finally broke, made the loudest sound ever heard in Andrews, according to some who remember that day. It is amazing to think that the old bridge could be demolished and the new one designed, financed, and built in only about nine months, but there were far fewer hoops to jump through then.

FACTORIES

Kitchen Maid was not content to continue with "just" the kitchen cabinet business. In November 1950, the company announced that they had formed a wholly owned subsidiary called Bath Maid, Inc., which would make standardized storage cabinets for the bathroom, just as Kitchen Maid made standardized cabinets for the kitchen. Their largest customer, at least at first, would be American Standard Company. One of the units that Bath Maid produced was designed in color and shape to fit the new "China Dresslyn Lavatory" sold by the American Standard Company. From the description and pictures, it appears that these bathrooms, except possibly for the color palette, would fit right into many bathrooms of today's homes.

Many Kitchen Maid employees had long terms of service with the company, and celebrating their milestones was an important part of Kitchen Maid culture. In 1951 employees with 25 or more years of service were Henry Yentes, Oliver Wade, Edward Reemer, Lowell Wilson, Bert Forst, Leroy Smith, Glen Campbell, Nellie Denney, E. M. Kitt, Cecil Jennings, Clarence Willets, and Lawrence Millman. Another 67 employees had worked for the company for 5, 10, 15, or 20 years. By this time, the annual banquet that had previously been enjoyed by employees had changed to refreshments and a program. Later a Christmas box or basket was given to each employee present, and an appearance by Santa Claus also became part of the tradition. Many of the same employees were honored at the 1958 Christmas party. It is remarkable that Clarence Willets and Bert Forst each had 47 years of service, Oliver Wade 44 years, and Glen Campbell and Ed Reemer 41 years. Another 10 employees had at least 25 years of service by that time. Kitchen Maid was blessed with faithful employees.

It was partly because of the work of the factory employees, as well as the sales department, that Kitchen Maid announced in January 1955 that they were both building a new building at the factory site and renovating the old Andrews opera house to use as office and sales space. Officers at the time of the expansion were A. F. Wasmuth, president; H. Kenneth Ware, secretary and director of manufacturing; C. E. Brady, treasurer; Robert E. Wasmuth, vice president; and J. W. O'Harrow Jr., vice president in charge of sales.

A picture in the newspaper of January 10, 1955, shows that there had apparently not been much done to the opera house building since it was constructed in 1895. It had full-length windows across the front, in what appears to be a division allowing for two businesses. Another set of windows appears toward the rear of the building, on Jefferson Street. There were exterior stairs to the second floor. Plans were to use the main floor as office space (executive, sales, and general) and the basement for the advertising department and sales meetings. The second floor, the location of the opera house, was to remain unused. The building front would be redone with brick and glass block windows. It would both update and change the appearance of downtown Andrews.

The new building at the factory site was 54 by 92 feet in size, two stories, and built of block and steel. The first floor was used as warehouse space and the second floor as a finishing room, opening up more space in the main building for actual construction work. Perhaps as a result of the expanded work space, the *Herald Press* published a "wanted" ad in the September 1955 issue. Men were needed immediately: three men for the trim room, two men for the shipping room, two men for the stockroom, four men for the machine room, and three men for the building room. (Sorry, ladies, but that's what the ad says!)

In 1958 business seems to have slumped a little, but A. E. Wasmuth expected it to come back in the third quarter of 1958. At this time, Kitchen Maid employed about 200 people, many of them Andrews residents. It was the largest, but not the only, factory in Andrews.

The "other factory" went by several names, including Huntington Manufacturing Company and the Hettrick Company. Some people called it "the tent place," even though their main product wasn't tents, at least not at first. The company's main building, the old Andrews Hotel on Main Street next to the library, was purchased in 1950, and in January 1951 plans were in place to begin production there. It was a three-story building that required quite a few internal changes to prepare it for production, but the changes were made. Other buildings were either leased or purchased (north of the hotel and up to the old opera house, where the Poehler restaurant had been), and a former garage on the west side of Main Street was purchased to use as a warehouse.

The Huntington plant had received a government contract for tents, so much of their other business was transferred to the Andrews location. One of those products was a line of hassocks, specialized for different functions. Some were nesting, to provide additional seating for television viewing, some were hollow for storage, and some had serving trays built in so that when the top was removed and turned over, it was useful for snacks and beverages. The plant also made plastic and Formica dinette sets. The quantities made were not small. They produced about 2,000 table tops a day and 120 train carloads of hassocks in a year. This was a thriving business.

Business was so good in 1952 that the company purchased 10 acres of land at the corner of California and Jackson streets, just north of the railroad tracks, in order to build a new facility. Several buildings were kept for storage, and the number of residences that had to be torn down was "not many." Steel was still regulated by the national production administration, so the company wasn't sure when building could begin, but since some of the company was involved in production of tents for the armed services, it was hoped that construction could begin soon. The building size would be 150 feet by 300 feet, so it would take a lot of steel, although the exterior walls were block.

According to his daughter Margaret Wallace, Earl Wallace began working for Hettrick Manufacturing in Toledo, Ohio, during the Depression. He came to Huntington to help start the Huntington Manufacturing branch of the business, and moved to Andrews in 1947. Earl Wallace had a great deal to do with the design and layout of the new building, and he became the plant manager. The plant at Andrews soon expanded the production line. They made above-ground swimming pools, also designed by Earl Wallace, and many who were young during the late 1950s and 1960s remember swimming in the Wallace swimming pool. The company also made outdoor furniture and owned the rights to some of the Disney characters. Their catalog features a children's picnic table with a picture of Mickey and Minnie Mouse on it and also features items that tied in with Davy Crockett. Some of the Hettrick catalogs specify that these items, among others, would be shipped from Andrews, Indiana.

In July 1957, the Huntington plant of Huntington Manufacturing announced that it was closing, with jobs to be transferred to Andrews. There was plenty of room in the Andrews plant to absorb both the machinery and the product lines so that all could be manufactured at the same location. At the time, the product line was said to consist of above-ground swimming pools, pool filters, cushions for summer furniture, children's playpens, hassocks, tractor umbrellas, upholstery specialty products, and custom plastic furniture. They were also producing tents and shelters under experimental contracts with the US Army. The challenge facing the company was to find products that would permit substantial year-round production, rather than mostly products for summertime use. In 1958 it was announced that Huntington Manufacturing had been purchased by a wholly owned subsidiary of Hettrick Manufacturing. It may have been at this time that the name was changed to General Engineering. Earl Wallace continued as plant manager.

Later the company moved into the production of seats for the vans of the day, and then into converting vans into true recreational vehicles. That came to an end when gas shortages depressed the market for big vans. It had been a good run for the company, which during the 1950s employed as many as 200 people.

Shortly after the end of World War II, Ivan McDaniel, Henry Crull, and Ira Belcher (of Markle) joined to form the MCB Manufacturing Corporation. This operated, at a loss, for several years out of the old Andrews Hotel on Main Street, building pumps of different types. By 1948 about 10 employees worked there. Ivan McDaniel had the good fortune to meet Earl Wallace, who at the time was looking for someplace to store both products and inventory for the Hettrick Manufacturing Company (see story above), and a week later the deal was done. Hettrick was in and the MCB Manufacturing Corporation was out. That meant the three men needed to find another location for their business, quickly. Fortunately, there was a building available at the corner of Market and Washington, formerly occupied by Antioch Machine and Tool Company, and MCB Manufacturing moved there. Although the company started out as a very small business, making pumps, they soon were building industrial machines for Hettrick Manufacturing, including tube-rolling and wire-straightening machines. Some of these were used at the hotel location and some at the new location on Jackson Street, when the new plant was built for Hettrick. Mr. McDaniel basically designed and helped build these machines from the ground up. When the other men left the business, McDaniel continued it for several years, but eventually he went to Fisher Engineering until his "retirement," when he started the business again, and finally, finally was able to show a profit. This time the business was known as the Andrews Tool and Machine Company. It's not clear how long it continued to operate, but it may have been about 1982 that it finally closed its doors, as that is when Mr. McDaniel's final term as township trustee ended.

OTHER BUSINESSES

Julius Poehler sold his building, the old opera house that housed his restaurant, in 1951, but we can almost take a trip down memory lane to visit the interior, because he held an auction, and many of the goods to be sold were listed in the newspaper advertisement of July 9, 1950. Other than purely kitchen equipment, he also auctioned a 17.7 by 13 foot maple dance floor, a shuffleboard, mirrors, chairs and tables, benches, six restaurant booths, a glass showcase 6 feet long, a 12-hole ice cream freezer, an antique table made of cherry and walnut that was 11 feet long, three counters, a maple counter, eight metal stools, and, from the walls, a deer head, deer horns, elk horns, and steer horns. Now that I've had a hint, I'd sure like to find a picture or two of the interior of that building!

As previously mentioned, tracing the history of Andrews newspapers is difficult, perhaps impossible. We know that the *Andrews Signal* quit publishing in 1923, except that it may have been published in 1926 and again in the 1930s. Or perhaps it was still publishing, and we just don't know about it. On July 8, 1950, the *Herald Press* said that the Lagro Press Publishing Company, publishers of the *Andrews Signal*, had been purchased from Mr. and Mrs. Lamonte H. Moore, who had moved "some time ago" to Florida. The new owners were Eugene Clare and Eugene Johnson. Kathleen Bickel Nichols shared a copy of the *Andrews Signal* of Friday, October 6, 1950. It is identified as volume five, number 35, which would indicate it had been published since January 1, 1946. We could learn so much more about Andrews if we had access to more of those papers.

Sometimes businesses did very little advertising, so it's hard to know how long they were in business, or even who the proprietors were. Marge's Cafe, mentioned in passing in a description of a birthday party held there in January 1951, is one. Another is Betty's Cafe, which advertised in a Cardinals booster ad on January 26, 1952. Other advertisers that year were North End Grocery, Andrews Phillips 66 (Pat and Charley), Hoffman Oil Co., Wasmuth Lumber and Supply Company, Blue Moon Cafe (John and E. H. Keefer), Chuck's Standard Service, Andrews Feed Store (Clyde R. Wilson), Frank's Home Store, Lew's Barbershop, Schaefer Drug Store, Andrews Elevator, Fults and Goodrich, and Powell's Garage. A short time later, Mr. and Mrs. Arnold Spencer, owners of the Andrews elevator, purchased the feed store, when Clyde Wilson took another job. The 1953 ad boosting the Andrews Cardinals included ads from Ward's Texaco Station and "Your Appliance Store," which suggested one should purchase a Philco television to view the state basketball finals.

It's hard to trace the bars in town, because they didn't often advertise. Even when the members of the Huntington County Retail Alcoholic Beverage Association advertised that minors who entered any of their establishments would be prosecuted, the Blue Moon is the only one listed from Andrews.

The Metz funeral home was sold to Mr. and Mrs. Robert Deal of Muncie in February 1953. The notice from Mr. and Mrs. Basil Metz stated, "We think Andrews is a wonderful community and has fine people. We dislike leaving very much."

Andrews residents must have been cheered to learn that the First National Bank in Huntington was opening a branch office in Andrews. The Andrews State Bank had been voluntarily liquidated in 1946 by men who had bought the bank for that express purpose, and it must have been inconvenient for many to have to go to Huntington for their banking needs. The building would be the same, but the personnel and the financial backing would be much different. The announcement was made on January 11, 1953, and the bank had its grand opening in August 1953. Max Wiley was in charge of the branch, with Miss Carol Hacker as clerk. In a "Welcome to Andrews" advertisement, Andrews Liquor Store, Deal Funeral Home, Hollowell Cities Service, Huntington Manufacturing Co., Inc., Keefer Greenhouses, Kitchen Maid, M.C.B. Manufacturing, E. R. Small Ready Mix Concrete, and J. R. Small & Co. advertised, as well as Marge's Cafe. The Andrews Texaco Service Station wasn't advertising at the time, but in 1954 it was owned by George Branstator and Max Boxell.

A 1955 Cardinals advertisement shows changes in two businesses. The Blue Moon Cafe was now run by Howard Stephan, and instead of "Fults and Goodrich" offering dry goods, the Goodrich Store now was offering "produce, meats, groceries and dry goods." Organic Soil Builders advertised on April 4, 1955. They were open seven days a week, but on weekdays they closed at 1:30. (It appears that the owner, Roy Gallaspie, also worked as a machine operator, but I'm not sure where his other place of employment was.) The 1958 Christmas issue of the *Huntington Herald Press* featured more changes. The Blue Moon Cafe was now under the management of Bob Tester and Carl Hoover. Florence's Beauty Shop and Delbert Snow each advertised in the paper for what I believe was the first time. Another big community ad welcomed shoppers back to Andrews when the bridge, which had been replaced following ice jams in the Wabash River, opened up in October 1959. "Willie's Texaco and Drive-In" advertised, as did the General Engineering and Manufacturing Co.

Kreigh's Cafe had their grand opening on July 15, 1955. Their special of the day was "Buy one, get one free" for sundaes, sodas, malts, shakes, and cones. They advertised "chicken dinners every Sunday." I've heard many stories about this business. Aside from all their other business, this was "the place" to go in Andrews after a ballgame or school dance, and any time at all during the summer months. They were in business for several years. There was a bowling lane in one corner of the building, and apparently a soda-fountain-type counter. It must have been a fun place!

Keefer's Greenhouse advertised from time to time, particularly around Christmas and Easter. By the middle 1950s, they were holding an annual Christmas open house, at which cameras were welcome. I've been told that it just "smelled like Christmas" at that time and that there were always beautiful displays of poinsettias. I sure would like to find a picture from someone who took advantage of that offer to "Bring your camera!" In 1957 the company made news for the development of a new color of carnation, a salmon-colored variety they named the "Cheri Sim," after the young daughter of Ned Keefer, who had developed the flower with his father, Edgar Keefer. They sold the rights to the plants to a large distributor in Indianapolis but received a royalty from the sales that company made, and in addition they were permitted to continue to sell the cut carnation.

Auctions came to town in late 1956. The opening of the Andrews Auction House in the "center of business district" was announced by Guy Friermood, owner. The first auction was on November 20, 1956, and every Tuesday thereafter. Rudicel, McIlravy, and Harris were the auctioneers. They accepted consignments up until 5:00 p.m the day of the auction, so one never really knew what to expect at the auction. By 1959 Homier Furniture was advertising Monday night auctions as well as their retail business. They were located at the corner of Main and Madison. It's not clear whether they had purchased the Friermood business or whether they were in direct competition with Friermood's Tuesday night auctions.

The Bulldog Drive-In was a business near and dear to the hearts of Andrews teenagers, and probably factory workers too. It opened about the first of August 1957, with a grand-opening special of hotdogs for 10 cents each. It was at the rear of the Texaco station, where gas was being sold that day for 26.9 cents a gallon. (Yes, those were the days.) The first owners were Willie and Donna Nunemaker, and then Crit Newsome owned it during the first half of the 1960s. Newsome also owned the Corner Tavern in the 1960s.

One of the oldest buildings in Andrews was torn down in October 1956. The Wabash rail station had been downsized through the years and had been only lightly renovated. The heating system was an old potbellied stove, which didn't keep the station warm in the winter, and other changes were needed also. The amount of freight being shipped through the station finally justified the cost of building a new station, and Andrews said goodbye to this particular landmark. The new station was 46 by 60 feet, made of concrete block, and would include an office and a restroom as well as storage and passenger facilities. It was scheduled to be completed by December 1.

While these were the businesses that were mentioned in the Huntington newspaper or are remembered by residents for these years, by no means were these the only way people earned money. Several women took in roomers, and some probably fed their renters, also. I found no evidence of a real rooming house, but I've been given the names of several who rented out a room or two in their home, generally to well-behaved young men or women. Teenagers earned money in a variety of ways. They mowed lawns, babysat, baled hay for farmers, shoveled snow, and generally hustled, if they didn't have a "steady" after-school or summer job. Andrews was full of workers of all ages.

When sharing memories of Andrews, many people have mentioned the movies that were shown downtown. The merchants of the town were generally the ones who provided the movie, a different, family-friendly movie each week, sometimes shown on a large sheet that may have been hung from a building or sometimes stretched across an alley. These were regular summer events during the 1950s and into the first few years of the 1960s, and the community enjoyed and appreciated this opportunity for family fun.

SCHOOL

The Andrews school turned out soldiers and sailors, and also factory workers and homemakers. It is amazing to look back and realize what a huge amount of good can come out of such a small school. The class of 1950 included 15 graduates, and classes stayed small during much of the decade. By 1959 there were 26 in the graduating class, one of the largest classes ever graduated.

Between those years, a lot was happening at the building on the hill. The school building itself was 20 years old now and still serving the town well. It went both ways. The town was also supporting the school, not only in sports but in many other areas of both academic and extracurricular life. Students continued to excel in areas such as music, for instance. In February 1950 Mary Edith McDaniel and

Colleen Reemer were rated excellent in a vocal contest held in Fort Wayne, and Kenneth Rittenhouse and Edgar Kitt were rated superior. The junior class put on their class play, in which Alfred Reust, James Fields, Madonna Garrison, James Blake, Joann Hunnicutt, Kenneth Rittenhouse, Norma Owens, Carol Hacker, and Joe Rupel all had active parts. Robert Smart was stage manager, and stage assistants were Larry McDaniel and Lester Keefer. At the same time, both juniors and seniors were raising money for a class trip, this time with a white-elephant auction. The senior class also held a variety show, highlighted by the crowning of the Queen of the Variety Show. Joann Smith, freshman; Dorothy Sands, sophomore; Joann Hunnicutt, junior; and Barbara Snyder, senior, competed to see who would sell the most tickets to the show. Barbara Snyder was the winner of the coveted crown. About 29 seniors and juniors from the school enjoyed the class trip to Washington, DC, which included a tour of Gettysburg and Annapolis. The trip lasted six days, but it's not stated whether they went by bus or train. Either way, they saw a lot in their days away.

One way to note what we don't know about Andrews school life is to consider Mary Jane Shaffer, who graduated in 1950 and was awarded the $200 Kitchen Maid scholarship for that year. She was secretary of her class, president of the Booster Club, and reporter of the Contabile club and also served the school as pianist and librarian. Although we can guess about the activities and purpose of the Booster Club, the Contabile club is new to me. (Dictionary definitions indicate it had to do with accounting, but I don't know if that is applicable in this situation). I also don't know about the term "librarian." No teacher has been identified with that position, so was Mary Jane the only one who carried out librarian responsibilities? How often could the library have been open, in that case?

The seventh grade, students who would graduate in 1955, held a party at the school. There were 36 students who attended. Only 25 students of that class would graduate. Those who attended the party were Barbara Beeks, Sharon Sandlin, Barbara Long, Barbara Hunnicutt, Janet Bare, Carolyn Fields, Lou Ann Rudig, Mary Ann Smart, Jim Smart, Leon Smith, Ann Kellam, Joe Keffer, Sharon Flaugh, Donna Smuts, Gerald Yentes, Louis Dickson, Shirley Garrison, Doneta Decker, Michael Garretson, Dea Hethcote, Frances Glass, Jack Millman, Shelby Millman, Frances Jones, Pauline Garrison, Janice Hammon, Wilma Miller, Alvin Huston, Darlene Ferrell, Joann Randolph, Nancy Mathews, Susie Percell, Pat Sands, Charles Penn, Ronnie Harvey, Billy Grossnickle, and the teacher, Mrs. Leakey.

The big event of 1950, however, was the spring election. Dallas Township and Polk Township voted on whether to merge into a metropolitan school district composed of both townships. Under the law as interpreted by the state attorney general, each township would have to have a majority vote in favor of the consolidation in order for such a plan to move forward. Each township had shown that there was interest in the proposed consolidation by filing petitions signed by at least 5 percent of its taxpayers. Polk Township voted "No" overwhelmingly: 178 against and 35 for the proposal. Dallas Township voted 231 for the proposal and 161 against. Monument City, the school in Polk Township, had only 25 students, could not meet state requirements for classes offered, had no gymnasium, and had no funds to maintain the school, but it seems the voters did have community spirit.

Teachers for the 1951-52 school year featured some new names. O. W. Beitelshees was principal. James J. Hughes would teach social studies and physical education; Garland B. Borden, science and social studies; Helen Burkhart, commerce; Ersell Leakey, mathematics and Latin; Ruth

Stookey, music and English; Mary Moore, home economics and physical education; Paul Sellenberger, band; and William McPherran, Lois Schilling, Doris Wall, Gertrude Goebel, Doris Walter, and Florence Schery would be elementary teachers. Later, "Mary Moore" was identified as Mrs. Mary M. Morehead, who resigned in the middle of the year to return to her home in South Carolina. Miss Madeline Salisbury was chosen to take her place.

One highlight of the school year for many students in grades one through three was the almost-yearly trip on the Wabash Railroad, leaving from Huntington and arriving in Wabash, where buses were waiting to bring them back to the school The students were shown how to buy tickets and had a short tour of the railroad cars during the trip. This was in conjunction with lessons on transportation and, for some of them, might have been the only time they rode the trains. The rest of the school year was full of the usual events of Christmas plays, the variety show, class parties, and then graduation events.

The 1951-52 school year opened with 336 students in the Andrews school, including 77 high school students. The building had improved heating, a new roof over most of the building, and new equipment in the lunch room. In addition, the usual more typical maintenance work had been done during the summer.

The juniors and seniors held an elaborate bazaar on November 17. It included 13 shopping booths, 5 entertainment booths, and 2 restaurants, set up to look like a town. The "businesses" included a toy shop, a general store, a fish pond, a flower pot, a workbasket, a bookstore, a butcher shop, a fruit market, a pantry shelf, a daisy maid bakeshop, a sweet shop, an apron bar, an opera house, a shoe-shine boy, a jukebox, cider, "freaks," and curios. A waffle supper was served in the cafeteria and short orders in the home economics room. A baton exhibition, a spelling

179

bee, and an amateur hour were also offered, followed at the end of the day by the crowning of the king and queen. Coelestine Keiser was chosen queen and Tom McDaniel, king. Surely the students and probably the parents worked a long time both before the big day and on the big day, to prepare the goods offered, make the decorations, and keep the booths running.

The junior play that year was *Rest Assured*, with a cast of characters comprised of Arden Hanselman, Phyllis Laymon, Jean Riley, Janis Tullis, Velma J. Goebel, Rudy Decker, Richard King, Sandra Garrison, George Plew, Bill Yahne, Edgar Kitt, Carol Ann Niblick, Ivan McDaniel, Roderick Goebel, and Norma Cocklin. Some of those listed for the junior play were actually seniors, as the list of graduates that year included Norma Cocklin, Richard Cundiff, DeWayne Fitch, Ruth Forst, Allen Hollowell, Nina King, Carol Niblick, Robert Oswalt, David Pratt, Betty Satchwill, Shirley Small, and Walter Stephan,

A new competition among the county schools was inaugurated in 1952 with a county spelling contest. Andrews walked away with five awards out of the 24 places, with a total of 13 schools represented. Diann Moore, third grade, was the first-place finisher for Andrews, and Karin Kelly, Marilyn Wallace, Paula Wilson, and Norma Cocklin took second or third place at their respective grade levels. Surely some students were already saying, "I'd like to be a part of this and will work harder next year."

Andrews was probably not happy when Coach Jim Hughes announced at the end of April 1952 that he was resigning to take a position as head basketball coach at Syracuse. The *Herald Press* described him as popular, having turned out many good ball clubs at Andrews during his six years there, and having won two-thirds of his basketball games during that period.

Two men from Andrews received scholarships for the freshman year of college. David Pratt, valedictorian, won the Kitchen Maid scholarship of $200 as well as a state scholarship for any state school in Indiana. He planned to attend Purdue to study electrical engineering. He lived in Andrews with his grandmother, Mrs. Ethel Pratt, while attending school here. James Stephan, salutatorian and son of Mrs. and Mrs. John Stephan, was awarded the Kitchen Maid sportsmanship trophy for the year, as well as a state scholarship to be used at any state school.

New teachers for the 1952-53 school year included Marvin F. Simons, social studies and English (although later it was stated he would be a sixth-grade teacher); Philip Hyman, physical education and industrial arts; and Gladys Putterbaugh, commerce. The fall of 1952 was apparently the first time that parents in Dallas Township would have the option of renting used text books for their students rather than purchasing new ones.

Janis Tullis, daughter of Mr. and Mrs. C. M. Tullis, won a county "Voice of Democracy" contest. She wrote her speech and then recorded it for judging, along with the speeches of four other contestants. Her speech would be forwarded to the state contest, where she would be competing with about 30 others. Janis was a yell leader and a member of the girls' athletic association, the Sunshine Society, and the Booster Club.

The Sunshine Society had gone quiet, at least in the newspaper, but in December 1953 members of the group and some members of the school choir went to the Wabash County Home to share a Christmas program. We don't know what else the group might have done. Their good deeds were supposed to be done mostly anonymously, so it is possible that much had been happening that we just don't know about.

It was time in the fall of 1953 to finish raising funds for the junior-senior class trip. In addition to the plays the classes usually put on, and concession sales, this year the students conducted a scrap drive, collecting scrap metal, papers, and rags in an early version of recycling. Class members would come to the donor's home or place of business to pick these items up.

The 1954 graduates were Morris Bitzer, Sondra Detamore, Jackie Ferrell, Eunice Gilbert, Hubert (LeRoy) Hackworth, Merritt Hethcote, Donna Lassiter, Helen Laymon, Larry Oswalt, Robert Reemer, Bud Tullis, and Marjorie Wallace.

Again in the 1954-55 school year there were faculty changes. Richard Hostetler would be teaching science and social science; Harry R. Bollinger, English and science; and Louis Durflinger, band. Ersell Leakey seems to be the longest-serving teacher at this time, but Ruth Stookey had also been teaching for several years. O. W. Beitelshees, the principal, was also a pastor who occasionally did pulpit fill-ins in the area. The school year featured the usual plays, music programs, spelling contests, and of course ball games, and probably (though not found in the newspapers) a junior-senior class trip. The graduating class was composed of Janet Bare, Carolyn Bitzer, Doneta Decker, Lois Dickson, Joseph Ferrara, Carolyn Fields, Michael Garretson, Francis Glass, Ronald Harvey, Dea C. Hethcote, Donna Hetler, Joe Keffer, Georgia Ann Kellam, Shelbylyn Millman, Philip Nettleton, Suzanne Percell, Nancy Reemer, Shirley Rittenhouse, Lou Ann Rudig, Sharon Sandlin, Patricia Sands, Mary Ann Smart, Lawrence Smith, Carolyn Thompson, and Gerald Yentes.

O. W. Beitelshees left at the end of the 1954-55 school year and was replaced as principal by Robert J. Hahn, who also taught science in the high school. He had been teaching math and science at the Salamonie school previously. Lucile

Phillips came from Markle to teach English and art at Andrews.

Contestants for the spelling bee that year, from grades 3 to 12, respectively, were Robert Flora, Cheryl Kester, Deborah Casey, Claudia Garretson, Ronnie Johnson, Arthur Stouffs, Anne Pilcher, Marilyn Wallace, Charlotte Glass, and Terry Buckles.

The school year ended with little noted in the newspaper, other than sports and a brief mention of the Christmas program. Graduates that year had doubtless been active in the usual school activities. They were Kay Beghtel, Terry Buckles, William Detamore, Phyllis Fearnow, Donna Hollowell, Evelyn Laymon, Arnold Miller, Shirley Owen, David Pearson, Carol Small, Esther Snyder, Suzette Stouder, Mary Wright, and Dwayne Ziegler. Suzette Stouder won the Kitchen Maid Scholarship and David Pearson the sportsmanship award.

We have more information about the 1956-57 school year. The senior class held a chili supper and later in the year a variety show. There was the usual Christmas program, involving almost every student of the school. The Sunshine Society had a caroling party, and 38 girls were in attendance. They included Paula Wilson, Joyce Wright, Marilyn Wallace, Jean Anne Beghtel, Jeannie Krile, Karen Millman, Sharon Cook, Kaye Groscost, Marilyn Groscost, Barbara McCullough, Sharon Bickel, Donna and Darlene Rodocker, Alice and Rose Marie Clements, Donna Primmer, Linda Garretson, Virginia Chapman, Elnora Schenkel, Merrilee Sands, Joyce Long, Beverly Turner, Mary Newsome, Connie Cones, Ann Wilson, Arretta Ragan, Jerrine Buzzard, Holly Millman, Betty Wright, Patsy Beghtel, Evangeline Hamman, Peggy Kreigh, Linda Beghtel, Marcia Reemer, Carol Garrison, Shirley Stephan, Phyllis Garrison, and Nancy Huston.

The Parent Teacher Association of the school put on a minstrel show as a fund-raiser. Today we shudder to hear of such a thing, but at the time it was a popular way to raise funds and wasn't considered demeaning. The all-male cast included Walt Collins, Roy Huston, Ralph Hunnicutt, Gene Wilson, Dave Pearson, Lester Stephan, John Bickel, Louis Durflinger, Ivan McDaniel, Edgar Keefer, Dean Bickel, Louis Goebel, Kyle Stouder, and Maurice Friedman, among others.

The junior class presented a play in late March, and later Louis L. Durflinger, band director, led the fourth-grade song-flute class, the sixth-grade junior band, and the senior band in an evening of instrumental music. The fourth-graders included Ronny Adams, Patsy Adamson, Barbara Beghtel, John Carpenter, Karen Clabaugh, Robert Flora, Sally Huston, Sharon Kennedy, Renee Kitt, Carol Krile, Carol Maxton, Bonnie McCullough, Teresa Miller, David Osborn, Michael Schaefer, Danny Smith, Rod Smith, David Stephan, LaMoine Theobald, Carolyn Thompson, John Wasmuth, and Keith Wilson. The sixth-grade band members were Deborah Casey, Ann Bare, Nancy Wilson, Pat Bomersback, Marie Garrison, Ricky Wilkinson, Dian Everroad, Susan Ward, Norman Urschel, Jill Flaugh, Terry Plasterer, Terry Close, and James Beghtel. Members of the senior band were Phylllis Garrison, Sue Schenkel, Kay Groscost, Donna Everroad, Sharon Cook, Donna Rodocker, Tom Schenkel, Jean Krile, James Johnson, Barbara McCullough, Sue Groscost, Daleen Rodocker, Billy Smith, Claudia Garretson, Pam Wilson, Wilma Gray, Mark Crain, James Miller, Rex Ziegler, Arreta Ragan, Douglas Chopson, Joyce Wright, Karen Millman, and Saundra McDaniel.

The *Herald Press* headlines said that the Andrews Sunshine Society held their annual formal dance, but this is the first time I noted it in the newspaper. It was held in the school gym, which was decorated with the theme of "April

Showers." Most if not all of the high school faculty attended, as well as 29 couples from the school.

Judith Stouder was the valedictorian and Paula Wilson the salutatorian for the class of 1957, which had just 19 graduates. Although this was the last class born at the end of the Depression, there may have been other factors at work, also. Andrews was a small enough school that a difference of just a few students was quite noticeable. Considering all that they did during the school year, "small but mighty" might have been their class motto.

The 1957-58 school year started with a new principal, Norman Cozad. Teachers were Eleanor Perry, Mary Schenkel, Belle Butler, Mary Gerdes, Fern Brown, and Vera Olson in the grade school. Teachers for the upper grades were Sanford Brueckheimer, physical education and social studies; Homer Kline, math and science; Lucille Phillips, art and geography; Alfred Piedmont, industrial arts and physical education; Gladys Putterbaugh, commerce; Frances Smith, home economics and physical education; Ruth Stookey, music and English; Louis Durflinger, band; and Marvin Simon, English, social studies, and mathematics. Looking at this list, one wonders what chance the students had to learn a foreign language. Latin hadn't been offered for several years, and it appears that the students had no opportunity to learn French or Spanish at this point. They may not have been sorry.

The school year was fairly quiet, if you judge by the newspapers, but we know there was a band concert and a Sunshine Society dance. The Brueckheimers held a party for the graduates, for the purpose of sharing pictures taken from the senior class trip to Washington, DC. This was apparently no longer a junior-senior trip, and we are given little sense of how hard the students worked to raise money for the trip. However, judging from other class efforts, they had worked since their freshmen year at various fund-raising activities in order to go on the trip. In many ways, this trip was the highlight of the school year for many of the students.

One interesting item about the Andrews school was in the April 1, 1958, *Herald Press*. Technology had come to Andrews, in one form. The fourth-grade class was able to receive supplemental material that was broadcast by radio station WVSH in Huntington. Several modules were available, and we don't know how many were used in Mrs. Gerdes's class. I've asked various members of the class what they remember about this education via radio, and the answer has been "nothing," so perhaps it was an experiment that was ahead of its time.

The 1958-59 school year started with a dispute that involved Andrews only indirectly. The Warren Township (Bippus) and Clear Creek Township trustees had entered an agreement that the seventh- and eighth-grade students from Clear Creek would go to the Bippus school, and the Bippus high school students would go to the Clear Creek School. That didn't meet with the approval of all of the parents, and 13 high school students enrolled at Andrews. I'm unable to track how many stayed at Andrews, but three of the five who enrolled as seniors graduated at Andrews that year, and at least two of those who started as juniors graduated from Andrews in 1960. So for at least some of the students, the change was permanent.

Religious education was provided in the public schools to fourth- and fifth-graders. Nancy Casey, Stephen Owens, Diana Osborn, James Nichols, Nancy Raney, and David Stephen (Stephan?) gave talks in the Andrews churches to explain the benefits of the classes.

For the first time, a list of the officers of the Dallas Township School Student Council (note the change in the name of the school) was provided to the *Huntington Herald Press*. Or perhaps this was the first year a student council had been selected. Roger Miller was president, Sharon Cook was vice president, and Nancy Stouder was secretary-treasurer. Other students on the council were Lu Ann Close, Lyle Laymon, and Larry Quinn, seniors; Kenny Wright, Lyle Garretson, and Joyce Long, juniors; Arden Campbell, Carolyn Garrison, and Ronnie Johnson, sophomores; Gary Fearnow and Jim Miller, freshmen; Terry Close, eighth grade; and Steve Kreigh, seventh grade.

Most if not all of the seniors were involved in the class play, *The Roaring Twenties*, presented on October 17, 1958. Cast members were Roger Miller, Betty Wright, LuAnn Close, Patsy Beghtel, Jerry Harvey, Ray Fearnow, Lyle Laymon, Nancy Stouder, Larry Casey, Rhett Ripplinger, Holly Millman, Sue Groscost, Beverly Turner, Sue Bitzer, Larry Quinn, and Ann Pilcher. Donat Forst, Dale Grade, and Jay Dee Rittenhouse were in charge of stage arrangements, and Philip Bitzer was the business manager.

The school again sent students to musical competitions. Andrews brought home four "excellents" in vocal and piano competitions and three "superiors" in instrumental competition. Donna Everroad and Sue Schenkel took "superior" with a clarinet duet, and Claudia Garretson and Sue Groscost each took a "superior" for their cornet solos. The new band director–teacher was Richard Whitacre.

The seniors again held a variety show in March, with proceeds to go into the senior trip fund. The trip would have been coming up quite quickly. Members of the cast included students from all 12 grades, and there was excitement over who would be crowned queen. Candidates were Claudia Garretson, Judy Prilaman, Holly Millman, and Judy Wegmann.

The Parent Teacher Association held what was at least their second minstrel show, one having been held two years earlier. Again the performers were all male, and they included Ed Buckles, Forest Bare, John Bickel, Paul

Warschko, Lester Stephan, Jake Schmalzried, Edgar Keefer, Robert Deal, Fred Beghtel, Tom Rudig, Gene Moore, Gordon Schaefer, Charles Rogers, Roy Huston, Ralph Hunnicutt, Kenneth Schenkel, George Bitzer, Ernest Schenkel, Howard Urschel, Harold Close, Garent Paul, Rhett Ripplinger, Lyle Laymon, Jay Kitt, Homer Bitzer, Marion Percell, Don Lassiter, Earl Laymon, Don Rodenbeck, Glynn Rudig, Walt Collins, J. D. Rittenhouse, Haskiel Clements, and Ned Keefer. We can assume it was a big success, and we can hope it was the last of those productions.

School opened in 1959 with the town bridge not yet completed. It had been destroyed by an ice jam in late January, and although construction was under way, the bridge was still about three months away from completion. So, as in the previous winter and spring, two of the three buses that Andrews used had to take a long alternate route, adding as much as 35 minutes to the bus trip for those who came in from the north. The merchants weren't the only ones who rejoiced when the bridge was finally opened.

The 1959-60 school year included parties and plays, ball games and concerts, Sunshine activities and probably an all-school Christmas program, although there is not a lot of information in the newspapers about that year. We do know the band traveled to Indiana University to participate in the High School Band Day festival there, which may have been the first time for that experience. Part of the thrill of the day was playing at halftime for the IU–Marquette University football game, as part of a large joint high school band.

The senior class play, *Headin' for the Hills*, was presented on October 16, The cast included Sharon Bickel, Ray Groscost, Tom Schenkel, Joyce Long, Sharon Cook, Jeanne Krile, Kenny Wright, Barbara McCullough, Judy Emley, Karen Millman, Jim Jennings, Charlie Flaugh, Donna

188

Everroad, John Bigelow, Judy Prilaman, Linda Beghtel, Norma Michaels, Dan Smart, and Jim Garrison. Phil Ruppert and Tom Clements were musicians.

As the year ended, there was the usual flurry of parties, along with baccalaureate and commencement, probably a senior trip, and an alumni banquet that welcomed the new crop of seniors. The school, and the graduates, had much to anticipate as they looked toward the next decade.

CHURCHES

Thriving churches were another part of the good memories people have from Andrews in the 1950s. There were four and then five churches to choose from, and attendance remained good for the big three, anyway.

One of the first big church events, on August 23, 1950, was sponsored by the four Andrews churches (Christian, Methodist, Church of the Brethren, and Pilgrim Holiness) and St Paul's Evangelical and Reformed Church, northwest of Andrews. The event featured Homer Rodeheaver, a nationally known song-leader and trombonist, with his pianist, Virgil Brock, and other members of his staff, in a musical program. Rodeheaver, who had been the song-leader for evangelist Billy Sunday, lived at Winona Lake. Proceeds from the event would go to the weekday religious education program that was offered in the Andrews school.

The next year the ministerial association sponsored a 90-minute movie, *The Pilgrimage Play—The Story of the Life of Jesus Christ*, at the school, with proceeds supporting "the work carried on by the ministers of the community." This may have been a benevolence fund used to help down-and-out people who came to the various parsonages to ask for help. Frequently the churches jointly sponsored Good Friday services, for which school would be dismissed, and vacation Bible schools, and they collected funds for UNICEF each fall.

Each church was busy on its own, too. They had men's groups, women's groups, missionary groups, youth groups, children's groups, and Sunday school classes. The groups met on a regular basis, if not weekly, and many times they sponsored fund-raising efforts of one sort or another to raise money for a special cause. They also met for parties and fellowship. Then, of course, the churches themselves had fund-raisers. The chicken barbecues on the lawn of the Methodist Church date from this period, and churches still held ice cream socials and bazaars as well. Some of the money raised, whether through dinners or by private donation, went toward improvements at the various churches. The Methodist Church got new carpeting and installed new front steps while enlarging the foyer of the building. The Christian Church reinforced the belfry of the steeple, which had been in danger of being condemned, and later in the decade replastered the walls, moved the baptistry, and constructed a new platform across the front of the sanctuary. The Church of the Brethren added a basement under their building, giving space for Sunday school classes, a kitchen, and restrooms.

A completely new-to-Andrews church was started in the 1950s. Rev. Homer Habegger came to town to establish a Nazarene congregation. Meetings for the first three months were held in the home of John Carpenter. Later, there was a tent revival meeting in September 1958, and on September 28, 1958, the church held a groundbreaking ceremony. A frame building was constructed to use as a sanctuary at first, and the plan was to use it later as the Sunday school chapel; it was designed so that brick or rock could be added later. A parsonage had already been purchased, next to the church grounds, which were at 333 W. McKeever. John Carpenter,

Frank Stephan, and Mrs. Ellen Owens were the first trustees of the church.

Church membership was serious business in Andrews, or perhaps churches had already begun to see a decline in membership, or at least in enthusiasm. The Methodist Church, the Church of the Brethren, and the Christian Church joined to conduct a survey of all members of the town and township on April 28, 1957. Members from each of the churches went door-to-door to obtain church membership or preference information. Each of the three churches would be provided with the information from the surveys, along with recommendations by Rev. Lonnie Hass of Indianapolis, who would analyze the data.

LODGES AND CLUBS

In addition to the busy schedules of the churches, there were still two lodges for men and two for women, plus one for girls, and the Lions Club, Victory Circle, home demonstration clubs, 4-H, Boy Scouts, Cub Scouts, Girl Scouts, Brownies, and of course the Parent Teacher Association at the school. One can easily envision the mothers who weren't working, as well as those who were, being almost too busy to turn around as they hurried from place to place. TV dinners may have become popular during the 1950s for reasons other than being able to easily eat them in front of a television.

The Free and Accepted Order of Masons appears to be somewhat ritualistic, but every member was obligated to contribute to charity, through the lodge. So certainly all the lodges did good things for Andrews. Officers in 1952 were William Garretson, Edgar Buckles, Arthur Hummer, Robert Spencer, Dorrence Cross, Charles Clements, Forest Bare, Earl Krile, Fred Warfel, and Claude Garretson.

Elected officers for the Order of the Eastern Star for 1950 were Sally Garretson, Eugene Moore, Lindel Buckles, Arthur Everhart, and Hazel Wasmuth. At the time, a member had to have a direct connection to a member of the Masonic Lodge to join the Order of the Eastern Star.

The Miriam Rebekah Lodge was also still active. The overall purpose of this group, loosely attached to the Odd Fellows, was to "live peaceably, do good unto all as we have opportunity and especially, to obey the Golden Rule." One did not have to have a connection to a member of the Odd Fellows Lodge in order to join. Officers in 1950 were Ruth Ellen Speicher, Ruth Prilaman, Alta Roberts, and Isabelle Krile, assisted by Mary Sandlin, Estella Clark, Norma Kitt, Maydean Wilson, Opal Bare, Margaret Stephan, Dorothea Smith, Marian Millman, Estella Clark, Mary Harshbarger, Isabelle Krile, Bernice Tyner, and Betty Kahlenback.

The Freedom Theta Rho Girls club was growing. In March 1950 they installed 11 new members, including Darlene Ferrell, Frances Jones, Jean Riley, Dixie Grossnickle, Peggy Smuts, Janet Bare, Nancy Mathews, Barbara Beeks, Donna Smuts, Doris Cook, and Bonnie Beeks.

Andrews continued to support the Red Cross through local blood drives, donations, and first aid classes. At a blood drive in August 1951, 121 pints of blood were donated. Mrs. Boyd Parks, Mrs. L. C. Schaefer, and Mrs. I. McDaniel were in charge of the local arrangements, including lining up the 164 persons who had agreed to donate. Doubtless some were found ineligible and some were unable to keep their appointments, but the need for blood was understood. With Andrews boys in harm's way in Korea, everyone wanted to do his or her part. Door-to-door campaigns for monetary donations were also an annual occurrence. The collectors for Andrews in March 1956 were Mrs. Edgar Casey, Mrs. George Kellam, Mrs. Ralph Dillon, Mrs. Gene

Moore, Mrs. Gene Knight, Mrs. Don Boone, Mrs. Forest Bare, Mrs. Pete Smith, Mrs. Bill Snyder, Mrs. Richard Wilkinson, Mrs. Ned Keefer, Mrs. John Hahn, Mrs. Leland Flickinger, Mrs. E. H. Roberts, and Mrs. Pearl James. Andrews's goal that year was $175. In 1955 the Red Cross sponsored first aid classes at Andrews. Earning certificates were Gene Wilson, Alta Roberts, Fred Warfel, Eva Wallace, Ethel Yeiter, Jewel Rider, Perdith Myers, Marie Gray, Aldah Tullis, Forrest Gray, Robert Harvey, Norma Bricker, Charles Clements, Mary McDaniel, Charles Fix, Sally Garretson, Claude Garretson, Leona Jennings, Ned Keefer, Flossie Keefer, Albert Moore, and Myron Jennings. Several of the men on this list were serving on the fire department at the time.

Door-to-door campaigns were also held for the Mothers March Against Polio, for UNICEF, and probably for other causes that didn't necessarily merit newspaper space.

The Andrews Lions Club was only a few years old in 1950, but already they were making a difference in the town and for the town. They held an annual fish fry, with proceeds targeting different causes. The 1950 fish fry, which featured Jay Gould of WOWO radio station in Fort Wayne as speaker, would support the remodeling of the government building purchased for the school. Another year, the proceeds went toward a public address system for the school. This particular fish fry was different from some. The home economics clubs would do the cooking, the Lions Club would serve, the Dallas Township Farm Bureau would sell tickets, the conservation club would have charge of the doors, and the Parent Teacher Association would decorate the gym and set up the tables and chairs. Doubtless there were other women who provided food, also. By the next year, the Akron Jonah club did the actual fish frying. The Lions Club has always given back to the community, with one of the big activities being the annual

Halloween parade and costume judging. Usually the high school band led the parade, and it was a time of fellowship over cider and doughnuts for the community, as well as for viewing the costumes and rooting for one's favorites. The Lions Club also sponsored a Christmas lighting contest each year.

Other Lions Club community fund-raising activities included at least two auctions and a circus. While it's not clear which events supported which items, the club supported Boy Scout troops and Little League teams, sponsored a canvas wading pool that was set up at the school, bought a resuscitator for the town, and installed linoleum tile in the "new" town building, while also contributing to district and state Lions Club projects. The wading pool, borrowed from Hettrick Manufacturing Company, was set up on the northeast corner of the school grounds. It had pumps and filters and was fenced, and when open during the summer of 1958, there was always a lifeguard on duty. Children and youth ages 6-14 were welcome to wade there.

Boy Scout, Cub Scout, Girl Scout, and Brownie troops, as well as an Explorer Post (older Boy Scouts) were part of Andrews life in the 1950s. The Boy Scouts mostly were reported in the newspapers for their camping activities, including the 1950 Jamboree at Valley Forge, Pennsylvania, which involved Dr. Omstead and his sons Drake and Harvey as well as others from the county. The Boy Scouts were responsible for paper drives and town cleanups, which provided some of the funds needed for their activities. The cleanup days were for the collection of paper, scrap iron, ashes, and tin cans. Residents were asked to donate generously in exchange for having these items removed from their homes and yards.

Rhett Ripplinger, son of Mrs. Darlene Hamer, earned the status of Eagle Scout in December 1956. It was a rare event even then for a scout to stay in the program long enough, and work hard enough, to earn this rank, and it was a proud moment for Fred Warfel, scoutmaster at the time. Two years later, Lawrence (Larry) Casey was one of the first scouts in the Fort Wayne area to earn the God and Country award. He completed more than a year of study and of service to his local church (the Christian Church) in order to qualify for the award. He was the son of Ed and Margaret Casey. Larry and Jimmy Garrison also earned Star Scout awards; a Star Scout appears to be somewhere between a First Class Scout and an Eagle Scout.

In August 1952, the Cub Scout rosters were long. Boys who took a daylong trip to several businesses in Fort Wayne were DeWayne Andrews, Larry Quinn, Dan Smart, David Tester, James Jennings, Billy Bitzer, Philip Bitzer, Tom Clements, Charles Wallace, Earl Wallace, James Long, Doug Chopson, Terry McDaniel, Tom Bomersback, Arthur Stouffs, Dan Stouffs, Max Kohr, Lyle Laymon, Jimmy Miller, Roger Miller, John Henson, Lyle Garretson, Dennis Middleton, Kenny Wright, Johnny Snider, Tom Tullis, Melvin Dinius, and Billy Smith. Den mothers were Mrs. Ben Garretson, Mrs. Pete Smith, Mrs. Charles Clements, Mrs. Edna Bitzer, Mrs. Hilbert Middleton, and Mrs. Arthur Stouffs.

Four Girl Scout and Brownie troops were organized in 1952. The Brownies leaders were Mrs. Garland Bamberlin and Mrs. Fred Beghtel; the leaders for younger intermediate girls, Mrs. Ed Casey and Mrs. Roy Huston; for intermediate girls, Mrs. Claude Garretson and Mrs. Fred Warfel; and for older intermediates, Mrs. Robert Warfel, Mrs. Howard Stephan, and Mrs. Earl Krile. Brownie troop members in 1953 were Pamela Chopson, Sandra Dinius, Debby Casey, Ann Bare, Patty Bomersback, Dian Everroad, Maria Garrison, Cheryl Dewert, Cheryl Chopson, Lindal Krile, and Kay Walters. Some of these troops were sponsored by the Home Demonstration Club, and some by various churches, but it is hard to keep a scorecard for them. Mrs. Robert Deal, Mrs. Gordon Schaefer, and Mrs. Earl Krile were leaders for a new group of Brownies in 1954. Two years later Mrs. Russell Clabaugh was the leader of a new Brownie group. By May 1956 there were six troops, three of Brownies and three intermediate groups. After that, there is no newspaper coverage of scouting, either boys or girls, although it's believed that the programs continued.

The Dallas Township Home Economics (Demonstration) Club was quite a large organization at the time. They held a mother-daughter banquet in 1951, attended by about 40 members, in addition to guests. These ladies liked to have fun. In November 1954 they held a Hard Times party, with costumes requested. The winners were Mrs. Belle Butler, Mrs. Lawrence Garretson, and Mrs. Guy Peters. It's nice to think that the Depression was far enough back in history that the ladies, having lived through it, could laugh about it.

The club, sometimes in conjunction with the Dallas Township Farm Bureau, also held banquets and programs honoring the achievements of the members of the 4-H clubs. In 1953, pins for achievement by girls were given to Lois Nettleton, Billie Schwartz, Sue Schenkel, Joann Kohr, Judy Emley, Donna Primmer, Donna Everroad, Linda Hackworth, Wilma Gray, Carlene Theobald, Francis Miller, Sam Tullis, Sharon Bickel, Dalene Rodocker, Wendy Fryer, Nancy Stouder, Donna Rodocker, Donna Lassiter, Lindel Beghtel, Sandra McDaniel, and Judy Stouder. Boys who received pins were Billy Bitzer, Richard Haley, Clair Lynn, Philip Bitzer, Richard Garrison, Francis Glass, Lyle Laymon, Roger Miller, Philip Schilling, and Donald Lassiter. The membership grew in the later 1950s, when in 1958 there were about 40 girls in the program and presumably many boys, too. The article I found, indicating that Mrs. Rudy Decker and Mrs. Earl Laymon were leaders, only mentioned girls: Patsy Beghtel, Andris Beghtel, Barbara Beghtel, Patty Bomersback, Melanie Campbell, Cheryl Chopson, Donna Chubbuck, Cheryl Duhammel, Donna Everroad, Dian Everroad, Claudia Garretson, Marie Garrison, Phyllis Garrison, Sharon Goebel, Barbara Hamer, Joyce Hollowell, Sharon Kennedy, Renee Kitt, Jean Krile, Carol Krile, Linda Krile, Kathy Kuschel, Barbara McCullough, Bonnie McCullough, Lois Nettleton, Daleen Rodocker, Sue Schenkel, Nancy Stouder, Diana Turner, Linda Turner, Kay Walters, Judy Wegmann, Mary Wehr, Pam Wilson, and Betty Wright. Each of these girls would have completed projects and participated in the county 4-H fair.

Clair Lynn was one boy who was involved in 4-H from the time he was nine years old. He signed up for six projects his first year in the organization, including poultry, barrow, gilt, garden, rabbit, and wild life. Clair had earlier participated in an essay contest, and his prize was 200 chickens. 4-H was in this family's blood, as his older brother Richard and his sister Carolyn had also entered many projects and won blue ribbons.

The Victory Circle had a renewed cause as the boys and men of Andrews went to Korea and other locations overseas. In November 1950, they sent Christmas boxes to the men in service. Members at that time included Viola Caster, Mary McDaniel, Leona Jennings, Sarah Hawes, Earl Lyons, Adah Tullis, Cleo Beeks, Blanche Wintrode, India Small, Edith Rittenhouse, Lulu Taylor, Alta Roberts, Vera Heitz, Bertha Stallings, Kate McDaniel, Minnie Reid, Anna King, and Myrtle Quinn, and probably others who weren't at the meeting that was in the news. By 1952 they had learned a little about sending the boxes. They held a bake sale and market on September 6, with proceeds to go toward Christmas boxes for the "boys in the service." They would get this year's boxes off early enough that they would actually be received by Christmas. For several years, the club sponsored a Memorial Day service at the plaque on the library grounds. Usually this included Boy Scout and Girl Scout formations, a presentation of some kind to represent the lives lost in World War II, and a speaker. The club made plans to add names to the plaque, but it's not clear whether or not that happened. In 1955 they purchased a hospital-type bed for the use of community members. It was kept at the Deal funeral home and was available to anyone upon request. In December 1958, the members of the club voted to disband. Membership had slipped as the international situation had quieted and fewer men and women were in the service. The women made a final trip to the County Home, and then donated their treasury to charity and their flag to the Boy Scouts.

There was one other club in Andrews, but it appears to have been of short duration. There is a single notice, on August 17, 1951, of the "Coffee Clatch club of Andrews." It met at the home of Mrs. Ella Goebel and included Mrs. George Stephan, Mrs. Elizabeth Wiedenhoet, Mrs. Julia Richards, Mrs. Katherine Goebel, and Mrs. Sophia Diefenbaugh. They planned another meeting for the next month, but that is the last that is heard about them. It may have been a social gathering rather than a club organized for a purpose.

CRIMES

People and businesses in Andrews continued to be a target of criminals. Mrs. Mildred Pohler, who operated a package liquor store in Andrews, was robbed of about $70 on April 25, 1950. She was alone in the store at the time, and was robbed at gunpoint by one man, who disappeared without being noticed by anyone else in town. The liquor store was located on Jefferson Street, a half block off Main Street, just behind the Blue Moon, in a white frame building. This occurred in the early evening, so presumably $70 would have been most of the day's receipts.

About six weeks later, thieves broke into the elevator, run by Parks and Spencer, but took only candy. They had probably hoped to find money in the safe, which was open, but there was no money there.

Other crimes committed in and around Andrews were solved when Darrell E. Briggs, 27, was arrested in Wabash County on other charges. He confessed to breaking in to the Bitzer service station three different times, stealing a vehicle belonging to Myron Jennings, ransacking "Eddie" Keefer's car, and slugging Keefer, on July 12, 1950. The confession came a few days later. This would help the town rest a little easier, even though the liquor store and elevator incidents were still unsolved.

Marlene Dickson Hendricks was 19 years old with two small children when she slipped out of her home in Huntington and went to visit her parents, who lived in Andrews. It's not clear what happened next, but her husband, Gerald Hendricks, found her in Andrews. Pushing and shoving ensued, and Gerald fired two shots with a revolver. One hit Marlene, and she was taken to the hospital. Authorities were called and Gerald was arrested back at his home in Huntington. He pled guilty to a charge of assault and battery and was sentenced to three months at the state penal farm, plus a small fine and costs. Marlene Hendricks filed for divorce.

Charles Breeding's service station, at the corner of US 24 and State Road 105, was hit again by robbers on October 31, 1952. Money belonging to bus companies was stolen, but the service station money was safe at home. The station sold tickets for the bus company, which made stops at or across from the station. November 17 brought a repeat of

199

the October 31 event, except that the Cities Service Station, located nearby and operated by Jack Nunemaker, was also broken into. A garage and filling station at South Whitley, also on State Road 105, had a break-in the same night, and that theft appeared to be connected to the ones at Andrews. Charles Breeding's service station was robbed again on December 12, 1953, but this time the loss was greater and the outcome was different. The thieves made off with about $100 worth of goods, including automobile batteries and accessories, candy, and cigarettes, but they were caught in Ohio later. These perpetrators were youths, who were not identified in the newspaper. The station was again the target of robbers on January 17, 1957. This was before the days of burglar alarm systems and security cameras, and Breeding couldn't seem to find a way to prevent the thefts.

A story about a youth from New Mexico who robbed SS Peter and Paul's Catholic Church in Huntington wouldn't belong in this book at all, except that he had briefly lived in Andrews and was arrested at "a rooming house in Andrews." He worked at one of the Andrews factories but had only been in town about seven weeks.

The saga of Edward M. Millican, which continues beyond the official scope of this book, begins in the 1950s. He was 18 years old when he was arrested on charges of being AWOL from the Air Force Base in Kansas where he was stationed, transporting a stolen auto across state lines, and theft of money from fellow servicemen. He was arrested near the Idle Hour quarry east of Huntington and was turned over to the US marshal. He would be heard from again. On March 11, 1957, he and his brother William broke into a home in the county and stole three revolvers and ammunition, and also broke into Frank Bomersback's grocery, where they stole 12 cartons of cigarettes, about $150 in "redeemable coupons," and six wristwatches. The coupons were later found in a steel box that had been dumped in the creek along Range Line Road, wet but undamaged. The cigarettes had been smoked and the watches disposed of, although one was recovered in an Andrews alley. Possibly Millican had been dishonorably discharged from the Air Force for his previous crimes and had returned to live in Andrews, but surely not happily ever after. I didn't find a disposition of the charges regarding the grocery store break-in, but for the theft of the guns and ammunition, reduced to a charge of grand larceny, he was found guilty, fined $10, sentenced to 1 to 10 years in the Indiana reformatory, disfranchised for five years, and ordered to pay costs.

I may be missing another crime, for on December 8, 1961, Millican walked away from a work detail at the Indiana State Reformatory. He was there for second-degree burglary and vehicle theft, which is not the charge from the grocery robbery. Millican was arrested again on December 23, 1961, in Terre Haute, having robbed a finance company in Logansport of $386. He had used a bus to make his escape and had dyed his hair black to help him elude police, but was arrested just three days later. He filed a guilty plea and was sentenced to 10-25 years in the reformatory, in addition to being disfranchised for 10 years. First, however, he would have to finish serving concurrent sentences of 1-10 years and 2-5 years for the charges that had put him into the reformatory previously.

Millican apparently was not happy at the Indiana State Prison in Michigan City, where he had been sent, and managed to escape on January 19, 1965. He made his way back to Huntington County and committed three robberies before local authorities were aware that he had gone missing from the prison. A truck stop, a service station, and a liquor store were all subjects of Millican's crimes. He also stole at least one vehicle and robbed the Stop and Go grocery store in Huntington on February 5. He hired a man

201

in Marion to take him to Kentucky and got as far as Madison, Indiana, where he was caught. The stolen car was recovered, along with evidence that tied him to a burglary at the Andrews school.

Then it gets confusing. There is a report on October 6, 1971, that Millican and another man had disarmed and handcuffed three Huntington city policemen, taking their revolvers and throwing their car keys on the roof of a downtown building. Millican had escaped on August 22 from Marion County General Hospital in Indianapolis, where he had been brought for treatment while serving a "one year term" at the Indiana State Reformatory. Arrested by two policemen in Marion, he pulled a gun on them when he was in a police vehicle. The officers rolled from their vehicle and shot at it, wounding Millican. I failed to find follow-up articles about the charges that undoubtedly resulted from these crimes, but Millican was surely sent back to finish his sentences from earlier crimes, and would have had additional time added for these.

So why was he out of prison again in June 1976? Despite a long list of crimes and several escapes, he had been paroled . Within days, he was wanted for questioning regarding a bank robbery in Kokomo. And on July 15, 1976, he became something of a notorious legend, or at least a celebrity, in Andrews when he tried to rob the First National Bank in town. The employees, Gilbert Shideler and Mary Brooks, saw him about to enter with a sawed-off shotgun and quickly made their way to the vault, closing the door and locking it from the inside. There were no customers in the bank, and the town marshal, Ray Williams, saw what was happening from his office window more or less across the street. He called to Millican that his getaway car had left (it had), that he was surrounded (he wasn't), and that he might just as well surrender (he did). Meanwhile, the getaway car left, and the accomplice ended up ditching it on

Leedy Lane. He then walked back toward town and persuaded Bert Forst, who lived on Leedy Lane, to take him to Wabash. Forst did so, never suspecting that he had a bank robber in his car, until he hit a roadblock in Wabash and his car was swarmed by Wabash police. Bert's wife had contacted police and told them that her husband was taking a stranger to Wabash, and she thought it might have something to do with the bank robbery. Eventually, the town stopped talking about the incident, and Millican was sentenced to 30 years for the bank robbery, the maximum sentence. Millican apparently ended his criminal career with four crimes as a juvenile, bank robberies, several vehicle thefts, three or more escapes, and several "miscellaneous" robberies.

Millican died in Indianapolis in 2002, and his obituary as well as his death certificate state only that he was a conservation officer in California. I am not able to verify this. I think it's safe to say that he led an interesting life, though not one worthy of emulation. He had six brothers and sisters, and as far as I have been able to learn, they were decent, law-abiding citizens for the most part. I can't tell you why one boy from Andrews went so wrong.

Eugene Newsome was found guilty of assault and battery after a jury trial in October 1956. The original charge had been assault and battery with attempt to commit rape, but a jury found him guilty of the lesser charge. He was identified as being 17 years old and from Andrews, but I found no details about the alleged crime other than that it involved a young girl. He was fined $100 and sentenced to the penal farm for 90 days.

OTHER TOWN NEWS AND HAPPENINGS

While Andrews obviously had people who were in the newspaper for all the wrong reasons, lots of Andrews people were featured there for good reasons. Among those in the 1950s:

Pfc. Wilbur Stallings's picture was on the cover of *Infantry Journal* magazine in March 1950. He was attending NCO school at the time, and the article that accompanied the photo was about "Frontline Fighters" in the Korean conflict.

Henry J. Crull of Andrews received a patent on June 5, 1956, for "a method and apparatus for producing fish bait." He had developed a new way of raising and packaging live bait, particularly bee moths. Many people still remember his shop, at the corner of Main Street and Madison, the current location of the Bethesda Freewill Baptist Church.

Frank Wade, son of Mr. and Mrs. Oliver Wade and a graduate of the class of 1934, was regional director of the southern district of Boys Clubs of America in April 1951 and was one of the most successful directors in the nation for developing the greatest number of clubs. It is reported that, not long before his death in 1969, he had his picture taken with President Richard Nixon, so he must have continued his success in that endeavor. Who knows how many lives Frank touched through his work?

Kenneth Cook of Andrews got his 15 minutes of fame when he was tagged as being the one-millionth person to attend a Chicago White Sox home game at the old Comiskey Field during the 1951 American League baseball season. As part of the honors, he and Mrs. Cook were introduced at home plate and were presented with a year's supply of beer, ice cream, and margarine; a three-month supply of gasoline; two season passes to the 1952 White Sox home games; a topcoat; 100 pounds of canned ham and barbecued beef; and a television set (perhaps one of the first in Andrews?). Mrs. Cook commented that if all the ice cream arrived at once, they would have an ice cream social on their front lawn, and they would give away the beer!

Homer Ross, of letters-to-the-editor fame, and his wife, identified only as "Mrs. Ross" in the newspaper article, celebrated their 50th wedding anniversary on September 28, 1951. As a tribute, Mr. Ross wrote this letter to the editor:

A girl lived across the street from our house. I was interested in that girl. That interest grew until it took me an hour to tell that girl good night. When that interest reached the stage that an hour was not time enough, I ask [*sic*] that all important question and she being in a reckless mood said yes and fifty years ago, across the breakfast table from me, was that girl. Other faces have appeared around that table, little faces that grew up and went away. To them, across the breakfast table from me today its Mom. To other little faces that are sometimes around that little table its grandmother. But to me it's still that girl.

Homer Ross

(published in the *Huntington Herald Press*, September 20, 1951)

Mr. Ross was still writing letters to the editor, mostly humorous but sometimes stepping on people's toes. Some didn't like it and wrote back, which probably increased the daily sales of the newspaper a little bit.

Judy Laugle made the front page of the *Herald Press* on April 6, 1952. She had been fitted with a hearing aid at age ten, purchased by the Huntington County Society for Crippled Children. The young girl had very little hearing before the aids were purchased, and she now had a chance to go on and lead a normal life. The hearing aids cost nearly $100, which was a significant sum for the society. Judy's story was presented as part of a fund-raising appeal.

The *Herald Press* listed the names of their newspaper carriers occasionally. In 1952, the special occasion was the issuance of a three-cent US postage stamp honoring "newspaperboys" (sorry, I know there were girl carriers, too). The newspaper carriers were each given a first-day issue of the stamp. Andrews carriers at the time were Larry Coldren, Robert Burnworth, and Tom Tullis.

Mr. and Mrs. George Gray of Andrews celebrated their 67th wedding anniversary on Sunday, April 19, 1953. They had lived on Colorado Street in Andrews for about 17 years after he "retired," but George had plowed gardens and helped build the Pilgrim Holiness Church and was still busy. Mrs. Gray still did all of her own housework and had made 12 quilts and pieced two silk ones in the previous year. But the Grays were known primarily for their gardens, which included 200 varieties of flowers. Mrs. Gray got the credit for the gardens, but I suppose Mr. Gray at least helped lay out the flower beds. It must have been quite a sight. Their son and daughter-in-law, Forest and Marie Gray, continued the tradition but perhaps not quite to the same extent.

Mr. and Mrs. Edgar Keefer attended a School of Floral Design in Seattle, Washington, in September 1955, and then fished for salmon in the Pacific Ocean before continuing to a remote Alaskan fishing camp near Bristol Bay on the Bering Sea. Their trip included stops in Victoria and Vancouver, British Columbia, as well as Juneau and Anchorage, Alaska. They flew to the fishing camp by bush plane and reported afterward that the trout fishing was unbelievably good.

Tennessee Ernie Ford stopped in Andrews sometime in the late 1950s. Or rather, the train he was riding on stopped here. Ron Inyart remembers that he greeted people at the depot and perhaps signed some autographs. I wonder if he "blessed their little pea pickin' hearts" as he left town. This would have been a big deal for the Andrews people who were lucky enough to see him. Celebrities in Andrews were few and far between.

Mrs. Irene Harris and Mrs. Elsa Louthan, both of Andrews, earned a footnote in history as being the last two people who were naturalized in Huntington County courts. They were granted citizenship on March 7, 1956. Irene, from Fichtenberg, Germany, had married E. L. Harris in 1948, but I was unable to locate additional information regarding Elsa. Future naturalizations took place in Fort Wayne.

Andrews, more than 100 years after its founding, still produced hunters. There were local fox drives, and deer season was important to many, but some men felt the need to drive about 1,200 miles to a camp near Douglas, Wyoming, for the opening of deer season in September 1958. Guy and Orange Powell, Ray Keel, John Brumbaugh, Joe Keffer, and Larry Luker were there in position to take shots at the first light. All six men had deer licenses and three had antelope licenses, and each man got his limit a short time after the season started. This wasn't the first, or the last, time that most of these men went hunting. They brought home game, but they also brought home stories.

PASSINGS

Other good men and women lived their last days during the 1950s. Thurman Eagleson, who had been a barber in town for about eight years, died May 30, 1950, at age 50. He had come to Andrews from Fort Wayne.

James (Bill) Haley died at age 79. He had worked as a machinist and millwright at the Wasmuth-Endicott

(Kitchen Maid) company for 25 years before taking employment in Huntington. He was 79 years old and had been retired for four years. As a 40-year resident of Andrews, a member of both the Masonic lodge and the Order of Eastern Star, and a member of the Christian Church, he would have been well known in town.

Lawrence Bitzer, who owned the Standard Oil station at State Road 105 and US 24, north of Andrews, died at the young age of 38. He belonged to the Andrews Lions Club and the Dallas Township Conservation Club.

Vesta Pearson had been town marshal of Andrews for several years when he retired in 1950 because of ill health. While visiting a sister in New York, he had become ill and was hospitalized at the Veteran's Hospital in Brooklyn, New York.

Charles Keefer died on February 22, 1953, at age 88. He had lived in Andrews for all 88 years and was a member of several lodges and the Andrews Methodist Church. He had two sons, Edgar and Noel, and a daughter, Rosemary, who was a career Army nurse.

Time marches on. Flora Bell Mower, a lifetime resident of Andrews, died at age 80. She was the last surviving charter member of the Order of Eastern Star and was a member of the Methodist Church.

Norma Owen, a member of the small but mighty Andrews High School class of 1951, died on March 3, 1954, in a traffic accident near Woodbridge, Virginia. She was a member of the Women's Air Force and was stationed at Fort Myers, Virginia.

Earl Lyons died March 21, 1954, at age 72. He had lived in Andrews for 45 years and was a member of the Andrews Lions Club. Andrews people had gone to him for his services in real estate and in insurance. He had offices at his home in Andrews and at the Odd Fellows lodge in Huntington.

Dr. J. P. Young had lived in Andrews for five years when he died on July 12, 1954. He was a chiropractor in Huntington but had come to Andrews to live when he married Mrs. Dessie Ross in 1949. He was a member of the Lions Club in Andrews.

Irvin M. Wiley, often referred to as "I. M. Wiley," passed away on May 12, 1955. He had lived in Andrews since the end of World War I, after serving in the US Army in France. He was a retired schoolteacher and had been a Dallas Township trustee for about two and a half terms. He was a member of the Christian Church and both the Masonic Lodge and the Andrews IOOF.

There would never again be a letter to the editor quite the same as those that Homer C. Ross wrote. He died January 5, 1956, after keeping area residents interested in his letters to the *Huntington Herald Press* for several years. He was a retired carpenter, an elder of the Christian Church, and a member of the Andrews library board. He was described as a retired carpenter, but he worked for many years at Kitchen Maid.

Town employee Walter Yeiter died August 12, 1951. Sadly, his death was not from natural causes; he committed suicide after taking a shot at Elias "Bud" Beeks, Andrews deputy marshal, following a domestic dispute with his ex-wife, who had just been granted a divorce.

Another sad suicide was that of Bernice Zimmerman, widow of Charles Zimmerman and formerly part of the Zimmerman funeral home in Andrews. She died March 3, 1952, in Huntington at the Jefferson Sanitarium.

Mary Harshbarger, wife of Cleveland Harshbarger and mother of three young children, died in a traffic accident just outside of Andrews. The funeral attendance was large, because Mary had a large family, she worked at Kitchen Maid, and Cleve worked at the Majestic factory in Huntington. The whole community mourned for Mary.

Clarence Keefer died at age 48 of a heart attack. His wife, Flossie Rector, had been raised in Andrews by her grandparents, and it may have been good that she lived among home folks when she became a widow. He had been employed at Kitchen Maid.

W. O. Taylor, who had been involved in several businesses earlier in the century (he was the "T" in Gets Manufacturing), died in July 1956 in Ann Arbor, Michigan. He had left Andrews in 1922, except for visits back, but was remembered especially for owning and operating the Lagro–Andrews–Mt. Etna telephone company.

Arthur Wasmuth died November 3, 1956, at age 84. He was a graduate of the IU law school and practiced law in Huntington. Later he entered the lumber, coal, and feed business and had lived in Andrews since 1937. He had a son, John, who lived in Andrews, and four other sons and a daughter. His sister, Mrs. Elizabeth Endicott, lived in Indianapolis, and a brother, Harry, lived in Mount Dora, Florida, at the time of Arthur's death.

Another "old-timer," John Chronister, died May 16, 1957. He lived and worked in Andrews from 1907 to 1954 as a harness maker and cobbler, retiring at age 88.

Daisy King, widow of Benjamin King, died August 2, 1957. She had been involved, with her husband, in operating a grocery store in Andrews for 20 years, ending about the time her husband died in 1933.

Frank Huston, who had operated a garage in Andrews, died March 3, 1957.

And then there is Andy Manson, who died March 2, 1959. He was born in 1876 in the same home at the north edge of Andrews that he lived in all his life. He was a retired Kitchen Maid employee and belonged to the Methodist Church in Andrews. He was, in a way, representative of the many residents of Andrews who lived most or all of their lives in Andrews and died a resident of the town, people who paid their taxes and stayed out of trouble with the law, whose only mention in the local newspapers was in the neighborhood columns, but who contributed in their own way to their town and to their country. There are probably more people like this than those who gained widespread recognition, and we owe them gratitude.

The 1950s, despite the loss of these good people, was a good time for the people of Andrews. If someone wanted to work, there were local jobs available. There were stores in town to supply basic needs, and gas stations. Something interesting was usually happening at the school. It was the last decade of what one would consider "idyllic times" in Andrews, although those who lived in town in the 1960s also had much for which to be thankful.

Chapter Seven
1960-1966

NATIONAL

The 1950s for the nation had been a fairly quiet time, despite the development of the hydrogen bomb, the mandate for racial integration in schools, the Space Race, the Korean War, and tensions in Germany and eastern Europe. The 1960s, nationally, was a decade of excitement and progress as well as of tensions and political assassinations. In 1961 the Russians and East Germans built the Berlin Wall, which they hoped would permanently separate East Germany from West Germany. It called for a strong military presence in Germany for the foreseeable future. By 1966 the United States was involved in the Vietnam War, which involved more of our young people. Most of that war is beyond the scope of this book, but we should acknowledge that young men from Andrews lost their lives in Vietnam, and they deserve our gratitude for serving their country. The town, along with the country, grieved as President Kennedy was shot down, and later would grieve again as other assassinations took place. Russia and the United States were in an arms race as well as a space race. It was discouraging at first as the Russians put the first man into orbit and set other space records while the United States seemed to be lagging behind. Andrews, along with the rest of the country, watched much of this on television, as many if not most residents had a black and white set at the start of the decade and perhaps a color TV by 1966.

America, and Andrews, was "invaded" by another country, too, in the 1960s. Music had changed a lot from even the music of the 1950s. It had more of a beat with perhaps less emphasis on lyrics. When the "Brits" music, and then groups, came to America, those factors were amplified, and the young people loved it! The Beatles, the Dave Clark 5, Herman's Hermits, and numerous other groups could be heard playing on many radios from many households as one walked through town. American music changed, too. Elvis Presley was in the Army and not recording new music, but the Beach Boys, Ricky Nelson, and others became frequent background music, even in Andrews.

Again, what I've found about persons who served overseas during this time period is only what was in the local newspaper. I am quite sure there are names that I've missed, but I want to at least acknowledge these men. Donal L. Forst was a lance corporal in the 8th Marine Division and served in the Mediterranean Sea area. From the single article I found, he had ample recreational opportunities as his ship docked in different ports. Not everyone was so blessed. Donald R. Hetler, son of Mrs. Barbara Huston, was in the US Navy stationed in Iceland. In 1961 he had been in the Navy for five years.

Airman First Class Morris Wade was stationed in France. James E. Hollowell was a private first class serving in the US Army in Germany in 1963. He was a gunner and participated in frequent training exercises, and was based in Mainz, Germany. Airman First Class David Pearson was stationed at Tokyo, Japan, where he was an announcer for the Eastern Network of Armed Forces Radio. He had voluntarily extended his tour of duty there. Pfc. Walter Rogers, US Army, was stationed with the First Cavalry

Division in Korea. According to the November 25, 1964, *Huntington Herald Press*, he had previously operated a barbershop in Andrews.

Marine Lance Corporal Carl W. Turner served with the Special Landing Force of the Seventh Fleet in the Far East. This mention was made on July 16, 1964, just weeks before the Gulf of Tonkin incident precipitated the American buildup in and off the coast of Vietnam. Tom Clements, newly promoted to private first class, was stationed on Okinawa in 1964. Private John W. Garrison was stationed in Germany in an artillery unit in 1965. Lt. Rhett Ripplinger was assigned to the US Army Depot near Germersheim, Germany, where he was an administrative officer and assistant adjutant. George Tourfille, husband of Carol Akers, was stationed in Guam. Everette D. Goings was stationed in Germany as of June 6, 1966.

Andrews men did not escape unscathed. Gary (Ladd or Laddie) Biehl attended the Andrews school most of his life but graduated from Northfield High School in Wabash County, because his family then lived just across the Huntington-Wabash County line. He was a member of the Andrews Boy Scouts and attended the Christian Church in Andrews. He enlisted in the Marines April 2, 1966, and was a lance corporal when he was killed in action in at Quang Tri, Vietnam, on May 3, 1967. Many people in Andrews knew and loved him, and it was a sad day when the news arrived and for many days thereafter.

Another young man with an Andrews connection, Roger Lee Egolf of Columbia City, had died earlier, on February 23, 1966, while fighting at Da Nang, Vietnam. He had worked at Essex Wire (formerly Precision Fittings) in Andrews before enlisting in the US Army.

TOWN GOVERNMENT AND INFRASTRUCTURE

Andrews was busy with several projects, not the least of which was trying to get the sewer building project moving again. It had failed earlier due to local opposition and the failure to find buyers for the bonds needed to finance the project. It would still take some doing. The Andrews Lions Club voted on July 14, 1960, to support the project by circulating information and obtaining signatures on a petition asking the town to install a system. About 80 percent of the water users in town signed the petition. The *Herald Press* article of July 15, 1960, quoted John Turpin of the State Department of Health as saying, "The need for sewers in Andrews is vital to the growth of the town. There is septic material in many of the town's drainage ditches and it is definitely a health problem." Dr. T. W. Omstead, county health officer, pointed out that during the time he practiced medicine in Andrews, there was always sickness after wet weather, which he related to the absence of a sewer system, since Huntington, with a sewer system and few if any open ditches, did not have the same health problems develop. Realtor Richard E. Beaty reported that it was practically impossible to obtain loans to build, or to buy, homes in Andrews due to the lack of a community sewer system.

It seemed that there might finally be enough support to get the system built, especially since a federal grant might be available to help with the expense. In August, Andrews had the top priority in the state for funds, in a list prepared by the Indiana Stream Pollution Control Board. The federal government came through with a grant for $43,464 out of a total project cost of $345,301. This would provide both a townwide sewage collection system and a primary-type sewage treatment plant. The charge for the sewer system to

215

water users would be $4.90 a month. Meanwhile, in June 1961 there were rumors of hepatitis (yellow jaundice) in Andrews, and a warning was issued for children, especially, to stay away from the creek, which it was feared was contaminated. Whether or not the hepatitis scare affected the vote or the bond sale, the bond sale was a success, and bids were accepted from two Fort Wayne companies to begin construction. The plant itself was scheduled to take 180 days to complete after starting, and the sewer lines, 270 days after starting. However, based on interviews with Andrews residents who remember large pipes being installed as late as 1964, it seems that it did not all go according to plan. Construction was probably completed in late 1964 or 1965, but I could not find documents that actually stated this.

The town board was busy with other concerns as well. In June 1960 it was decided that the speed limit on three streets that led to the school grounds was too high. Consequently, Jefferson Street from Main Street to the school, McKeever Street from Main Street to the school, and Leedy Lane from the town limits to the school would now have a maximum speed limit of 20 miles per hour. It's very possible that the impetus for this change was the death of a young school boy who rode his bicycle into the path of an automobile while trying to cross McKeever Street near the school. The accident had occurred on December 29, 1959.

Some problems are constant, it seems. Fifty-five years ago, in 1964, dog owners were warned to keep their dogs tied or on a leash when the animals were outside, citing a town ordinance that was on the books. Town Marshal Ed Bigelow said that several children had suffered dogbites, and property owners were also complaining that their yards were being damaged by animals running loose. When dogs started attacking sheep in areas neighboring Andrews, town and county law enforcement officials began a drive on stray dogs. Any dogs they picked up were subject to being "disposed of," as the law permitted. A few years later, in 1966, it was junk, particularly junk cars, that was a problem. Burl Millman, Pete Smith, and John Wright were town board members who passed an ordinance making junk cars, car parts, trash, and other debris that was visible from either roads or other property a nuisance. Town residents would be fined $10 for each day that the situation was allowed to continue. It was a misdemeanor, but it could bring an expensive fine. Townspeople took notice and removed 77 autos from the town in just two months, leaving 15 still to be hauled off, whether by the property owners or by the town.

A mystery: Early in 1966, the trustees of Andrews asked Judge Ray Ade to appoint appraisers to determine the value of a piece of land in which the town had an undivided half-interest. The appraisers appointed were Edgar Casey, Robert Deal, and Wilbur Beeks. I didn't locate any follow-up information to this, but it's interesting to speculate. Was this Kitchen Maid property, or perhaps the future town park, or perhaps the old town-township town hall? The men appointed had little or no real estate experience, so it's puzzling.

The *Herald Press* published a photograph of members of the Andrews volunteer fire department in October 1960. Members at that time were (Chief) Gene Wilson, Leland Flickinger, Henry Miller, Earl Ellet, Charles Clements, Roy Huston, Edwin Bigelow, Myron Jennings, Charles Kuschel, Ned Keefer, Gene Moore (assistant chief), Forrest Gray, Howard Wright, and Orlo Gephart. Little else was found concerning the fire department, but townspeople always knew when a call went out, because the siren was sounded, and immediately many curious people would trail the fire truck to the location, to watch the action. Residents would talk about the incident for days afterward. At this time, and for a number of years later (into the 1980s), the fire chief and a few others had a "fire phone" in their home. Residents, and also the police and sheriff's departments, called the fire number to report a fire, and the person answering the phone would throw a switch to set off the siren from their home, then stay on the phone until someone arrived at the fire station to take down directions to get to the fire. Of course, this system meant that someone needed to be near the fire phone at all times, including weekends and holidays.

In July 1963, it was announced that for the "first" time, flags would be flown in the downtown business district for the Fourth of July and subsequent patriotic holidays. This was actually a tradition that was being brought back, so perhaps the more correct wording would have been "for the first time in recent memory." The town supplied the brackets, and the Business Men's Association of Andrews purchased 14 flags, 3 by 5 feet each, for the display. George Wintrode, president of the Business Men's group, headed the committee to raise the funds for this project, assisted by Mrs. L. C. Schaeifer, Eugene Moore, Frank Bomersback, and John E. Wright.

The last information about the town board, from November 6, 1963, shows that Andrews had elected an all-Democrat board, consisting of Pete N. Smith, John Wright, Burl Millman, and Barbara Boone (clerk-treasurer). The Republicans had run a slate of Richard L. Holmes, J. Frank Stouder, Earl Wallace, and Clyde Wilson. The last information regarding other offices was in an article stating that certain candidates had not replied to a request for information from the *Herald Press*. Charles F. Homier, running for justice of the peace in Andrews, was listed in that May 1, 1966, article.

Finally, much of the middle years of the 1960s was involved with residents wondering why it was taking so long to build the post office. After about 30 years, the brick building on Main Street was no longer able to carry the volume of mail that came to and went from Andrews. Plans were announced for the building on February 2, 1964, and bids were requested, to be opened June 19, 1964. The specifications called for a building of 2,225 square feet, with 144 square feet for the "platform" and 7,528 square feet of pavement area. The building would be constructed at the southeast corner of Jefferson and Snowden streets, and an "old home," formerly the residence of Stella Coss, would be torn down to make room for the construction. The Aten Construction Company of Fremont, Ohio, won the bid, but they were in no apparent hurry to complete the construction. The post office was originally scheduled to be completed in November 1964, but a picture in the April 21, 1965, *Herald Press* shows that the brick was just starting to be laid at that time, and there was still no roof and only a bit of the brick veneer added by November of that year. Dedication of the new building did not occur until 1967.

Telephone communications improved between Huntington and Andrews, due to investments by the Indiana Bell Company. Local passenger service for the railroad ended in 1963, and the last connection of the town to its beloved—and despised—railroad ended when the freight agency was closed sometime in 1965. Before that time, the trains were accepting only carloads of freight, and after Kitchen Maid closed, there were few shipments that large made from Andrews.

FACTORIES

Meanwhile, Andrews life continued. People worked, and were honored by their employers. People worked, decided they weren't paid enough, and went on strike. With as many as three factories in town, merchants, restaurants, and service businesses in Andrews had a broad customer base; they could keep their businesses going for as long as the factories continued.

Kitchen Maid still held their annual Christmas employee parties. In 1960 it was a dinner held at the Masonic Lodge. Service award winners that year were Roy Huston, Jack Barnhisel, John Wasmuth, Burl Millman, Walter Collins, Marvin Earley, Lawrence Holmes, Charles Harvey Sr., Louis Griggs, Clarence Roberts, Shirl Clements, Catherine Blacketor, Thelma Collins, Flossie Yeiter, Mildred Hendricks, Richard Fluke, Loyd Heck, Frank Strange, Veva Frazee, William Sunderman, Homer Botkins, Bryce Clinger, Mike Luker, and George Kellam. Employees with more than 25 years of service were Clarence Willets, Bert Forst, Ed Reemer, Glen Campbell, A. F. Wasmuth, Nellie Denny, Cecil Jennings, E. M. Kitt, Lowell Wilson, Everett Bigelow, R. E. Wasmuth, A. B. Ware, H. K. Ware, Marvin Harris, Charles Clements, and Owen Burkhart.

The highlight of the 1961 Christmas dinner was the presentation of a gold watch to Bert Forst, who had completed 50 years of service. This meant he had been with the company since before the Wasmuths had owned it. He would have been a walking encyclopedia of Kitchen Maid history!

In February 1961, Kitchen Maid introduced their first new line of cabinets in several years. Called the "Superba" line, this one was available in five stain colors as well as four new enamel colors. Since it was the early 1960s, the colors that were offered were Glacier White, Sunrise Pink, Daffodil Yellow, and Bermuda Turquoise. New types of hardware were offered, there was an option for a built-in sewing machine cabinet, and shelves were now adjustable, only needing to be tilted to move them up or down in a cabinet. An ad by "Kitchen Maid Service," with the location shown as Andrews, now said they had 9 designs and 14 finishes to choose from. The picture in the *Huntington Herald Press* appears to show an early example of the now-ubiquitous kitchen island, and it also directs customers to the Andrews location.

Kitchen Maid was purchased by a new group known as Kitchen Maid, International (previously the official name was Kitchen Maid Corporation). The new chairman and CEO was James W. Charbonnier; other officers were A. F. Wasmuth, president; Edmund Wasmuth, secretary; M. G. Weisse, assistant secretary and treasurer; and Robert Powers, vice president of sales. The newspaper article of September 22, 1964, indicated that the company would begin to produce new lines of cabinets as well as the traditional lines and that production would start "as seasonal sales conditions permit." However, the factory did not reopen.

Glenna Brown of Andrews is reported to have told the story of how she locked up Kitchen Maid for the last time and took the key to Gilbert Shideler at the First National Bank, Andrews branch, herself, on May 5, 1964. It's not clear what the purpose of the sale was. Did the Wasmuths know that the factory would not be able to reopen? Were they hoping that an influx of capital from Mr. Charbonnier would be enough to help the company, which had been struggling for at least a couple of years? Top pay at the company was reportedly $1.95 an hour, so perhaps Kitchen Maid was losing good workers to companies that provided a higher wage. Regardless of what was expected and of what happened, the loss of this factory, after over 50 years, was a blow to the town's morale, to the people who worked there and their families, and to the finances of the town, since the factory would be taken off the tax base and would no longer be paying bills for the town utilities.

For a brief period of time, a company known as Hoosier Wood Products Corporation operated out of the Kitchen

Maid building. Pamela Mahan advised that she worked there only a few weeks, in the fall of 1966, and that the company made wooden TV stands. It's unknown what became of the company, but operations in Andrews didn't last long.

By June 1961 Hettrick Manufacturing Company had vacated the large factory building they had constructed at the corner of Jackson and California streets. A company known as Fittings, Inc., had either rented or purchased the Hettrick building, which was now in use as a factory that made industrial fittings. James M. Baker had recently purchased a controlling interest in the factory, and he and several other former employees of the Weatherhead Company were the officers and key employees. At this early stage, it employed about 40 workers, but more were expected to be hired. About 15 months later, in April 1962, the company, now known as Precision Fittings, purchased a line of hydraulic hose assemblies, as well as more fittings, from the Flextronics Division of Calumet and Hecla, of Chicago. Increased production was possible because the company had just built a 37,000-square-foot foundry in Andrews, which allowed production from raw material to finished product there.

It seems that the employees may not have taken kindly to the new ownership and to changes they may have implemented. On July 24, 1962, a strike was called by Plant Local number 302 of Allied Industrial Workers of America, citing intolerable working conditions, including a lack of ventilation in the foundry. In July, that could well have been an issue. Low wages were also a primary focus of the strikers, even though their five-year contract was not up until 1965. Starting wages for the factory ranged from $1.25 to $2.09 per hour. Interestingly, female machine operators started at 20 cents an hour less than male operators. Some jobs were specifically listed as female, and all women would

222

receive a 5-cent-an-hour pay raise in October, with male employee wages to increase in 1963. Officers of the local were Allen Randall, Raymond Tackett, and Mrs. Norma Brown. The strike was not entirely nonviolent; at least two men were arrested for driving cars that hit striking workers, as the drivers left work for the day. Fear seems to have been a component of the strike, since some said they went out because they were afraid of their co-workers. Max Schoeff, plant manager, is reported to have said that as far as he was concerned, the strikers no longer had jobs. The plant had a total employee force of about 200 people at this time. The strikers went back to work on July 31, with no promises of either a pay raise or better working conditions.

Sometime between 1962 and April 29, 1964, C. P. Fittings became the C-P Fittings Division of the Essex Wire Corporation. Another new line was purchased from Cobra Metals, and the company now was in a position to manufacture flexible metal hose connectors for appliance, water heater, and radiant baseboard heater applications, as well as the automobile lines they were currently producing. There was a short wildcat strike at the foundry over seniority rights in 1965, which had nothing to do with wages. We aren't told what happened with the contract talks in 1965, but in March 1966 the plant was accepting applications for factory work, offering "paid vacation, 8 paid holidays, free life and hospitalization insurance, excellent wages, and a training program."

I found little in the newspapers about General Engineering, Gemco, during the 1960s, other than want ads. They were still operating in downtown Andrews, in the old hotel and other nearby buildings. All of these plants, for as long as they were in business, offered Andrews residents the chance to work in town, eliminating the need for transportation and letting parents spend more time with their children. It was a win-win for the town, until they shut down.

OTHER BUSINESSES

For the smaller businesses of town, the 1960s started out well. The Blue Moon Cafe and Tavern closed, but Robert Warfel applied for a beer and wine retailer's permit for that same location. The Indiana Alcoholic Beverage Commission gave tentative approval to his application but said the Indiana State Board of Health and the State Fire Marshal's department would have to give their approval, and the federal stamp would have to be purchased. This permit was more contentious than most in Andrews. Rev. Daniel Bengston and Rev. Glenn Raney, along with other local residents, appeared at the hearing by the local Alcoholic Beverage Board and raised so many objections that the county board asked the state board to decide after the local board's vote ended up as a tie. The local residents made several trips to Indianapolis but were never able to determine when the state would hold its hearing, so they did not appear to restate their objections.

Keefer Greenhouses continued their year-round operations, with special emphasis and advertising at Christmas, Easter, Mother's Day, and Memorial Day. Their Christmas Open House in 1960 extended over three days, with Santa Claus present, and attenders were invited to "Bring Your Friends and a Camera."

There were still several other businesses in town at the start of the 1960s, including grocery stores, restaurants, bars, and service stations, as well as the elevator and even a coal yard. Roy Gallaspie expanded his Organic Soil Builders business and went to a Lawn-Boy factory school in Missouri to learn how to service their lawn-mowing equipment. Ed and Margaret Casey still operated Casey's Print Shop, although much of their business came from Huntington. There was one "Andrews Pest Control Co." advertisement for termite control, but I haven't located the business owner's name. Schaefer's Corner Store was still open, and doubtless there were other businesses, too, that have been lost to written memory. The Crulls bee-moth and bait business was also still active, in what at one time had been the Pilgrim Holiness Church building.

SCHOOL

Up until May 1966, one of the unifying factors of Andrews was the school. Most people had some connection to it. They had attended school in Andrews, or their children did, or their neighbors and their neighbor's children were students there, or all of the above. What happened on the hill mattered to people in the town. That may be one reason the town paid close attention to what was happening with the "County School Reorganization Plan" study group. Frank Stouder, Mrs. Charles Rogers, J. D. Miller, Ben Garretson, Kenneth Schenkel, James Johnson, and Robert Deal were named to a county committee that would eventually report to the county school board on the best way to move forward. That does not, however, mean that all of Andrews was in agreement as to what should happen.

But in the school itself, the normal events were planned as usual, with the expectation that they would be carried out, and carried on. The Andrews School chorus participated in the Huntington County Music Festival on March 25, 1960, at the Community Gym in Huntington. Members of the chorus, directed by Mrs. Ruth Stookey, were Lois Nettleton, Sharon Cook, Diann Moore, Kaye Groscost, Sharon Bickel, Barbara McCullough, Frances Miller, Marie Garrison, Glynna Biehl, Dian Everroad, Patty Bomerstack, Joyce Hollowell, Andris Beghtel, Deana

Clements, Claudia Garretson, Carolyn Garrison, Lois Cecil, Nancy Wilson, Ann Bare, Lindal Crile, Sharon Turner, Pam Wilson, Sue Schenkel, Jeannie Krile, Karen Millman, Donna Everroad, Sharon Goebel, Diana Johnson, Jill Flaugh, Debby Casey, Helen Wright, Cathy Fearnow, Lyle Garretson, Terry Plasterer, Steve Kreigh, Ned Lewis, Wendell Holbrook, Andy Sutton, Duane Glass, King Ryan, Tom Schenkel, Kenneth Wright, Jim Garrison, and Nelson Pearson. This list probably includes more than 25 percent of the high school population for that year. Remarkably, 27 high school students also participated in the annual spring band concert. We often think that Andrews only cared about sports, but clearly music was also a large part of Andrews school life and received great support from the parents and community.

In 1960, 26 students graduated from Andrews High School. Sharon Bickel was valedictorian of the class and also received the Kitchen Maid Scholarship award. Barbara McCullough was salutatorian. Tom Schenkel received the Kitchen Maid Good Sportsmanship Award and a special award for outstanding leadership. Sharon Cook received the DAR Good Citizens award and a special award for outstanding leadership.

All too soon, it must have seemed, the 1960-61 school year was under way. Class officers were elected, and the senior play, *Quit Your Kidding*, was presented by the cast of Lois Nettleton, Sue Schenkel, Hugh Sutton, Sharon Goebel, Richard King, Glynna Biehl, Carolyn Garrison, Bill Bitzer, Arden Campbell, Ron Johnson, Dorcas Paul, and Pam Wilson. The annual Christmas program this year was, appropriately, called *Christmas*, and all of the songs told the story of the first Christmas.

Fourteen students received "excellent" ratings in the annual Northern Indiana Instrumental Solos and Ensembles Contest in Fort Wayne the following February.

226

Jacqueline Sutton, Donna Everroad, Sue Schenkel, Sally Huston, Judy Flora, Diana Osborn, Linda Turner, Marie Garrison, Lindal Krile, Larry Bickel, Dian Everroad, Claudia Garretson, Rodger Smith, and Sam Goebel earned those ratings. Lonna Harvey, Lois Bengston, Larry Bickel, Lana Garrison, Steve Turner, Robert Flora, David Osborn, Susan Ward, and Duane Glass received "superior" ratings. Some of these winners competed at the state level also, and seven of them brought home an "excellent" rating.

School spelling champions were John Wegmann, Marcia Harshbarger, Carolyn Ellet, Lonna Harvey, Mary Murray, Robert Flora, Lana Garrison, Nancy Wilson, Alan Maxton, and Lois Nettleton, for grades 3-12, respectively.

The Sunshine Society attended the state convention and held their annual dance. The seniors had a variety show. The Andrews GAA (Girls Athletic Association) elected new officers. I've not been able to determine when this organization started.

At graduation, 28 seniors suddenly became adults, or college freshmen, or whatever the future held for them. Graduates were Glynna Biehl, William Bitzer, Thomas Bomersback, Arden Campbell, Douglas Chopson, Donna Everroad, John Fearnow, Dennis Flaugh, Carolyn Garrison, Sharon Goebel, Wilma Gray, Ronald Johnson, Richard King, Pamela Kulb, Diann Moore, Terry McDaniel, Lois Nettleton, Nancy Niblick, Dorcas Paul, Christine Piel, Charles Porter, Sue Schenkel, John Snyder, Hugh Sutton, Carlene Theobald, Judith Wegmann, Pamela Wilson, and Larry Yeiter. Lois Nettleton was the valedictorian, having a straight-A average for all of her school career. Charles Porter Jr. was the salutatorian, barely edging out Nancy Niblick for that honor. He had transferred to Andrews from Rossville during his junior year.

The 1961-62 school year had the same sort of wonderful, time-honored routine to it. The Sunshine Society initiated new members Barbara Beghtel, Karen Clabaugh, Patty Dickson, Sally Huston, Ann Jersey, Sharon Kennedy, Renee Kitt, Carol Krile, Cheryl Poteet, and Mary Sue Urbanek. The senior class presented a play on October 21, 1961, with Deana Clements, Andris Beghtel, James Rougeau, Carl Turner, Joyce Hollowell, Jim Dillon, Randy Laugle, Ron Ruppert, Jim Miller, Claudia Garretson, Mary Wehr, Shirley Glass, and Asa Ellet as members of the cast.. Kenneth Stoffel directed the junior class play, with Kay Walters, Joe Wegmann, Lindal Krile, Debby Casey, Terry Close, Jan Buckles, Dianna Johnson, Cindy Porter, Veva Murray, Jim Beghtel, Helen Wright, Dian Everroad, Terry Plasterer, and Nancy Wilson in the cast. There were music contests and spelling contests, a Sunshine Society dance and a band concert. There was probably a music program, too, although I didn't find note of that.

Soon enough, the class of 1962 graduated, with 18 graduates. Andris Beghtel, Deana Clements, James Dillon, Asa Ellet, Camella Fearnow, Emma Holbrook Fearnow, Claudia Garretson, Shirley Glass, Elaine Goings, Joyce Hollowell, Randy Laugle, Alan Maxton, James Miller, James Rougeau, Ron Ruppert, Carl Stewart, Mary Wehr, and Rex Ziegler were the graduates, with Alan Maxton valedictorian and James Miller salutatorian.

Vera Deal had been operating a kindergarten in the Deal Funeral Home, and perhaps it was felt that it was time for the school to step up and offer it as a public school class, rather than the private school that it had been. Steve Keefer remembers going to kindergarten at the funeral home. I asked him whether the children had desks or tables there, or books, or writing materials. He replied that they had no desks, tables, books, or writing materials. "We had toys, and usually a body in the casket," he wrote. Attendance was 8-10 kids, the best he could recall. Whether the low attendance was due to tuition cost, transportation difficulties because it was half a day, or just the decision of parents to "let kids be kids," kindergarten was not perceived by all as being necessary. Until the school decreed it so.

When the 1962-63 school year started, Norman Cozad, the school principal, announced a meeting for parents of children who were eligible to attend kindergarten. It appears that this was a meeting to gauge interest in offering kindergarten for the first time. The kindergarten was approved for the 1962-63 school year, with a last-minute enrollment on Wednesday, September 4. Classes would start at 8:15 and dismissal was at 11:15. Tuition was $3.50. Presumably the children would have desks or tables, books, and toys at their disposal. Kindergarten at that time was much less about academics than it seems to be today.

The school year otherwise seems to have been about as normal. Plays were presented by the senior class in the fall and the junior class in early spring. The Christmas musical program was centered around the birth of Christ. This may have been the first year that the high school choir sang the "Hallelujah Chorus" from Handel's *Messiah*, but it wasn't the last. There was a band concert, and outside of public performances, Lonna Harvey rated a "superior" in the Northern Indiana School Band Orchestra and Vocal Association competition for her piano solo. Diane Wintrode won the county spelling bee for grade seven, and Linda Carpenter won the competition for the eighth grade. The Sunshine Society held their spring prom, as well as their "annual tea," the term implying that this was not the first year for the event. Each girl attending the tea was to bring as a guest a woman who had been influential in her life. Sometimes this was a mother or other relative. but it seems that sometimes it was a church member or a neighbor. It takes a small town to raise a young woman.

The graduating class of 1963 had 23 members: Terry Close, Jim Beghtel, Dian Everroad, Rick Wilkinson, Ann

Bare, Pat Bomersback, Jan Buckles, Deborah Casey, Jill Flaugh, Marie Garrison, Dianna Johnson, Lindal Krile, Tim Millman, Terry Plasterer, Cindy Porter, Yetive Ruppert, Sharon Turner, Norman Urschel, Kay Walters, Susan Ward, Jim Wegmann, Nancy Wilson, and Helen Wright. Nancy Wilson and Deborah Casey were the valedictorian and salutatorian, respectively. Each young woman had a scholarship as they headed off to Manchester College (Nancy) and Butler University (Deborah).

The 1963-64 school year started out with a new principal. Willard Barnes, who had taught at Monument City and then at Van Buren, was appointed principal by Fred Warfel, township trustee. Other teachers were Mark Crain, biology and coach; Rosemary Douglas, music; Nyle Fox, science and driver training; Gene Kaufman, commerce and golf coach; Don Kline, English and French; James Meadows, math and chemistry; Gladys Putterbaugh, commerce; Anna Robrock, homemaking; Kenneth Stoffel, English and social studies; Richard Whitacre, band; and Herbert Yake, industrial arts. Grade school teachers were Robert Fulton, Vera Deal, Elaine Schenkel, Belle Butler, Corinne Horrell, Mary Miller, and Opal Sharp (kindergarten teacher). Cooks were Esther Kreigh, Dorothy Plasterer, and Thelma Lamprecht. Bus drivers were John Brumbaugh, Kenneth Quinn, and Lloyd Stewart, and Richard Thorne was the custodian. An open house was held September 16 to allow patrons to meet the teachers, at which refreshments were served and a cake walk was held.

Two sixth-grade girls, Debbie Laymon and Judy Chapman, wrote to Congressman J. Edward Roush and asked for a flag for their classroom. Not only did he present them with a flag, but he managed to get one that had flown over the US Capitol building.

Angie Garrison, Steve Turner, Ned Lewis, Larry Bickel, Linda Clement, Linda Oswalt, Ron Inyart, and Luke Ellet were the cast of the senior class play, *Tattletale*, performed on Wednesday, October 23. The junior class play, *Antics of Andrew*, included Sally Huston, Barb Beghtel, Cheryl Poteet, Carole Krile, Bob Flora, John Wasmuth, Dave Stephan, Keith Wilson, John Teague, Ron Adams, Renee Kitt, Dan Smith, Rod Smith, Mike Schaefer, Mike France, and David Osborn in the cast. Sue Ferguson was the valedictorian and Steve Kreigh the salutatorian for the class of 1964. Steve planned to major in mathematics, and Sue in business, in college.

The 1964-65 school year went by quickly. New teachers were Homer Peterson and David Verbeck in the high school. Plays were presented, and presumably there were musical programs, dances, perhaps a bonfire, spelling and musical competitions, and a variety show. Somehow the students found time for lessons, too, as well as for ball games.

Bob Flora was valedictorian for the class of 1965, planning to enter Huntington College, and Sally Huston was the salutatorian, planning to work as a secretary at the General Engineering Company. Other seniors were Ron Adams, Judy Fisher, Sharon Kennedy, Cheryl Poteet, David Stephan, Barbara Beghtel, Renee Kitt, Michael Schaefer, Christina Street, John Carpenter, Mike France, Carol Maxton, Dan Smith, John Wasmuth, Karen Clabaugh, David Osborn, Rodger Smith, and John Teague.

Perhaps if it had been known at the start of the 1965-66 school year that this would be the last year of the existence of Andrews High Sschool, students and teachers might have done even more to make it a memorable year. As it was, there were a junior class play and a senior class play, a variety show, a music program at Christmas, and competitions and other activities all year long. The Student Council, the Sunshine Society, and the Girls Athletic

Association all continued with their normal service and fun activities.

The graduating class of 1966, the last set of names to enter the history of Andrews High School, included Pam Adams, Joyce Burk, Melanie Campbell, Beverly Carpenter, Bob Crunk, Judy Flora, Phil Garrison, Gene Grimm, Sam Goebel, Larry Kennedy, Roy Hamer, John Harshbarger, Dennis Hendricks, Kay Ferguson, Allen Jacoby, Judy Karst, Paul Lamprecht, Bonnie McCullough, Jim Nichols, Pam Notestone, Terry Pepper, Mike Rogers, Roger Speicher, Jim Teague, Pam Thorn, Linda Turner, and Mary Sue Urbanek. Nancy Casey, valedictorian, had plans to attend Butler University to study languages, and Joyce Schenkel, salutatorian, planned to go to Manchester College to major in elementary education.

It would probably have been acknowledged by many school patrons by 1964 that there were ways the high school could be improved. One way was by the addition of more languages, chemistry and physics, and other electives. Those changes were made. But the school wasn't in control of its own destiny. There were state requirements, and sometimes the county school boards were not imaginative nor thoughtful in their response to criticisms. In 1966 two schools in the county school system, Rock Creek and Union High schools, lost their commissions entirely, and several other schools, including Andrews, were certified for one additional year only, for various reasons. As of April 3, 1966, the only thing certain was that something would have to be done about Rock Creek and Union schools, but by April 21, the county school board decided that the only solution was to consolidate all the high schools in the county into one, and of course that high school (actually two buildings, for a couple of years) would be in Huntington. The county school board felt "under the gun" to arrive at a solution and barely listened to the howls from Andrews and other small towns, whose residents were disheartened at the thought of losing their high school. The only reason that Andrews was "certified" for just one year appeared to be overcrowding at the facility. While that could have been addressed by other methods, such as bringing in temporary classrooms or finding space for students in other buildings, the school board chose not to address the individual community's concerns, but to come up with a one-size-fits-all solution.

The loss of Andrews High School was a real blow to the town, and animosity about the change persisted for decades. Merchants and restaurants felt the loss. There was pressure on parents to transport their children to Huntington for one reason or another much more often than previously, and some students were no longer able to participate in extracurricular activities because doing so would have meant not getting home until about 5:30 in the evening. It affected family life, too, and introduced stresses that the students who consolidated must endure. It was a culture shock to go from a very small school to one with about 2,000 students at the two campuses.

CHURCHES

All of the churches in Andrews, now numbering five, recognized major milestones during the 1960s. The churches seem to have been holding their own, as far as membership goes, but they were aware that they'd need to make special efforts in order to be able to continue to serve God and their community.

Sometimes it was nice to stop and take a look back, and both the Methodist and the Christian churches were able to do that as they celebrated major events. December 4, 1960, the Methodist Church celebrated their centennial anniversary, with a carry-in dinner and a special service in the afternoon. Several former pastors were in attendance.

Although their celebration wasn't as elaborate as the celebration for their 75th anniversary, it was still a day to remember. Officers of the Women's Society of Christian Service that year were Mrs. Hazel Slagle, Mrs. Vera Deal, Mrs. Mary Haupert, Mrs. Pauline Wilson, Mrs. Inez McBride, Mrs. Ersell Leakey, Mrs. Mamie Schmalzreid, Mrs. Leona Jennings, Mrs. Fern Johnson, Mrs. Vivian Garrison, Mrs. Bette Clements, Mrs. Mabel Kitt, Mrs. Belle Campbell, Mrs. Loretta Smith, and Mrs. Lila Beghtel.

The Christian Church held a dedication service for their new piano, organ, and communion-ware in October 1960. Their new pastor, R. Clayton Kendall, was installed at the same time. Two years later, Wayne Johnson was the pastor when the church celebrated their centennial anniversary. It had been 100 years since the church was constructed, and although many changes had taken place over the years, it was still at the same location and the original part of the building was used regularly for worship. The building was rewired and newly painted, ready for service over the next century.

The Church of the Nazarene had a new pastor, Elder Orville Rees. He was welcomed with a reception at the home of Mr. and Mrs. Claude Glass.

The Church of the Brethren held a dedication service in 1966, in connection with the acquisition of "new" pews, purchased from the Huntington Church of the Brethren and then modified to fit the needs of the Andrews congregation. Church members had done the hauling and refurbishing of the pews.

The Pilgrim Holiness church was able to burn their mortgage in June 1966, not many years after the building was constructed.

A varying number of churches participated in various "union" programs, also. There were Good Friday and Thanksgiving services held, with churches rotating in "host" duties, and with pastors generally sharing the "preaching" duties. The churches also sponsored joint Vacation Bible School classes, some years held at the churches and at least once (1963) at the school. These were not small undertakings. The list of teachers and helpers from 1961 included oat least 26 names. Perhaps the most ambitious undertaking the Andrews Ministerial Association sponsored was the "Greater Andrews Area Evangelistic Campaign," which was scheduled for June 13-27, 1965, at the school gymnasium. It was moved to the Methodist Church, however, after "acoustical problems" at the school proved too difficult to overcome. The speaker was evangelist Billy Springfield from Marion, Indiana, with organist Maurice McKenzie of Belfast, Ireland; Virgil Trucks, song leader; and Professor Jack Patton of Taylor University did chalk drawings. Finally, at least two of the churches cooperated annually in "Trick or Treat for UNICEF" drives, raising money for children in disadvantaged countries.

LODGES AND CLUBS

Lodges and clubs continued to help further the well-being of the town. Mrs. Raleigh Sandlin, of Miriam Rebekah Lodge 37, received a chivalry award from the Patriarchs Militant, an auxiliary of the Rebekah Lodge. This was for outstanding service to the local lodge, and it was the first time in many years that a Huntington County member had been awarded the designation. Mrs. Alta Roberts was presented her 50-year pin in 1963. She had been a member of the lodge since shortly after the fires of 1909 and 1911.

The Miriam Rebekah Lodge of Andrews intended to reactivate the Theta Rho girls club, which had been active in the 1940s but had apparently disappeared into the sunset. The Order of the Eastern Star was also active, with Worthy Matrons during this time including June Wintrode, Susan

Hackworth. Mildred Reemer, Pat Garrison, and Devota Smith.

We know that the men's lodges were also active. The IOOF sponsored the tractor pulls, and Antioch Lodge number 410 of the Free and Accepted Masons was occasionally mentioned in the newspaper, mostly when officers were installed. In 1960 the officers were Robert Deal, Claude Garretson, Raleigh Sandlin, Dale Mansbarger, Mark Fisher, Robert Mayne, Dorrence Cross, Eugene Wilson, Edgar Keefer, Roy Sandlin, and Darl Richardson.

The Lions Club was here, there, and everywhere, it seemed. There were annual fish-fry dinners, some of which drew 800-900 people. It took about 35 members, plus the behind-the-scenes work of many wives, to make the event a success, but it seems that it always was just that—a successful fund-raiser for the club and a successful morale-builder for the community. Various types of programs were held during the dinners, from the Chain O'Lakes Barbershop Quartet to Jack Underwood of WOWO radio station fame. In 1965 the club earmarked $200 of the profits from the event to go toward a scholarship to be awarded to a high school senior.

The Lions Club and the IOOF partnered for tractor-pulling contests for several years. A six-inch-thick concrete slab was to be built for the first occasion. Proceeds from the pull were to go toward the development of a recreational area for the town. In 1961 a pony ring was added to keep the children somewhat occupied during the event.

Each year the Lions Club scheduled a Ladies Night, where service awards were given to the men. It was also a tradition to honor the teachers of the school at this event. Halloween celebrations continued, with parades of costumed children (and adults); winners would receive a silver dollar. In 1960 there was also a record hop at the school. The money raised by the Lions Club was not only devoted to state and national Lions Club projects; much of it supported local projects. In 1960 they presented new 50-star flags to the town library and Boy Scout Troop 120 after Hawaii was admitted to the United States the previous year. They planted 16 shrubs around the library building in April 1962, and purchased hospital and invalid equipment for townspeople's use, kept at the Deal funeral home. They sponsored a Little League team, Boy Scout Troop number 120, and "saw to some of the town's welfare needs." For example, they purchased roofing material for retired Andrews fire chief James Russell. After suffering a heart attack, Mr. Russell was unable to work or to maintain his home. During a recent rain his roof had "leaked like a sieve," and the fire department provided the labor to install the roof for their former chief. The Lions Club also provided and installed Christmas decorations for the three-block downtown area every year and, for a time, provided and planted ornamental flowers in downtown Andrews during the spring and summer. They sponsored Spring Clean Up–Fix Up days, and in 1966 sponsored a summer "Park Program" for two hours a day at the school. Rick Wilkerson was in charge of the program that year.

A partial list of members in 1965, when the Lions Club celebrated their 20th "official" anniversary, included Mark Anson, Richard Allen, Glynn Rudig, Paul Warschko, Lawrence Kennedy, Dallas Theobald, Ned Keefer, J. D. Miller, Robert Deal, Carl Stephan, George Wintrode, Ben Garretson, Max Schoeff, John Garrison, Russell Ferguson, John Spry, Jackie Ferrell, Eugene Moore, Homer Bitzer, Ed Goodrich, and Norman Nightengale.

There are still quite a few men living who remember the good times that Boy Scout Troop 120 enjoyed. The boys worked hard to learn camping skills and earn merit badges. An article in the March 22, 1960, *Herald Press* mentioned the following scouts: Earl Murray, Terry France, Mike Schaefer,

James Biehl, Gary Biehl, Keith Wilson, Ron Adams, John Wasmuth, John Harshbarger, David Osborn, Paul Lamprecht Jr., Danny Smith, Philip Bengston, Robert Pilcher, Chuck Kuschel, and William Groscost. The Scout Master was Haskiel Clements, and Scotty Huffman was the assistant Scout Master. In a further article, the names Rod Smith and Ival Gressley Jr. appear. Many of these people remember participating in the Klondike Derby, which taught survival skills in winter weather and included outdoor camping, in tents, despite the occasional snow on the ground.

However, It wasn't all fun and games. Some of these young men worked extremely hard to earn the highest accolades scouting had to offer. Danny Smith earned an Eagle Scout ranking, having earned 34 merit badges and served as leader of a Patrol. Ron Adams, at the same April 21, 1961, meeting, earned a Star award, which also noted a significant accomplishment in the scouting world.

There was also an active Cub Scout Pack, number 3120. Those attending a meeting in December 1962 included Stanley Percell, Fred Osborn, Jeffrey Grodian, Mark Weyler, Jeff Wintrode, Doug Burkhart, Terry Rittenhouse, Fred Smith, David Rittenhouse, Keith Miller, Jerry Hysong, Randy Day, Arthur Strange, Randy Buzzard, Charles Garrison, Steve Keefer, Peter Deal, Ricky Day, Jesse Dyer, and Lynn Harris.

I found no mention of Girl Scout or Brownie troops during the 1960s, although several women remember being in Brownie troops during this time. There was probably a Girl Scout troop, too, at least in the earlier years of the decade.

The Andrews Homemakers met all during these years and held fund-raisers such as bake sales. Members who attended a meeting on March 19, 1962, were Mrs. John Bickel, Mrs. Gordon Schaefer, Mrs. Willis Nunemaker, Mrs.

George Wintrode, Mrs. Jay Kitt, Mrs. Fred Warfel, Mrs. Wayne Notestone, Mrs. Arlin Johnson, Mrs. Richard Holmes, Mrs. Charles Harvey, Mrs. Don Hammel, Mrs. Jay Nichols, Mrs. Jay Kitt, Mrs. Max Schoeff, Mrs. Leroy Hackworth, Mrs. Paul Garrison, Mrs. Pete Smith, Mrs. Henry Miller, Mrs. Don Saluke, Mrs. Charles Garrison, Mrs. James Brown, and Mrs. Don Reed.

4-H Club members entered projects at the 4-H Fair, and celebrated their honors at annual banquets that were sponsored by the Farm Bureau. Whether the members were "farm kids" or "town kids," and whether their projects were related to agriculture or represented hobbies, they all worked hard, learned much, and had a little bit of fun along the way.

CRIMES

Criminal activity involving Andrews businesses and residents during the 1960s seems to have been minimal. Chuck Breeding's gas station was broken into, perhaps more than once. Vandals again destroyed several headstones in the Riverside Cemetery, knocking some over and breaking three of them in half, prompting a warning that anyone found in a cemetery after dark was subject to prosecution. A bank containing loose change was stolen from the Nazarene church, and Christmas lights were stolen from several locations in 1960. Four unnamed juveniles, ages 12-15, admitted to break-ins at Precision Fittings, involving vandalism the first time and theft the second time.

Donald Beeks, accused of following a former landlady in Huntington and taking the money she had collected in rent that day, was charged with robbery with force.

Good citizens Howard Ward and Virgil Shultz were summoned by the Andrews town marshal, Ed Bigelow, to assist in a high-speed chase on September 23, 1964. The suspect had refused to pull over for Bigelow in Andrews, and Bigelow, knowing that Ward's car was faster than his, requested assistance. The chase came to an unfortunate end, however, when Ward's car hit loose gravel about four miles south and a mile west of Andrews. The car ended up on its top in a creek, and only the prompt actions of Bigelow and another unit involved in the pursuit kept the two men from drowning. The car they were pursuing made its escape.

Seven young men, runaways from White's Institute in Wabash County, were not so lucky. They broke into Lew Skinner's laundromat and took the units to a nearby field to remove the coins from them. Later tracked down in Huntington, they confessed to the Andrews break-in. Nancy Scharding reports that she found a comment in a letter received from her mother, Irene Niblick, stating that pencils from White's Institute were found in the alley behind the laundromat.

The small fires that Andrews had during this time period went unreported in the newspaper, but the *Herald Press* did report on the fire at the home of Mr. and Mrs. Edward Bigelow on December 4, 1962. It heavily damaged the home where the Bigelows lived with their three children, Noralyn, Shannon, and an infant unnamed in the news story. There was no insurance, but a fund was started to help the family with their expenses, and a home was quickly found for them. The only other mention of the fire department in action was a fire September 30, 1964, at the House of Furniture in Huntington. The Andrews fire department responded, along with units from Bippus, Warren, and Roanoke, and the newspaper noted that the help of all was greatly appreciated. We know there must have been other fires, but mostly the fire siren sounded just twice a day, at 6:00 a.m and 6:00 p.m.

OTHER TOWN NEWS AND HAPPENINGS

As part of good citizenship, Andrews participated in the "Stop Polio Sunday" on November 21, 1965. The Huntington County Medical Society campaigned to have every person over six weeks old in Huntington County take the oral vaccine, even those who had received the Salk vaccine in the 1950s. There had been another effort two months earlier, but a follow-up was needed. A donation of 75 cents per dose was requested but not required. The Andrews location for receipt of the vaccine was at the school.

It should be noted that Andrews children and youth were students even outside of the classroom. There were sports leagues and 4-H clubs, and more than a few took music lessons (piano, instrumental, or vocal), either in Andrews or in Huntington. There were probably piano recitals every year, but the last one I found was in 1960, given by the students of Mrs. George Kellam. Deborah Clements, John Garrison, Michael Korrecht, John Fearnow, Karen Raney, Jackie Kellam, Gail Fulhart, Margaret Fearnow, Alberta Michaelson, Nancy Casey, Rosetta Campbell, Connie Hethcote, Janet Andrew, Deborah Casey, Ann Bare, and Nancy Wilson each performed a solo, to what was probably a full house at the First Christian Church.

Edgar Keefer had long been involved in the activities of the Red Cross, having served as a first aid instructor and a water safety instructor, as well as sitting on the board for two terms as the representative from Dallas Township. In September 1962, he had recently "retired" from Keefer Greenhouse and was now going to serve as Disaster Chairman for the county chapter of the Red Cross. Keefer had helped set up the disaster service and knew how it needed to work. What he didn't know was how often the Disaster Committee would be called into use, both in Huntington County and beyond. The Red Cross conducted blood drives in Andrews as late as 1965.

There were accidents, too. Two boxcars and a tanker derailed just west of Market Street in Andrews on February 14, 1963, We don't know whether the residents were in any danger, because the contents of the tanker car were not known. One boxcar carried ore and the other rice, so it's possible that there was a mess left at the accident site. The only visible damage to the railroad tracks was to the "crossing planks" at Market Street.

Jerry Hysong had a story to tell for the rest of his life. A crane owned by the railroad had hit an electric wire, and the Public Service Company had been notified that there was a wire down, in an alley between the coal yard and the railroad tracks. Darwin Cox, owner of the Andrews Elevator, along with Russell Morford, Charles Kuschel, and Harold Miller, were keeping an eye on the situation and saw Hysong on his bicycle, preparing to deliver his newspapers. The men yelled in unison, "Stop!" and whether or not Hysong heard them, he jumped from the bicycle just as the bike made contact with the live wire. The rear tire, fender, and chain guard on the bike were scorched, and a hole was burned in the newspaper bag, but Hysong was not seriously hurt. The eleven-year-old boy lived to ride again, and to continue delivering the *Herald Press*.

Both youth and adults from Andrews had accomplishments that got them mentioned in the newspaper for good reasons, also. Andris Beghtel in 1960 was the 4-H Grand Champion of the Garden Club. She was one of five females who were selected to attend the Garden Camp at Indianapolis, one of the five outstanding Garden Camp representatives, and the first Huntington County delegate to attend the National Jr. Vegetable Growers

Association Convention in Washington, DC. It was an all-expense-paid trip. Besides all that, her family enjoyed vegetables she had canned, at Christmastime.

Vera Deal, who had a long list of civic accomplishments to her name, was appointed Province Officer of the Chi Chapter of Tri Kappa Sorority, the first person from Huntington County to be so honored. A. E. Moore, known to the town as "Dinty," was one of ten Indiana members of the Christian churches (Disciples of Christ) to be honored with an award for churchmanship in 1962. Ronald Collins, a graduate of Andrews High School and a senior at Lincoln Christian College in Lincoln, Illinois, was ordained as a minister in 1962. Mr. and Mrs. Paul Haller (she was the former Neva Stouder), both graduates of the Andrews High School class of 1915, retired after teaching for a combined total of 77 years in the Fort Wayne school system. Ben Garretson was Governor of Lions International District 25-B, which at the time had 61 clubs with more than 2,500 Lions. Mrs. Eugene Smith, the former Maxine Wintrode, received first place in a poetry contest for students at the South Bend Campus of Indiana University. She was class valedictorian at Andrews in 1946 and was working toward her college degree in 1966.

PASSINGS

While many Andrews residents were in the middle of their life stories, others came to the end of their lives, some much sooner than they had anticipated. During the period from January 1, 1960, to May 12, 1961, a period of less than 18 months, Andrews lost four boys to traffic accidents. This must have been crushing for the town, to say nothing of the families involved. Jimmy Hendricks, nine years old, was the first victim. He rode his bicycle into the path of a truck on McKeever Street, just a few hundred feet from his home and a few hundred feet from his destination. He was a fourth-grader at the school, the son of Gerald Hendricks and Mrs. Robert Pearson. His family, his school, and his church mourned his death.

Less than 11 months later, on November 21, LaMoine Theobald, the 13-year-old son of Mr. and Mrs. Dallas Theobald, stepped off the school bus and into the path of a truck that failed to stop for the bus. His three siblings were in the driveway of the house when the accident occurred. There were 32 children on the bus who presumably witnessed the accident, or at least its aftermath. It must have been a terrible day for all involved, but especially for the family. LeMoine had been active in 4-H and at the Andrews Methodist Church and was an eighth-grader at the school.

Andrews was not yet done mourning. On December 9, 1960, not even three weeks after the death of Theobald, 16-year-old Ronald Wright lost control of the car he was driving at the north edge of Andrews, The car hit a utility pole and overturned. Wright died instantly. Two passengers, Ronald Ruppert and James Garrison, were seriously hurt in this accident. Wright was a junior at the high school and a member of the Andrews Christian church. He was the son of Mr. and Mrs. Howard Wright and had two sisters and a brother.

Then came the death of 17-year-old John Chapman on May 12, 1961. He was driving home from a trip to Huntington and lost control at the intersection of US 24 and County Road 750W. The car overturned and he was thrown from the vehicle. Chapman's parents were Wayne and Doris Schultz Chapman, and he had two sisters and a brother. He was a junior at Andrews High School and worked at Zahm Greenhouse near Huntington. Once again the town grieved, and supported the families in their sorrow. It was a lot for a small town to endure. But finally, finally the string of disasters had ended.

Other deaths in town, while sorrowful, were less unexpected. Charles Glaze, who had lived in Andrews for much of his life, died on September 18, 1960. He was a brother of Bruce Glaze and had worked at Gets Spark Plug Manufacturing Company. He married Fannie Wendell in Andrews in 1924, and had been employed at Kitchen Maid for 15 years before retiring in 1958, at age 81.

Bruce Glaze, the better known of the two Glaze brothers, died February 17, 1962, in a nursing home in Panama City, Florida. He had a long history in Andrews also, having arrived by 1910. He was first employed by the Wasmuth-Endicott company but left there to found the Gets Spark Plug Company and later the Glaze Manufacturing Company. After a long marriage to Olive Brenneman, as a widower he married a widow, Mary Elizabeth Gleason, in Andrews in 1949. (She was the widow of Otto (O. K.) Gleason, so she had long connections to Andrews also.) Glaze was described in his obituary as a "retired machinist, manufacturer, and inventor."

Dr. Grover Nie was reported to have been a graduate of Andrews High School, although I didn't locate his name in the *Memories: Andrews Schools and Dallas Township Schools 1844-1976* book that is more or less the official record of the school. He was born in 1896 so probably graduated around 1914, and there are no records listed for that year. He had been a practicing physician in Huntington for many years and had served as Huntington County coroner, but he kept some ties to Andrews, because at his death he was a member of the Antioch Lodge 410 of the Free and Accepted Masons.

Huel Goodrich died June 19, 1962, at age 65. He had run a grocery store in Andrews for many years and was a member of the Andrews Methodist Church, Lodge 410 of the Free and Accepted Masons, and the Andrews Lions Club. He was also a veteran of World War I.

Goodrich's former partner, J. Arthur Fults, died June 15, 1963, in Wabash. He had been a partner in the store for many years before he moved to Wabash, the home of his wife. He had been a member of the Andrews Lions Club and a deputy district governor.

Another former businessman, Russell Leakey, died December 23, 1964. He had worked as a plumber and electrician in the Andrews area since at least 1922, when he married Ersell Streit. He was a veteran of World War I and a member of Antioch Lodge 410 of the Masons, the Order of Eastern Star #189, and the Andrews Methodist Church.

Rev. John Bare died at age 82. He had first lived in Andrews from 1929 to 1936, when he pastored the First Christian Church. After serving other pastorates, he and his wife came to Andrews to live in 1956, and he became a member of the First Christian Church. Elizabeth Moore and Forest Bare, both of Andrews, were two of his children.

Dr. Samuel Frybarger was still a familiar name in Andrews when he died on December 5, 1962. He had practiced medicine in Andrews from soon after World War I until 1941, when he moved to Converse. In 1962 people still remembered that he made house calls, which by then were becoming rare.

Another former Andrews physician, Dr. T. W. Omstead, died June 23, 1964. He had practiced in Andrews for three years after World War II, before moving to Huntington. He still was a member of Antioch Lodge 410 of the Masons and the Andrews OES at the time of his death. He was 64 years old. Dr. Omstead is also well remembered for making house calls and for his bedside manner.

Stella Coss, widow of Dr. Roy J. Coss, died February 1, 1963. She had worked as an office secretary for two Huntington attorneys, but her life was in Andrews. Before her retirement, she was the town clerk of Andrews. She was also a member of the Andrews Christian Church and the Order of the Eastern Star.

Robert Wasmuth was not a resident of the town, but he was a part of Andrews life. He had worked at Kitchen Maid since 1929, and when he died September 3, 1963, he was vice president and director of engineering there. He died at a relatively young age, 56. He had never lived in Andrews, but by virtue of his employment and his part in the Wasmuth family story, he was a part of Andrews.

Another former business owner, Floris (Mrs. Edgar) Keefer died December 23, 1963. She had recently retired from her position with Keefer Greenhouse. She was a member of the Methodist Church and the Order of Eastern Star and had lived in Andrews about 40 years. She was just 62 years old at her death, so had lived in Andrews most of her adult life.

Yet another business owner died May 25, 1964. Robert Howard Warfel, who had owned and operated the Corner Cafe since 1960, died May 24, 1964. Earlier he had worked at Kitchen Maid for 34 years. He was a member of the Andrews Christian Church.

Sheridan Tibbals had not died yet, but a March 25, 1965, article about him in the *Huntington Herald Press* gave more information than his obituary over three years later did. At the time of his interview, Tibbals was 99 years old. He had lived around the Monument City area for most of his life but had moved to Andrews in 1955, He had far earlier connections to Andrews, though, because he had worked at the Wabash Railroad yards in Andrews before his marriage. He also remembered Thad Butler and the earliest days of the *Andrews Signal*. (It's hard to imagine that there was still someone in Andrews with memories of the railroad yard, at the time this second book of Andrews history is ending.) Tibbals had been a farmer since he'd married, "retiring" at age 89. At the time of the article, he was in good health "except for his deafness" and read the newspaper every day with the help of a magnifying glass. In his first 99 years, he had been hospitalized once, for an appendectomy. Sheridan Tibbals died July 14, 1968.

William Millican died May 3, 1966. A resident of Andrews since 1939, he had earned the Purple Heart in World War I. He left a widow and eight children, including Edward "of Michigan City."

Pearl James, who had lived in Andrews since 1901, died May 15, 1965. He had worked with his father in the grocery business, then was a timekeeper for the Wabash Railroad. He had worked 25 years at Kitchen Maid before retiring in 1962 (at age 75).

And finally, Frank Brown, who had operated the Brown Vault Company and was a cement contractor in Andrews for many years, died on February 26, 1966.

This ends the story of Andrews from 1916 to 1966, except for one glaring omission and one important addition. So—next up, Sports!

Chapter Eight
Sports

Ever since the earliest days of Antioch, Andrews has loved its sports. I have not studied other small towns, so I don't know whether all small towns had a love affair this great, but it seems remarkable to me. Andrews was committed to having a thriving town, successful factories, churches, lodges, and a good school, but the talk on the Liar's Bench, in the barber shops, at the restaurants and bars, and even in the beauty salons, often was about sports. In researching for this book, I printed a stack of newspaper articles about 2½ inches thick that is just about high school basketball, and I didn't print everything. If it was a sad and losing season, I printed very little from that year. "If you can't say something nice," I figured, "don't say anything at all." Obviously, even in a whole chapter devoted to sports, I will only be able to hit the highlights. But together we can almost hear the crowds cheering in the backgrounds, see the school parking lot (or the streets of downtown Andrews) crowded with cars from the various decades, and feel the excitement of a good game, well fought with lessons learned.

BASKETBALL

We don't have a lot of information about high school basketball during the early years of this time period. We do know that ball games were played in 1917 and that all home ball games were played at the opera house until the "new" school was finished in 1930. The opera house was "heated" by an old potbellied stove, and the stage was still in place from the days when entertainments of various sorts were presented there. Games at the opera house, according to Glynn Rudig, routinely saw spectators standing on their portable chairs in their excitement. As a hometown crowd, Andrews was great!

The team doesn't really seem to have a name, or at least wasn't referred to by their team name, until the 1920s, when they were known as the Red Devils for a time. Usually the combined score, based on different rules than current ones, would not total 50 points, and often a final score would be something like 15-12. If a team won by more than 5 points, it was considered pretty much a runaway. I didn't always find names of players, and when I did, often only the last name was used, but the 1920-21 team included Earl Stouder, Floyd DePoy, Earl Taylor, Albert Ross, Karl Bailey, Ivan McDaniel, and Leslie Streit. In a typewritten manuscript, Ivan McDaniel wrote that in the 1920-21 school year,

we played a total of twenty four games for the season. I can remember one game with Lagro in which the final score was 98 to 5, and we were the team which received the credit for the 5. Well, we just never gave up until the season ended. And when we tallied up the score for the year, we won all of our games but twenty. Nevertheless, we had a lot of fun, and at times we could not tell whether our fans were laughing at us or something else, so we just laughed with them. As long as we could get some fans to continue to come and pay 10 or 15 cents to watch us play we just kept on, because after all, we had to pay rent for our fine goal hall and we also had coal and light bills to pay.

The team the next year included William Bellam, Karl Bailey, Paul Warschko, Albert Ross, Robert Elward, Charles Jeffrey, Eugene Fox, and Clarence Wisner. It seems that these teams were good and got better. By late February 1924, Andrews had played 17 games, winning 14 of them. There was a "district" tournament that year, held over two days, and Andrews was defeated only in the final game. Andrews was proud enough that a supper was held at the Scott restaurant for the team when they returned to town on Saturday evening.

It will perhaps surprise no one, given earlier comments about how enthusiastic Andrews was about sports, that in February 1924, Edgar R. Keefer felt it necessary to write a letter to the editor in defense of the officiating at some of the games. Apparently, unfair aspersions had been cast on the referee at the Union Center–Andrews game, and Keefer charged to the defense of Mr. Notter. From the editor's own comments, it seems that perhaps the officiating at the recent Peru-Andrews game had not been the best, but the Andrews team had said not a word about it. Some things never change!

One of the confusing things about Andrews sports, or the reporting of Andrews sports, is trying to figure out whether the team the newspaper is reporting on is an independent team or a school team. The name "Andrews Athletics" may have been used for both, at different times. By 1927, though, the school team was definitely known as the Red Devils.

During the excitement of November 1924, attendance at a Clear Creek–Andrews ball game was expected to be so high that the game was moved to the Huntington College gym. The *Huntington Press* quoted someone from Andrews as saying, "All of Andrews is going to move over to Huntington that night," and Clear Creek was also expected to provide quite a crowd. Despite the buildup to the game,

Andrews lost this game 42-29. The paper gave last names only of those who played for Andrews: Knight, Bare, Wire, Haley, Wisner, Bixby, Bellam, Andrew, and Garretson. This appears to be "Rip" Knight, Art Bare, James Wire, Bob Haley, Howard Wisner, Robert Bixby, Clarence (Bebe) Bellam, Charles Andrew, and Claude Garretson, based on an undated picture in *Andrews Schools and Dallas Township Schools 1844-1976*. The teams for the next three years appear to have been good but not at the top of the standings. Again, it seems that Clear Creek was a strong rival.

That rivalry was honored at the first game played in the new high school gym, on January 8, 1930. It was a huge event for the town, but those who remember the "new" school may be a little skeptical of the report in the *Huntington Herald* the next day that 1,200 people packed the gym for the dedication and game. Players on that team were Burl Millman, Art Bare, Clarence Bellam, Willard Knight, Kenneth Shaffer, John Wintrode, and William Small. These teams were still playing under the name of "Red Devils," but a new team name was to be chosen for the 1931-32 school year, and by November 2, the team was officially known as the "Andrews Cardinals."

Several times during the 1930s, Andrews hosted a "blind" basketball tournament. The four teams who were playing would not draw their opponents until a half hour before game time, so each had to be prepared for any of the other three teams. Games must not have lasted long, because the first game was scheduled for 1:30 and the second for 2:30, with a consolation game preceding the championship game in the evening. An 18-inch trophy donated by Main Auto Supply Company in Fort Wayne would go to the tournament champions.

Andrews had to cancel two basketball games in February 1932 due to "an epidemic of sickness at the Dallas township consolidated school." It was planned to make those games up before sectional tournament time in March. Players for the tournament were Louis Notter, Wilbur Akers, Dean Wintrode, Hale Harvey, Herbert Yentes, Floyd Andrew, Nelson Latta, Louis Slagel, Waymond Wintrode, Kenneth Quinn, Carl Shoemaker, and Kenneth Flora. Schools were allowed to name twelve players and then had to eliminate two of them the Friday morning before the tournament began. Presumably, ill or injured players would be the first to be "scratched," but this rule also kept all the players at their competitive best, as everyone wanted to play in the sectional. Nothing much was expected from this team since only one was a returning player, and sure enough, the Andrews team came in at the bottom of the rankings when the season was finished.

The team did improve in the 1932-33 school year, but once again games had to be canceled due to illness in the Andrews school. This time, it was an epidemic of mumps that had people on edge. The season ended with slightly better results—12th in the county standings, despite having 10 wins against 11 losses.

When the 1934 sectional tourney was played, Andrews was ninth in county standings. The team was on its way up. Wilbur Akers, Louis Notter, Hale Harvey, Franklin Wade, Dean Wintrode, and Carl Shoemaker each had three years of varsity experience. Other members of the team were Kenneth Quinn, Gilbert Yentes, Orval Plasterer, Dallas Theobald, John Dunn, and Kenneth Fitch. Andrews won the first two games of the sectional, losing to the Huntington Vikings in the semifinal, so it was a good end to the year.

The year 1934-35 was a rebuilding one, as the team had lost most of its players and there was a low turnout of players. (It may be that, because of the Depression, boys were needed to work after school, not play ball.) At any rate, things got worse for the team in early December, when Carl Shoemaker was suffering from appendicitis, Dallas

253

Theobald had ligaments torn in a leg, and John Dunn had an infection in his foot. By the time of the "blind tourney" a month later, Andrews had won 3 games of the 10 they had played, but they recovered and were in eighth place in the county when the sectional tournament was played.

The 1936 ball team included Alfred Campbell, Gilbert Yentes, John Dunn, Robert Flora, Wallace Goebel, Kenneth Schenkel, Raymond Myers, and Ben Garretson, among others. The team ended with a winning season of 12 wins and 9 losses.

The team had another rebuilding year in 1936-37, as there were 6 returning players and 13 newcomers, 3 of them transfers from other schools. The team rebuilt quickly and was third in the county when the sectional was played. Andrews succeeded in going all the way to the final in that sectional, beating the Huntington Vikings in the semifinal.

The 1937-38 ball team finished with a winning percentage of .333, putting them 11th in the county. Certified players for the sectional were Robert Flora, Wallace Goebel, Kenneth Schenkel, John Hefner, Charles Eckman, Lester Stephan, George Stallings, Carl Flora, Clarence McDaniel, James Wintrode, Junior Bradburn, and Richard Schenkel. That was the last year that Edward Cleaver coached.

In 1938, Clifford Murphy took over as coach. The main players (a lot of young men turned out for this team) were Charles Eckman, Wallace Goebel, John Hefner, Marcus Myers, Kenneth Schenkel, Lester Stephan, Carl Owen, Leland Flickenger, John Bickel, Louis Haley, George Stallings, and Herbert Wintrode. The team worked hard but still finished in the same 11th spot, with the same percentage won, as in the previous year.

The 1939-40 school year saw the addition of three men with the last name of Clark, who would put the name of Andrews on the map for years to come, as well as a new coach, C. Dean Snider. Andrews won the four-way tourney at Huntington Township. Certified players for the 1940 sectional tourney were Ross Clark, George Stallings, Clarence McDaniel, Dick Schenkel, Rex Smuts, Meredith Hanselman, James Wintrode, Eugene Smith, Douglas Spencer, Wallace Yentes, and Gordon Schaefer. This team, which had won 11 games up to this point, defeated the defending champions, Union Center, in their first game of the sectional, and also defeated Rock Creek in the second round.

The Andrews Cardinals team of 1940-41 had won 12 games by the time of the sectional tourney. Players certified for the tourney were Richard Schenkel, Don Clark, Meredith Hanselman, John Isenberger, Eugene Smith, Douglas Spencer, Wallace Yentes, Dale Clark, James Clark, Dale Leakey, Gordon Schaefer, and Marion Schenkel.

The 1941-42 team had a better record than had been seen for many years, with a record of 12 wins and 4 losses by early February. They defeated Lancaster by a score of 41 to 30 in the sectional tourney, and then defeated South Whitley before falling to Roanoke in the semifinals. Even worse than the defeat was that Gordon Schaefer had suffered a broken ankle during the game and continued to play on it. He was put in a large, heavy cast and confined to home for several weeks, but was able to keep up with his schoolwork during the rest of his junior year.

The next year, 1942-43, was one for the books, as they say. With 15 veteran players back for another year and a few new players besides, Coach Snider was hopeful about prospects for the team. The team started strong and ended stronger. Week after week the headlines were "Andrews keeps record intact," "Andrews wins 13 straight," "Andrews keeps perfect slate," "Cardinals Ring Up Season's Highest," "Andrews Wins Final Game to Go Undefeated," and finally—yes, the big one—"Andrews Takes Sectional Final."

Certified players for the sectional were Dale Clark, James Clark, Dale Leakey, Gordon Schaefer, Herbert Smuts, Gale Eller, Rex Myers, Nelson Yentes, Joe Clark, Roger Leakey, Oliver Wade, and Bill Wasmuth. Dale Leakey scored 87 points during the sectional tourney games. The record the Cardinals had earned made them the regional favorites, but Monroe didn't read the statistics and defeated Andrews in the final game. Still, it was a never-to-be-forgotten thrill for the coach, team, school, and community. It was a welcome relief from the worry of the war, even though many of these men went on to serve their country in later months and years.

All of the "first five" of the team graduated, but Coach Snider had three players who had three years' experience and seven with two years' experience to start the 1943-44 season. The team did well, with a 10 win and 7 loss record, ranking seventh out of 15 teams in the sectional. Certified players were Claire Austill, Gale Eller, James Tullis, Nelson Yentes, Joe Clark, John Goebel, Roger Leakey, Bill Snyder, Bill Wasmuth, Doyal Wright, Frank Korreckt, and Wilbur Stallings.

There was hope for the 1944-45 team, as all of the returning team had experience playing basketball. The team, with seniors Joe Clark, Roger Leakey, John Goebel, Bill Snyder, Bill Wasmuth, Doyal Wright, and juniors James Keel, Robert Pinkerton, Floyd Priser, and William Stallings, won 14 of their games that year.

The 1945-46 team had a new coach, Bill McPherren, and there was only one senior on the roster. It was a difficult year for the team, as they won only one game. As always, the hopes for the sectional were high, at home if nowhere else. Certified players for the 1946 county tournament were Charles Garrison, Phillip Keefer, Dick Quinn, Jay Kitt, C. Miltonberger, Ray Quinn, William Quinn, Orville Rupel, Charles Snyder, Bob Smuts, and Robert Tullis.

Jim Hughes was the new coach for the 1946-47 year. The team greatly improved their record from the previous year, winning nine games, but they were still below the .500 mark for the year.

The 1947-48 year was even better, with Andrews in fourth place in county rankings as they headed to the sectional. Players for the biggest games of the year were Les Stallings, Charles Garrison, Orville Rupel, Jim Haley, Dick Quinn, Max Hethcote, Drake Omstead, Jim Fields, Phil Keefer, Joe Rupel, Mark Anson, and Harold Schlemmer.

Ivan McDaniel's manuscript reminds us that we should never forget the efforts put forth by not only the parents of the ballplayers, but also the cheerleaders for these teams. For the 1947-48 team, the cheerleaders included Mary McDaniel and Louella Decker.

It was time for the final basketball game of the year 1948, and Mary Edith had been very faithful to practice yells with her partner, Louella Decker, who lived a mile east of Andrews, and it was about a quarter of a mile south along the east side of the woods to her house. At times it seemed to be a regular occurrence when mother would meet me at the door when I would arrive home for supper and say, "Don't take your coat off yet, you have to go out to Louella's and get Mary," or take Louella home. Well, it was a must that we keep our Andrews Cardinals in the winning column. So, as usual, at game time I sought my most preferred seat on the top of the bleachers toward the east end of the floor. Here I could lean back against the south wall.

The 1948-49 ball team was exceptionally good, placing first in the county going into the sectional. They had 17 games in the win column and only 3 in the loss column, and added another win in the sectional. Players on that team were Jim Fields, Dick Quinn, Charles Garrison, Dick Fields, Phil Keefer, Joe Rupel, Ed Goodrich, Bill Mundy, Drake Omstead, Glen Rittenhouse, and Jim Stephan.

Of course, with five seniors gone, 1949-50 was another rebuilding year. It didn't turn out as expected, or feared, however. The Andrews team won 13 games during the year. Players certified for the sectional were James Fields, Ed Goodrich, Les Keefer, Edgar Kitt, Billy Mundy, Al Reust, Glenn Rittenhouse, Joe Rupel, Bob Smart, James Stephan, and Bill Yahne.

By now, Coach Hughes was in fairly comfortable territory. His teams were doing well, and for the 1950-51 year, there were six returning lettermen, including the team that had played as the first five the previous year. In fact, Andrews didn't lose a game until they were badly beaten by Lancaster on January 13, 1951. That was the first year for the county tournament to be played, and Andrews won their first game of the tourney. This new tournament was regarded as a tune-up for the sectional, when only a few additional teams were added to the schedule. Andrews played more good ball, but was upset by Roanoke when the first sectional game was played. They ended the season with a record of 17 wins and 3 losses.

Coach Hughes planned that 1951-52 basketball would be a building year, bringing underclassmen into the team, since the team had again lost several seniors to graduation. An added feature to this year's games would be fighting for possession of the "Shoe" trophy, sponsored by the *Herald Press*. Union Center was given the first possession of the trophy, and for another team to claim the trophy, they would have to defeat Union Center. It was designed to be a traveling trophy, and to generate extra interest in games where the trophy was at stake. It doesn't appear that Andrews had a shot at the "shoe" that first year, but the team was doing fairly well when the county tourney came around, with a seven and four record. By sectional time, Andrews was second in county standings but sixth in conference standings. They ended the year with 14 wins and

9 losses. Players that year were Bob Reemer, Larry Oswalt, Dave Pratt, Edgar Kitt, Arden Hanselman, Gerald Yentes, Merritt Hethcote, Jim Stephan, Dewayne Fitch, Bill Yahne, Carl Stephan, and Alan Hollowell.

The 1952-53 team had a new coach, Phil Hyman, and a shortage of tall ballplayers. Sophomore Gerald Yentes was already 6 feet 2 inches tall and the coach had hopes that he would play well in the center position. The team was off to a good start, having won their first three games, when they played Warren for possession of the coveted "shoe" trophy. Andrews took the trophy and held on to it for about six weeks, until losing to Huntington Township on December 23. Andrews had won nine games and lost just three when the county tourney was played. By the time of the sectional, their overall record was 14 wins out of 19 games played. Players for the sectional were Jack Ferrell, Morris Bitzer, Carl Stephan, Bill Yahne, Eugene McDaniel, Gerald Yentes, Arden Hanselman, Edgar Kitt, Jim Smart, Larry Oswalt, Joe Ferrara, and Bob Reemer.

Andrews had several tall ballplayers for the 1953-54 season, replacing some of the speed and experience of the previous year's team. This team also worked well together, having a record of nine wins and two losses going into the county tournament. They again won the "shoe" trophy and defended it for the final game of the season, thus retaining bragging rights until the following November. Players for the sectional tournament were Merritt Hethcote, Jack Ferrell, Morris Bitzer, Gerald Yentes, Bob Reemer, Bob Tullis, Dea Hethcote, Michael Garretson, Joe Ferrara, Harold Keefer, Jim Smart, and Dave Pearson. The team ended with a record of 16 wins and 6 losses.

For the 1954-55 year, there was another new coach, Don Hammel. He started out with six returning lettermen for the team, including Gerald Yentes, who was now at 6 feet 4 inches, and Dave Pearson, who was the county 100-yard-dash champion. One of the highlights of the year was watching Yentes score, and score, and score. He scored his 1,000th varsity point in a game on December 13, 1955, and by the time of the sectional tourney was credited with over 1,300 points. Games that year were generally high-scoring, with points scored by the winning team usually in the 65-to-85-point range. People remember those games with a smile. Players for the sectional game were Joe Ferrara, Dave Pearson, Mickey Garretson, Charles Harvey, Joe Keffer, Ron Collins, Gerald Yentes, Terry Buckles, Jim Smart, and Dea Hethcote. Andrews defeated Warren in an overtime first game but was defeated in the second game. They ended the season with a record of 18 wins and 7 losses.

Little was expected of the 1955-56 Cardinals. They had lost four starters, including Gerald Yentes and a substitute, to graduation, and prospects looked better for future teams than for this team. They did, however, win 6 of their 21 games, and Ron Collins was the high scorer for the county for the year.

A change in coaches took place for the 1956-57 year, when Stan Brueckheimer became the new coach for the Cardinals. It was a serious loss for the team when Ron Collins severely gashed his arm in late November. He missed over two months of the basketball season while his arm healed. The team won nine games that season. Sectional players were Dick Garrison, Delbert Fitch, Chuck Harvey, Tom Rudig, Mark Crain, Ron Collins, John Bigelow, Rhett Ripplinger, Don Lassiter, and Duane Andrew.

The 1957-58 year started out well and got better. Andrews raised their record to seven and one in the middle of December 1957. More importantly, the December 14 victory over Clear Creek gave them the traveling "shoe" trophy, after Clear Creek had "owned" it for about a year. Mark Crain, John Bigelow, and Tom Rudig were frequently mentioned as top players that year, with Rhett Ripplinger, Duane Andrew, Delbert Fitch, Ted Campbell, and Jay Dee Rittenhouse also contributing. They ended the season with 16 wins and 5 losses.

The 1958-59 year was another rebuilding year, as the Cardinals lost six of the top seven players to graduation or, in the case of Mark Crain, to a family move. Even so, the team started out by winning 11 games straight before being beaten by Clear Creek in the county tourney. It was the only loss they had, going into the sectional tournament. They ended the season with an outstanding record of 17 wins and just 2 losses, the best record in the county. Again, this team was a high-scoring team, fun to watch and remember. The first five for most of the year was composed of Rhett Ripplinger, Jay Dee Rittenhouse, John Bigelow, Monte Schenkel, and Tom Schenkel.

The Cardinals' winning ways continued into the last year of the decade. They started out with possession of the "shoe" trophy from the previous December, and despite the loss of several key ballplayers, they still had John Bigelow. Halfway through the season, Andrews was number one in the county, and they continued to win in regular play until they lost to Laketon on February 3, 1960. They did, however, repeat as Huntington County Conference Champions. Players for the sectional were Rick Wilkinson, Ron Ruppert, Rich King, Tom Schenkel, Charles Flaugh, Steve Fearnow, Dan Smart, John Bigelow, Bill Smith, and Tom Clements. Stan Brueckheimer had gone from the coach with the worst record in the county, at Markle, to the team with the best record in the county two years running, at Andrews. Andrews didn't always do well in tournaments, but their regular season record was stellar.

Once again, the 1960-61 season started off looking difficult, at best. John Bigelow had graduated, as had Dan Smart, Tom Schenkel, and Tom Clements. The young men

261

on the new team were fast, and they were good shooters, but there was little height on the team. Some of the players were just 5 feet 6 inches tall. Coach Brueckheimer thought they could "maybe" win three or four games that year. Andrews started out by winning three games in a row, but all good things must come to an end. The team had "owned" the "shoe" trophy for almost 23 months when they finally lost a conference game and turned the trophy over to Union. Andrews won 11 of their games that season, losing 9. That wasn't at all bad for a team the coach had thought could win three or four "maybe." Players for the sectional were Yetive Ruppert, Ron Ruppert (who had returned after suffering a broken pelvis and more in a car accident), Richard King, Tim Millman, John Snyder, Ron Johnson, Terry Plasterer, Terry Close, Jim Beghtel, Rick Wilkinson, and Steve Fearnow.

The 1961-62 team was short on seniors, but it included players who had played well in junior high games, and the future looked somewhat hopeful. In fact, they finished the year tied for second in the conference, winning 12 games. Players for the sectional were Jim Beghtel, Terry Close, Rick Wilkinson, Ron Ruppert, Yetive Ruppert, Asa Ellet, Tim Millman, Terry Plasterer, Steve Kreigh, and Mike France. This team beat Huntington Township and almost beat Roanoke in the second round of the sectional.

Coach Brueckheimer had several reasons for hoping for a good season in 1962-63. Only one of the previous year's players, Ron Ruppert, had been lost to graduation, and the team was experienced and eager. The question seemed to be whether the team would live up to the expectations held for it. The team did live up to expectations, winning several games and at one time winning the "shoe" trophy. This was the fifth time the Cardinals had held it. They won the county tournament in January, which was such a cause for celebration that school met for only a half day on Monday.

The semifinal game also put Coach Brueckheimer's wins with the Cardinals at 100, in just seven years. The team went on to win the Huntington County Conference Crown for the third time in five years and ended the year still in possession of the famed "shoe" trophy. Players for the team were Jim Beghtel, Tim Millman, Rick Wilkinson, Yetive Ruppert, Terry Close, Wendell Holbrook, Mike Schaefer, Terry Plasterer, Steve Kreigh, and Mike France.

For years, the coach had been saying it would be a rebuilding year, and much of the time the team had done better than expected. For the 1963-64 year, there was a new coach, Mark Crain, who had played on the team up until his senior year. It was truly a year for the players and coach to get to know each other and to learn to play better defense, since they no longer had high-scoring players on the team. By the time of the sectional, they had won just 2 games while dropping 17. The players had heart and desire, but they were short in stature and in topnotch shooting ability. Those who were eligible for the sectional were Tom Plasterer, Steve Kreigh, Roy Hamer, Rod Smith, Mike Schaefer, Mike France, Sam Goebel, Wendell Holbrook, and Dan Smith.

Many of those team members were back for Crain's second year as coach. They were able to improve on the previous season's record, winning more games, including the annual four-way tourney that had eluded them for years. They beat both Rock Creek and Clear Creek to take that championship. Going into the sectional tournament, the team had a record of 7 wins against 11 losses, a good improvement over the previous year. Players for the sectional tournament were Dan Smith, Rodger Smith, John Rogers, Sam Goebel, Mike France, Ron Stambaugh, Mike Schaefer, Roger Speicher, Mike Rogers, Roy Hamer, and Terry France.

The final year for the Andrews Cardinals started with another new coach, Nyle Fox. Coach Fox thought the main thing Andrews needed was to learn how to beat a zone. The team worked hard at that but had another rough year, winning 3 games and losing 15, ending up in the basement in the ratings. Those who played on the last sectional team before consolidation were Steve Hacker, Sam Goebel, Monte Barnes, Ron Stambaugh, Rick Fritz, Dan Ryan, Bob Clabaugh, John Rogers, and Mike Rogers. It should be remembered that even though the team had a rough few years, the crowds and the excitement were still there, the band played for the home games, the cheerleaders cheered, and if one didn't look at the scoreboard, there would have been little difference noticed between a winning year and a losing year.

It wasn't until April 1951 that an association was formed of both Huntington County principals and coaches. The purpose seems to have been to set regulations for games, such as when and how many could be played, but also to set limits for the junior high teams. Seventh- and eighth-grade players only were eligible for the junior high teams, and players were no longer eligible to play on those teams once they reached their 16th birthday. Reading between the lines, it may have been time for some guidelines to be put in place.

As an aside, the official high school games weren't the only games the high school teams played. They played alumni teams almost every year, as fund-raisers for the school or for charities, and sometimes played in other "exhibition" type games. So they had a chance to test themselves against not only other high schools, but also other, older teams. Fortunately, those other, older teams didn't practice as rigorously as the high school team did, and the Cardinals often won. It must have been a real boost to the 1937-38 team, who defeated the alumni who had members on the team who had defeated Huntington in the sectional that spring. Junior high and grade school teams played during most if not all of this time, and many of those players went on to play on the varsity teams. Andrews always had some ball team they could root on to victory.

Some of the boys who played basketball went on to college or the military and had outstanding careers. Some of those who stayed in Andrews, however, continued playing the game in various leagues or for benefit games, or wherever someone might let them play. Up until 1931, the home games were played in the opera house, with the same challenges that the high school teams faced in the beginning as far as seating and heat go. For instance, on March 3, 1917, the *Huntington Press* reported that the "Andrews Athletes" and the Dudlo shop team from Fort Wayne would play at the opera house, and the "Athlete Seconds" would play the Huntington College team as a preliminary. We are given the last names of the players for the first team: Shinkel, Reamer, Keefer, Gerard, Parks, and Wire.

Kitchen Maid sponsored a team for several years in the 1920s. The men wore dark green jerseys, black trunks, and gray sweatshirts, we're told. It's not clear whether the players came from the factory or from outside the factory, but they were referred to as "former college and professional players." They were identified as McClanahan, Stouder, Leaf, Bailey, Jones, Elward, and Swearingen. On February 6, 1925, the Andrews Kitchen Maids played the Huntington Knights of Pythias at the Coliseum (in Huntington), for the Huntington County championship. It would be a "battle Royal," said the advertisement. Teams played after the "championship" game included the American Legion at Chili, the YMCA at Peru, the Pierceton Regulars, the Greentown Independents, and the Fort Wayne Ben Hurs.

265

In 1926 the Gets factory took over the sponsorship and management of the team. The new team name was the "Gets Spark Plugs," and it included some of the same players who had been on the Kitchen Maid team at the end of the 1925 season. Names are given as Wisner, McClennahan, Elward, Leaf, James, Bailey, and Kocher, and all were former high school stars, though not necessarily at Andrews.

By 1929, there was a team known as the Andrews Independents, who had fun but were apparently less newsworthy.

Andrews still played strong ball. In March 1932, the Spencer's Bakery team of Andrews defeated the industrial league champions of Wabash County, Linco Oil, by a score of 40 to 17. Players on that team were Barnhisel, Carroll, Rudicel, Wire, Millman, and Briggs.

Six years later there was a team known as the Kitchen Maids again, this time in the Y Industrial Basketball league. Yentes, Notter, Riggers, Millman, Akers, Louis, and Kelly played on that team. In 1939 and again in 1940 there was a Kitchen Maid team playing in the same league. Players that year were A. Campbell, Yentes, Johnson, G. Stallings, R. Stallings, and Wasmuth. Some of these men were answering the call of their country within another year or two, but they could first savor the joy of earning the league crown for the 1940-41 season.

There seems to have been little league or independent play during the war, but after the war it didn't take long to get back in the swing of things. The Andrews Fire Association played a team from the Rural Fire Association in a fund-raiser to raise money for a new fire truck. And the Kitchen Maid team in the Y league was back at it again. Players in December 1946 were Joe Clark, Eller, Leakey, Smuts, Jim Clark, and Tullis. The team won a four-way independent tourney held at the high school gym, and league play may have continued after that season.

Andrews had the opportunity, two years in a row, to see how the Andrews Merchants team would fare against a team from the "All-American Red Heads" women's basketball organization. These games were fund-raisers for the Lions Club, and because the women played by men's rules, it was a novelty. The professional team was roughly akin to the Harlem Globetrotters in scope, as they played all over the country and even overseas. Andrews put up an "all star " team of their own, including Dale, Jim, and Joe Clark; Rex Smuts; Gordon Schaefer; Joe Keffer; Bill Yahne; Morris Bitzer; and Carl Stephan. Those must have been entertaining nights, and I hope the gym was full. Andrews always loved basketball.

BASEBALL

Andrews also loved baseball. The crowds may not have been as large, and the cheering may not have been as loud, but baseball was played by men as early as the 1880s. The earliest mention I found of a high school baseball game was in 1927, when Andrews and Monument City played each other. There were fall teams, spring teams, and later in the century even some summer high school teams, but newspaper coverage was sporadic. In 1929, we're given the last names of the players who, as the Red Devils, defeated Huntington Township. The players, most of whom also played basketball, were Knight, Wintrode, Shaeffer, Latta, Bellam, Botkins, Millman, Lakey (possibly Leakey?), and Bare. Some members of the 1931 team apparently played a little too much baseball and paid too little attention to their studies. The last three games of the schedule were "postponed indefinitely" because several players were placed on the academic ineligibility list. That probably got the attention of the players, and their parents. The spring 1932 team included Notter, Yentes, Andrews, Akers, Shoemaker, Latta, Caster, Harvey, and Wintrode. The 1934 team included Flora, Yentes, Shoemaker, Quinn, Dunn, Walker, Theobold, Slagel, Eberhart, and Russell. The fall 1935 team included Flora, Loy, Dunn, Campbell, Schenkel, Yentes, Wintrode, Herman, Garrison, Eckman, and Owens. Most years, it was hard to find a ranking, but in October 1938 the Cardinals were next to the last in the county standings, having won one game out of six. The fall 1939 team, however, was good enough to win the county championship. The players were Yentes, Wintrode, Smuts, Smith, Spencer, Stallings, Schaefer, Hanselman, Schenkel, and R. Clark.

The following year, the Cardinals made it to the play-off, losing to Warren in that game. In a repeat of the championship game in 1941, Andrews won. The newspaper article mentioned that Cardinals pitcher Don Clark had been ill for the 1940 game but was back, pitching at his best, for the 1941 game. Clark was never defeated in a regular season game during his high school career, but of course, baseball may not have been his first choice. He played a bit of basketball, too. Don Clark was still pitching in high school games in the summer of 1942, so apparently he was considered a senior until school started again in the fall. (Did I mention that this was confusing?) The Cardinals won the fall 1942 county championship with team members Yentes, Smuts, Dale Leakey, Schaefer, Dale Clark, Myers, Wasmuth, Joe Clark, and Goebel.

Either baseball took a rest until after the war, or the newspaper didn't print the results, or I overlooked them, because the next records I have begin in 1947. Players for that fall season included Stallings, Rittenhouse, Quinn, Rupel, Anson, Schlemmer, Fields, Garrison, Smart, Finton, Halen (Haley?), and Garrison. Andrews earned the county championship title for baseball in the fall 1948 season. Players were Dick Quinn, Glen Rittenhouse, Lester Keefer, Phil Keefer, Jim Fields, Joe Rupel, Harold Schlemmer, Bob Smart, Dick Fields, Drake Omstead, Les Stallings, and Dewayne Fitch.

The Cardinals continued playing good ball, and in 1950 again were the county baseball champions. Players were Fields, Rupel, Kitt, Yahne, Keefer, Smart, Hollowell, Reemer, and Hanselman. The 1952 team ended up in second place in the county. Players on that team were Stephan, Hanselman, Ferrara, Kitt, Reemer, Yahne, Yentis, Ferrell, Tullis, Decker, and Bitzer. The *Herald Press* reported on October 5 that "The summer sport had hardly gasped its last breath for 1952 in Huntington county before county school aggregations spun their attention to the Hoosier's delight—basketball." After 1952, the team must have had some rebuilding years. Although the Cardinals won games each season, they were not back on top again. The 1954 team included Pearson, Rudig, Smart, Yentes, Ferrara, Collins, Keefer, Hethcote, and Harvey. Collins, Ripplinger, Rudig, Harvey, Crain, Laymon, Schenkel, Bigelow, and Andrew played in 1956. The 1958 team was made up of Ruppert, T. Schenkel, Ripplinger, Smith, Bigelow, Laymon, Quinn, Schenkel, and Harvey.

Holbrook, Ruppert, Green, Wilkinson, Fearnow, Close, Campbell, Kreigh, and Plasterer comprised the 1960 team. The 1962 team included Schaefer, Millman, Close, Wilkinson, Kreigh, Hamer, Holbrook, Goebel, and Plasterer. During the 1963 summer season, Roy Hamer pitched two straight no-hitters. In the fall 1964 season, he struck out 17 players in one game, and the team tied Clear Creek for the best record that same year. Clear Creek won in the play-off. Andrews and Warren were cochampions in 1965, with Roy Hamer, Mike Rogers, Ron Stambaugh, and John Rogers chosen for the county "All Star" team. That was the last year baseball was played in the county conference. School consolidation took place in August 1966.

Although Andrews had good ballplayers through the years, Roy Hamer proved that he was in a class by himself. He won a baseball scholarship to Purdue in the fall and was scouted for the Detroit Tigers, among others. A shoulder injury may have cut his career short, according to Dave Ripplinger and Rod Wilkinson.

Men—after high school and for as long as they wished—played some sort of baseball or softball all through the years of this book. My stack of newspaper clippings about three-fourths of an inch thick attests to that, and by no means did I print all of the reports or reports of all of the games. I hope I am conveying a feeling for the games and teams, and some of the names involved, but this is not a comprehensive history of the game. The 1916 season was the first to be played before the "new bleachers that have been erected and almost completed." We don't know which ballfield this refers to. It may have been one east of town. Players for the unnamed team (possibly a team from Wasmuth-Endicott) were Wasson, Frakes, Withers, Sprowl, G. Frakes, Stalling, Notter, Grimes, Williams, and Collier, who was the pitcher and captain. An advertisement in the *Huntington Press* on July 1, 1916, advertised "Baseball, Sunday, July 2 Andrews vs. Specials Fairgrounds. Ad. 25 cents Ladies 15 cents, Game called at 3." Wasmuth-Endicott morphed into Kitchen Maid, and the teams played on.

In 1923 the Andrews team and the Orton-Steinbrenner team played for top place in the Industrial league. It must not have gone well for Andrews, because the *Huntington Press* printed a short article on September 20, 1923: "Andrews citizen says: 'The Huntington Industrial baseball league could not stand for a small town like Andrews winning their pennant so they brought up a kick to move Andrews town out of the league or forfeit enough games to put them in last place. Then after Andrews quit, some of the teams wanted to get their players. Andrews was leading the league when they quit and would have won the pennant if allowed to continue.'" This shows two things: Andrews cared about its baseball, and there are questions we won't be able to answer about what caused the "Andrews citizen" to write this letter.

By 1930 all had been forgiven, more or less. A team from Andrews played the Huntington Aces. The Andrews players' names were given as Millman, Wintrode, Bare, Stouder, Ballard, Wire, Anson, Ross, and Blaine. It was noted that Ballard and Anson had been players on the DePauw University squad. The Andrews Business men played a three-game series against the high school baseball team in October 1931. The Andrews Merchants sponsored a good team in 1932, with members including Benson, Wintrode, W. Wintrode, Notter, Smith, Anson, Bunker, Millman, and B. Millman.

The Andrews Independents (not sure if this is the same team as the Merchants) dedicated their new ballfield on the west side of North Main Street in Andrews in July 1932. Two weeks later, the ballfield is described as "on old US 24." So far, I've not located a picture nor a person with a memory that would help clarify this location. The 1932 season also featured a game with the "Hoosier Pirates," made up of "colored" men from Marion and Peru. The Andrews Kitchen Maid team and "a squad of picked players" were going to entertain a crowd in 1936 "at an Andrews diamond." The item that made this newsworthy was that all players would be riding donkeys. Admission was charged, but just to cover the cost of bringing the trained donkeys to town.

Kitchen Maid teams played in 1936, but by 1938 the team that was mentioned in the newspaper was the Andrews Fire Chiefs. J. Huston, G. Yentes, B. Stallings,

Campbell, Householder, Quinn, G. Stallings, H. Yentes, R. Huston, Millman, and Stouder played on this team, which defeated a team from the Lagro Civilian Conservation Corps, among others. John Wintrode pitched a no-hit, no-run victory over the Markle Boosters on August 27, 1938, on the Andrews diamond. Again, Andrews may have cared too much about their ball games. In 1939, an Andrews player, Lewis Notter, perhaps got carried away in an argument with an umpire. The umpire filed charges of assault, which were later withdrawn.

Players for the Kitchen Maid team in 1941 were Kern, J. Altman, Millman, Bunker, Stallings, Gray, Haines, Millican, Andrews, Fisher, Boe, Benson, Smuts, and Yentes. There also seems to have been a team of "Andrews Independents" that year. A 1947 team called "Andrews Church" lost 16 straight games before defeating "Bell Cafe." Players on this team were Keefer, Yentes, D. Quinn, Hughes, Haley, Bostel, R. Quinn, Kitt, and Hendricks.

The Andrews Lions Club started a tradition in 1948 when they sponsored a countywide softball tournament at the Andrews High School diamond. Sixteen teams took part in that first tournament, with 13 more typical in the ensuing years, as competition was limited to teams from Huntington County.

The Lions also had a team made up of club members and played the Bippus Lions for their first game, where a "fumbling good time" was expected. Players on the Lions Club team in 1950 included J. Clark, Rittenhouse, Schaeffer, Sunderman, Keefer, Fleckinger, D. Clark, Campbell, and Cowden. The Vim league was sponsored by Vim of Fort Wayne, apparently a sporting goods business.

In 1951 there were eight teams in the league, and two of them, the Andrews Lions managed by John Wintrode, and the Hoffman Oilers managed by Emory First, were based in Andrews. The Lions Club still sponsored their annual baseball tournament. In 1951 Schacht's defeated Andrews for the tourney championship. Players for Andrews were Yentes, Schaefer, Kitt, Draper, Byrd, Clark, Henson, Dalton, and Millman.

In addition to the high school and post–high school teams of all sorts, Little League and Pony League teams played during at least the 1950s and 1960s. There was a 4-H league and a Boy Scout league and probably others that played just a game or two and disappeared. Baseball or softball were probably available for watching any day of the week during the spring and summer months.

SPORTS FOR WOMEN

So far, I haven't mentioned the women. If you've never heard of the Andrews Cardinalettes, perhaps you can be forgiven. A lot of people don't know about the Andrews Cornet band, all women, of the 1880s, either. These ladies, in both centuries, were doing things that women didn't often do, and they were doing them in small-town Indiana. The Andrews Cardinalettes began playing baseball in 1948, with Lloyd Stewart as their coach and Eldon Stephan as assistant coach. The players on this team were Mary Yentes, Lily Harris, Enid Bobbitt, Joan Haley, Joan Slagle, Devota Scott, Marcella Stephan, Barbara Snyder, Estella Kelley, Marie Campbell, Joanne Bare, Norma Bucker (maybe Bricker), Doris Clark, and Marjorie Bitzer. Wilma Snyder was the manager. Most of the members of the team had graduated from Andrews High School, but their pitcher was "a negro hurler from Wabash," said the *Herald Press* of June 16, 1948. They traveled all over the area, including Fort Wayne, and had a good overall record in their "girls' league." They were season and tournament champions of the Tri-County league in 1948. After league play was finished for the 1948 season, they played a team from

Marion known as the Marion Blue Blazers, a "colored nine." The team may have changed their name in 1949, because a women's softball team known as the Andrews Cities Service team, sponsored by Gene Wilson, played that year. The same coaches were instructing the girls, and some of the same players were mentioned. This was identified as a softball rather than a baseball team, This team was part of the Vim Tri-County girls league. Seven teams entered the Invitational Girls' Softball tournament in 1949, sponsored by the Lions Club, but that is the last news I found of them. Perhaps the girls who had played for two years were getting married and no longer could make such a time commitment to the sport. That's what happened to the Cornet Band, all those years ago.

OTHER SPORTS

As important as basketball and baseball were to Andrews, often other sports drew participants and fans, too. Although newspaper records are spotty, Andrews High School had a long tradition of track and field athletes. The earliest reference I found was from March 25, 1927, when "one candidate is said to be able to make five feet eight inches on the high jump." Runners for the various "dashes" were expected to be plentiful, if not fast. Tryouts were also being held for shotput and pole-vault competitors. The next time track and field seems to be referenced is 21 years later, in 1948, when the first annual county track meet was conducted. Andrews took third place out of seven competitors in that meet, and they were determined to do better. They stayed in pretty much the middle of the pack until 1953, when it seems that only one Cardinal, Edgar Kitt, placed in the county meet. There were outstanding individual efforts over the next years, but the team couldn't accumulate enough points to challenge the various champs for several years.

In 1960 Andrews was involved in a three-way meet with Township and Union. The Ruppert brothers—Phil, Ron, and Yetive—together won five of the events, which put Andrews in second place. I wonder if there was a bit of celebration around that family dinner table later in the evening? By 1962, the relay teams of Andrews were starting to gel, and other efforts by Ron Ruppert resulted in an Andrews win over Huntington Township in a two-way meet. There were only two or possibly three meets held each year before the county track meet. Andrews won two of those in 1964 and then went on to win the county track and field championship in the closest meet of the series. That team included Luke Ellet, Ron Stambaugh, Sam Goebel, Larry Kennedy, Duane Glass, Dave Osborn, Bob Harrell, Wendell Holbrook, Rod Smith, Dan Smith, Roy Hamer, King Ryan, Mike Schaefer, John Teague, Roland Urschel, Keith Wilson, Jim Nichols, Steve Kreigh, Mike Rogers, Ken Quakenbush, Terry Starbuck, and Dennis Hendricks. Jim Meadows was the coach. They repeated as champions in 1965, with Nyle Fox as coach.

The first Andrews golf team, coached by Gene Kaufman, played in 1964. Fifteen young men tried out for the team, and an astounding 45 young women tried out for the girls' team. I found no further record of girls playing golf, but the boys played for three years. That first year, the team made a bet with the track team, that the track team would not win the county meet. See results above. As the losers of the bet, the golf team took turns hitting a golf ball from the Andrews school to the Huntington Township school. Although five miles sounds like a bit of a walk, Coach Kaufman assured the newspaper that it wasn't any longer than an 18-hole golf course. Those who made good the bet were Steve Turner, Ron Inyart, Wendell Holbrook, Chuck

275

Kuschel, Don Ludwig, John Harshbarger, Rick Fritz, and Monte Barnes.

Other brief mentions I found of sports were a tennis team in 1927, with members Clarence Bellam, Robert Warfel, Willard Knight, and Dean Stouder; cross-country in 1964; and a county volleyball tourney in 1949 and 1950. Girls also had their volleyball team in 1962, and possibly in other years. Although it's certainly possible that these or other sports were played for longer than just the seasons I found referenced, these seem to be one- or two-season wonders.

One sport that attracted some Andrews men in 1940 was boxing. Three men from Andrews entered a Golden Gloves tournament in Fort Wayne. Richard Owens, welterweight; Bob Flora, middleweight; and Carl Owen, lightweight, competed in that meet. We don't know how much other experience the men had, but there was considerable interest in boxing in Andrews down through the years. Probably a good crowd of people went to Fort Wayne for the event.

Andrews men tried to form a volleyball team in 1950, and then opened it to also include youth when they didn't get enough men to compete. The record is silent as to whether they actually played games.

The final sports action in the time period for this book actually took place right outside the town of Andrews, on what is now the old US 24, just a few hundred feet east of State Road 105. The facility was first owned by Ray Manning, Dan Hiatt, John Bickel, and Morris and Joyce Wade. A racetrack was designed so that two cars could drive abreast, and speeds of 70 miles an hour could be reached on the straightaways. Cars had to meet the specifications of the Hoosier Hot Rods Racing Association, but anyone was welcome to race if they could qualify. The public was invited and expected to attend. Bleachers were set into the side of a hill, providing seating for 800 to 1,000 people. If one were lucky enough to live across the street from the track, the race could easily be viewed from one's rooftop. I'm told that it was easy to hear the announcers, Charlie and Mandy Homier, from that vantage point. The only thing missed there was the dust!

Although as many as 50 cars showed up for the first races, the Hoosier Hot Rods soon bowed out of the management of the race, and a new group, the Andrews Racing Association, was formed. Ted Newsome of Andrews became a regular in the racing seat. He won often, and said that on his best night, his prize was $42. Demolition derbies were added to the card, and figure-8 races, and the crowds seemed to really enjoy those. Women weren't normally allowed in the pit area or on the track, but occasionally there was a competition among the wives of the drivers, otherwise known as a powder puff derby. They were given a chance to see what they could do behind the wheel, and they drove like they had something to prove. At the risk of leaving someone out, I'll also mention, as Andrews men who raced, Junior Schultz, Lloyd Flaugh, John Bickel, Jim Long, Daryl Milican, Ron North, Charlie Flaugh, Bob Newsome, Max Funderburg, and Everett Goins. Some of these men raced their own cars, and some drove autos owned by others. Both stock cars and go-karts raced on this track. Sometimes the roar of the cars was loud enough to be heard in Andrews, but I don't remember anyone complaining about the noise. The racetrack quit operating sometime in the late 1960s.

Sports of all kinds helped define Andrews during these years before television, computers, and smartphones changed society, even in Andrews.

Chapter Nine
Andrews's High Achievers

Andrews has a rich history. Most people who remember living in Andrews during the 40s, 50s, and 60s describe it in idyllic, almost lyrical terms. Whether speaking of the bustling business of the day, of hours spent playing in and around Loon Creek, of sports or school or parents or churches or Boy Scouts or any of the many other wonderful things that have made up our town, residents and former residents draw strength from their roots here. Some of those men and women, nurtured by their hometown roots, have taken their talents elsewhere to live remarkable lives. Some of them have been forgotten, and they should be remembered.

For instance, Louise Satterthwaite Fults Agnew was an Andrews schoolgirl who had an interest in art. She was an Andrews High School graduate and married Arthur Fults (of the "Fults and Goodrich" store). Louise was one woman who was recognized not just locally but throughout the Midwest and even nationally, for her art work. She had exhibits at the courthouse, and some of her individual paintings were accepted by the Hoosier Art Salon in Indianapolis. She also had a lithograph shown at an annual exhibition in Oklahoma City, and other oil paintings were shown at the Pennsylvania Academy of Fine Arts in Philadelphia. She was an art instructor at Huntington College.

It shouldn't surprise us that in the 1943 *Mnemosyne*, the Huntington College yearbook, Louise is described as "enthusiastic and really peppy, spends all available time working in the studio two flights up, and has won recognition from her paintings exhibited at art shows."

Later, Arthur and Louise divorced, and Louise ended up in Chicago. She met her second husband, Wallace Agnew, while doing some sketching. They struck up a conversation, he carried her supplies to the train station, and the rest is history. She became quite a talented photographer and gave talks all over the Chicago area about photography and especially some of the techniques she had developed for color slides. Louise Agnew was well known for her photos of the San Blas Indians of Panama and Colombia. She became fascinated by their textile arts and eventually wrote her doctoral dissertation on molas, a form of colorful layered embroidery practiced by the tribal women. As she continued her artwork and her teaching, she earned a master's degree from the Art Institute of Chicago and then her doctorate in visual design from the Illinois Institute of Technology. Louise Satterthwaite Fults Agnew made a name for herself, and she started from Andrews.

The *Huntington Herald Press* of July 24, 1959, carried a story about Dr. Louis E. Haley, an Andrews graduate in the class of 1940. It told only part of his story; I've been able to piece together just a little more, but I'm sure there is yet more to be told. The article was about the return of the family (wife Norma Whinery and sons Michael and Jerry) to the United States on furlough from Dr. Haley's position as a soils adviser with the International Cooperation Administration in Thailand. The ICA was a predecessor to the US Agency for International Development. Dr. Haley had earned his BS and MS degrees from Purdue University and his PhD in soil chemistry from the University of Illinois, and after working as an instructor at North Dakota

Agricultural College and Purdue University, and as a research assistant at the University of Illinois, he had joined the government program and gone to Thailand. There he used his expertise to help Thai farmers better fertilize their soil and possibly develop new crops.

The newspaper article didn't mention this, but Dr. Haley also had served in World War II, enlisting as a private. When he was wounded, he was already a staff sergeant. I've not been able to trace his military career, but when he passed away in 2011 in San Antonio, Texas, he was a colonel. His headstone lists "DSM BSM PH." DSM stands for Distinguished Service Medal, BSM for Bronze Star Medal, and PH for Purple Heart. Chances are, he had other medals that wouldn't fit on the headstone.

Norma Whinery Haley wrote a 30-page biography of her life, which Mike Haley, Louis and Norma's son, generously shared with me. Their story was fascinating. Every few years, the family would pull up roots and go to a different assignment. Norma seems to have fit in easily with whatever culture she was in, and it sounds like her sons also adjusted well to a life some might consider extraordinary. Their first assignment was in Bangkok, and immediately Louis was "whisked away up country."

They were later assigned to Cambodia; Jakarta, Indonesia; and Jayapura, New Guinea. They had another tour of duty in Thailand, one in the Philippines, and one in Colombo, Sri Lanka, as well as in Secunderabad, India. In between assignments and new companies, the family lived in Florida, Colorado, and other places in the United States. They traveled around the world and saw many sites and many cultures, sometimes staying for just a few days and sometimes for years at a time. Louis made a list of all the places he lived during his life, including a few hotel stays, and they added up to 44 address changes. Some of the time Norma lived separately at other addresses as she fulfilled a job contract, waited for the school year to end, or did some house-hunting. As this family learned and taught all over the world, Dr. Haley took a bit of Andrews with him.

E. P. Cubberly has been mentioned briefly before. He lived in Andrews from his birth in 1868 (at that time the town was known as Antioch) until he finished the 11 years of schooling then available in Andrews. He later graduated from Indiana University and taught at Ridgeville College, then served as president of Vincennes University, as superintendent of the San Diego, California, Public Schools, and eventually as Dean of the School of Education at Stanford University in Palo Alto, California. All of this has little to do with Andrews, but his "side job," writing educational text books, influenced Andrews directly. With money set aside from his royalties, he liked to help libraries, and when Andrews was at risk of losing the library building the ladies had worked so hard to have built, Dr. Cubberly came through with a timely donation. He also strongly suggested that the library be turned over to the town or township, to be funded by taxpayers so that bake sales and other fund-raisers would not be needed. After some thought, and negotiations, the change in ownership was made. Cubberly also was able to donate enough money from his "side job" to build a library on the Stanford campus that is still standing to this day. Andrews has produced some remarkable men.

I couldn't finish the story of Andrews without telling a little of the story of the Clark twins. Each time I have talked to a longtime resident and asked what I should be sure to include in this book, they've said "Be sure to tell about the Clark twins." Much of their story could better fit in chapter 8, about sports, but because they traveled so many places and were representatives of Andrews to so many people, I've chosen to include them in this chapter. Harvey and Gertrude Clark had four sets of twins—Ross and Robert

(Bob), Don and Dale, Joe and Jim, and Mildred and Margaret. Bob graduated from Union High School of Wells County in 1940, and Ross graduated from Andrews that same year. Don and Dale graduated from Andrews in 1943 and 1944, respectively, and Joe and Jim graduated in 1943 and 1945. Don, Dale, Jim, and Ross all served in the military during World War II, and when they all got back home, they started playing basketball together. Bob played for Huntington College for four years as well as with some local teams. Ross played for Andrews, and Don, Dale, Jim, and Joe all played on the Andrews team that won the Huntington sectional tournament in 1943 and almost won the regional title. Don also played basketball while in the army. Dale was regarded as being the best shot on the team, was all-county forward in 1943, and also played basketball in the service. Jim was the shortest player on the team at 5 feet 9 inches but the scrappiest member, and Joe, at 6 feet 2 inches, was the center, good at tip-ins and rebounds.

The Clark men all played on various teams such as Kitchen Maid and Markle Boosters in 1946, but for the 1947-48 basketball year, they planned to play together as a team, including some extended road trips. They played very well that year and ended the season with a record of 40 wins and 10 losses. That's a lot of basketball, but their manager, Vi Caldwell, wanted to keep them booked up. They won the national family team championship in both 1946 and 1947, defeating several teams that were expected to beat them. During these early years, Mildred and Margaret often traveled along as cheerleaders for their brothers and may have played an occasional game also. It was very much a family team.

By late 1948, the fame of the Clark twins was spreading. Spectators wanted to see one of the unique teams in basketball, and other teams wanted to have bragging rights to having played them, even if they couldn't beat the twins.

Abe Sapperstein, a booking agent in Chicago, scheduled a nine-day tour for the men, playing two games in Indiana, three in New York, and one each in Pennsylvania, Massachusetts, Maryland, and Washington, DC. After returning from that trip, they played a couple of games locally, and then played in Springfield, Missouri; Tulsa, Oklahoma; and Joplin, Missouri. At this time, they were playing opposite either the Harlem Globetrotters or the Kansas City All Stars on their games away. Later in the season, they toured in the western United States, where they battled the weather as much as they did the opposing teams. Winter blizzards, white-out conditions, and flooded roads were just a few of the adventures the men reported.

The Clark Twins traveled again with the Abe Sapperstein syndicate, playing all over the country against various other teams controlled by Sapperstein, including the New York Renaissance, who appeared in Huntington against the Twins. The team would not be quite the same for this season, since Bob Clark decided to stay home and continue coaching at Huntington Township high school. To fill the vacancy on this six-man team, Jack Walton of Wells County would join the team. Beginning in May 1951, the team, apparently including Bob, left for a three-month tour of Europe, playing the Harlem Globetrotters 96 different times in England, Scotland, Ireland, France, Belgium, Holland, Switzerland, Spain, Portugal, Morocco, Algiers, Italy, Austria, and Germany. Three months and 96 games, and all that traveling besides! One would need to be an athlete to follow that kind of a schedule. The men reported meeting several notable people, including King Farouk, Pope Pius XII, and famed photographer Robert Capa. Bob Clark played again the following season, with a team that toured with the Harlem Globetrotters. They played "around the world," from London to Japan, and many points in between.

After that, the twins settled down. Five of them were already married, and it was time to start families and move on with life. But for those few years, the Clark twins had a great time, and showed their fans a great time, too. And Andrews remembers.

In Closing

Every town has memories, but not every town is fortunate enough to remember them. It has been a privilege for me to find and especially now to share these stories, although I'm sure there are many more than I've found. I need to thank enough people to fill a book, but especially Mary Snyder, Meredith Hanselman, Ron and Janet Ruppert, and Ted Newsome, for talking with me at length about this town. I've had shorter conversations with many people. Phyllis Brumbaugh provided me with a map of the town in 1943, which was very helpful. Probably dozens of people have helped me when I asked a question on the Facebook page, "If you grew up in Andrews you remember . . . :" administered by Duane Glass. They are just the best people there, and I thank each and every one of them. Ken Interval helped me uncover the story of Roy Eastes, blacksmith and violin maker, which I found to be intriguing.

As much as I appreciate all the help I've been given, I accept full responsibility for any and all errors in the book. Names are probably misspelled in places, and for that I humbly apologize. Items I've stated as facts may not be correct, and surely this book contains strong opinions, most of them mine. I regret all the stories I know that I haven't been able to share, and I regret all of the stories that I don't know.

I've used the *Huntington Herald Press* and the *Andrews Signal* and other Andrews newspapers as my primary references. I've also used a manuscript written by Ivan McDaniel, one written by Elva Fults, and another by Lawrence Wade, as well as that of Norma Whinery Haley. With the kind permission of Nancy Casey Lewis and Larry Casey, I've referenced *Memories: Andrews Schools and Dallas Township Schools 1844-1976* many times while writing this book. Tim Deal, Connie Kline, and Shirley Stephan Fisher have shared pictures with me and given permission to use them. And dozens of current and former "Andronians" have shared memories with me, so many that I couldn't include them all. Every story and every memory, however, is greatly appreciated.

As always, the women who serve in the Indiana Room at the Huntington Public Library have gone above and beyond in helping me locate material, in answering questions, and in printing hundreds, or probably thousands, of newspaper articles for me. Sarah Kirby and Julie Theobald deserve thanks for all they have done to help find the stories.

Special thanks to Lois Crum, who has spent hours turning this manuscript into something even better—a book. Her editorial assistance has been invaluable.

Most emphatically, I can't thank my family enough for their help and encouragement. Melinda Harshbarger Marshall has improved the photos and prepared them for the book. Donovan Harshbarger formatted the book and designed the cover. John Harshbarger has both encouraged me and known when to stay out of my way. He is one of the reasons I wrote this book.

Even in Andrews, it takes a village to write a book.

Personal Names

Abernathy, John
Abernathy, Mary Jane
Abernethy, Herbert
Abernethy, John
Adams, Charles
Adams, Orval
Adams, Orville
Adams, Pam
Adams, Ron
Adams, Ronny
Adamson, Patsy
Ade, Judge Ray
Agnew, Louise Satterthwaite
  Fults
Akers, Carol
Akers, F.
Akers, Wilbur
Aldridge, Bernice
Aldridge, Frank (Mr. & Mrs.)
Alford, Mrs. Joseph
Allen, Richard
Alpaugh, D. R. (David)
Alpaugh, Hannah
Altman, J.
Altoan, Joy
Anderson, Charles (Mr. &
  Mrs.)
Andrew, Charles
Andrew, Duane
Andrew, Floyd

Andrew, Janet
Andrews, Charles
Andrews, DeWayne
Andrews, E. E. "Abe"
Anson, Bert
Anson, Mabel
Anson, Mark
Auman, Cheri Keefer
Austill, Claire
Austill, Lloyd
Austill, Mrs. Lloyd
Bailey, Alberta
Bailey, Brice L.
Bailey, Harriet
Bailey, Karl
Bailey, L. P.
Bailey, Lena
Bailey, P. E. (Pearl)
Baker, Anna
Baker, Eddie
Baker, James M.
Baker, Joseph
Ball, Rev. Kenneth
Ballard
Bamberlin, Mrs. Garland
Bammerlin, Mrs. Fred
Bannister, Joe
Barcus, George N.
Bare, Ann
Bare, Arthur

Bare, Elizabeth
Bare, Forest
Bare, Janet
Bare, Joan (Joanna, Joanne)
Bare, Mrs. Forest
Bare, Opal
Bare, Paul
Bare, Rev. John (J. J.)
Barlier, William J.
Barnes, Monte
Barnes, Willard
Barnhisel, Jack
Barron, Robert
Bauer, Paul (may be Bare)
Beamer, John
Beaty, Richard E.
Beauchamp, George
Beauchamp, Simon S.
Beedy, Bertha
Beeks, Barbara
Beeks, Bonnie
Beeks, Chester
Beeks, Cleo
Beeks, Donald
Beeks, Elias "Bud"
Beeks, James R.
Beeks, Leonard
Beeks, Norman
Beeks, Wilbur
Beghtel, Andris
Beghtel, Barbara (Barb)
Beghtel, Fred
Beghtel, James (Jim)
Beghtel, Jean Anne
Beghtel, Kay
Beghtel, Lila
Beghtel, Linda
Beghtel, Lindel
Beghtel, Mrs. Fred
Beghtel, Patsy
Beitelshees, O. C.

Beitelshees, O. W.
Belcher, Ira
Bellam, Clarence (Bebe)
Bellam, Swanora
Bellam, William (Bill)
Bellrose, K. W.
Bellrose, Martha
Bengston, Lois
Bengston, Philip
Bengston, Rev. Daniel
Benson, Kenneth
Benton, Doris
Bickel, Dean
Bickel, John
Bickel, John Lewis
Bickel, Larry
Bickel, Mrs. Dean
Bickel, Mrs. John
Bickel, Sharon
Bickel, Verna
Biehl, Gary (Ladd or Laddie)
Biehl, Glynna
Biehl, James
Bigelow, Carolyn
Bigelow, Edward (Ed); Mr. &
    Mrs. Edward Bigelow
Bigelow, Edwin
Bigelow, Evan; Mr. & Mrs.
    Evan Bigelow
Bigelow, Everett; Mr. & Mrs.
    Everett Bigelow; Mrs.
    Everett Bigelow
Bigelow, John
Bigelow, Lewis
Bigelow, Louis (probably
    Lewis)
Bigelow, Noralyn
Bigelow, Phyllis
Bigelow, Robert
Bigelow, Shannon
Bitzer, Carolyn

Bitzer, Edna
Bitzer, George
Bitzer, Homer
Bitzer, L. J.
Bitzer, Lawrence
Bitzer, Marjorie
Bitzer, Morris
Bitzer, Nondas
Bitzer, Philip
Bitzer, Sue
Bitzer, William (Bill Billy)
Bixby, Mrs. R. O.
Bixby, Raymond O. (R. O.)
Bixby, Richard
Bixby, Robert
Blacketor, Catherine
Blaine
Blake, James
Blake, Rev. Donald
Blose, Mrs. John
Bobbitt, Enid
Bodkin, Arlin
Bodkin, Nina
Boe
Bolinger, David
Bollinger, Harry R.
Bolton, Earl
Bomersback, Frank
Bomersback, Pat (Patty)
Bomersback, Thomas (Tom)
Boone, Barbara
Boone, Betty Lou
Boone, David
Boone, Fred
Boone, L. H.
Boone, Mrs. Don
Borden, Garland B.
Borders, Pauline
Borders, Rev. J. W.
Bostel
Botkin, Edith

Botkin, Floyd L.
Botkin, Max
Botkin, Noah
Botkins, Homer
Bowles, Emma
Bowles, H. G. (Bert)
Bowles, John
Bowles, Verne
Boxell, Max
Boyer, Arliss
Bradburn, Junior
Bradburn, Mary
Brady, C. E.
Bragg, Evelyn
Branstator, George
Braun, John (Mr. & Mrs.)
Breeding, Charles (Chuck)
Brenaman, Earl
Brenneman, Olive
Brewer, Charles
Brewer, Charlotte
Brewer, Grace
Brewer, Helen
Bricker, Charles
Bricker, Norma
Briggs, Darrell E.
Brindle, Buff
Brock, Virgil
Brooks, Mary
Brown, Fern
Brown, Frank C.
Brown, Glenna
Brown, Jerry
Brown, Mabel
Brown, Mrs.
Brown, Mrs. James
Brown, Norma
Brueckheimer, Sanford
Brueckheimer, Stan
Brumbaugh, Carl
Brumbaugh, Joe

Brumbaugh, John
Bruss, Howard
Bucker, Norma (maybe
   Bricker),
Buckles, Ed
Buckles, Edgar
Buckles, Jan
Buckles, Lindel
Bullinger, Grover Lee
Bunker, Waneta
Burch, A. V.
Burget, Mrs. Lewis
Burk, Joyce
Burkart, Vivian
Burkhart, Barbara
Burkhart, Doug
Burkhart, Helen
Burkhart, Keith
Burkhart, Laveda
Burkhart, Owen
Burkhart, Pauline
Burkhart, Thelma
Burnworth, Robert
Burtnet, Elmer
Butler, Belle
Butler, Thad
Butt, Don
Butt, Mary
Buzzard, Jerrine
Buzzard, Randy
Byerly, Arthur
Byerly, Fred (Mr. & Mrs.)
Byerly, Wava
Byrd
Caldwell, Vi
Calvert, H. A.
Calvert, Homer
Calvert, William
Campbell, A.
Campbell, Alfred
Campbell, Arden

Campbell, Belle
Campbell, Bill
Campbell, Everett E.
Campbell, Glen
Campbell, Glenna
Campbell, Helen
Campbell, Marie
Campbell, Melanie
Campbell, Pauline
Campbell, Rosetta
Campbell, Ted
Capa, Robert
Carpenter, Beverly
Carpenter, John
Carpenter, Linda
Carroll
Carson, Ezra H.
Casey, Deborah (Debby)
Casey, Edgar (Edgar)
Casey, Larry
Casey, Lawrence (Larry)
Casey, Margaret (Mrs. Edgar,
   Mrs. Ed)
Casey, Nancy
Cassady, Ralph
Caster, Howard
Caster, Thada
Caster, Viola
Caylor, Rev. & Mrs. R. C.
Cecil, Lois
Chapman, Doris Schultz
Chapman, John
Chapman, Johnny Wayne
Chapman, Judy
Chapman, Robert Leroy
Chapman, Teddy
Chapman, Virginia
Chapman, Wayne; Mr. & Mrs.
   Wayne Chapman
Charbonnier, James W.
Chenoweth, Mrs. A. C.

Chenowith, Dr. Albert
Chesman, R.
Chopson, Cheryl
Chopson, Douglas (Doug)
Chopson, Pamela
Chronister, Carrie
Chronister, Edward (Ed); Mr.
  & Mrs. Edward Chronister
Chronister, John
Chubb, Delmar
Chubbuck, Donna
Clabaugh, Bob
Clabaugh, Karen
Clabaugh, Mrs. Russell
Clare, Eugene
Clark, Charles
Clark, D.
Clark, Dale
Clark, Don
Clark, Doris
Clark, Estella
Clark, Gertrude
Clark, Harvey
Clark, J.
Clark, James (Jim)
Clark, Joe
Clark, Margaret
Clark, Mildred
Clark, R.
Clark, Robert (Bob)
Clark, Ross Thomas
Clark, Verne
Cleaver, Edward T.
Cleaver, Nina
Clement, Linda
Clements, Alice
Clements, Bette
Clements, Charles
Clements, Deana
Clements, Deborah
Clements, Haskiel

Clements, Mary
Clements, Mrs. Charles
Clements, Rose Marie
Clements, Shirl
Clements, Susan
Clements, Tom
Clemmons, Roy (Mr. & Mrs.)
Cline, Beulah
Cline, Mrs. Lynn
Clingel, Almira
Clinger, Bryce
Close, Dick
Close, Harold
Close, Lu Ann
Close, Max
Close, Terry
Clymer, Dr. Russell (R. S.)
Cocklin, Norma
Cogswell, Walter
Colbert, E. R.
Coldren, Larry
Cole, C.
Cole, Jerome
Cole, W. D.
Cole, William
Collier, Mel
Collins, Ronald (Ron)
Collins, Thelma
Collins, Walter
Cones, Connie
Cook, Doris
Cook, Kenneth (Mr. & Mrs.)
Cook, Lucinda Mae
Cook, Sharon
Cooper, E. H.
Cooper, Sidney
Cortle, Peter
Coss, Roy J. (Dr.)
Coss, Stella
Cowden
Cox, Darwin

Cozad, Norman
Crain, Mark
Crile, Lindal
Cross, D. W.
Cross, Dorrance (Dorrence)
Cross, Foster M.
Cross, H. T.
Cross, Henry
Cross, Lawrence
Cross, Phyllis
Crull, Anna Mae
Crull, Henry J.
Crunk, Bob
Cubberly, E. P.
Cummings, Laura
Cundiff, Richard
Dalton
Day, Randy
Day, Ricky
Deal, Peter
Deal, Robert; Mr. & Mrs.
  Robert Deal
Deal, Vera
Debuchananne, B. L.
Debuchananne, J. D.
Decker, Doneta
Decker, Louella
Decker, Mrs. Rudy
Decker, Rudy
Declan, Roy G.
Denman, Ward
Denney, C. M.
Denney, Nellie
Denny, Merle
Denton, Doris
Denton, Dorothy
DePoy, Floyd
Detamore, Sondra
Detamore, William
Dewert, Cheryl
Dickey, Burton

Dickey, Galen
Dickey, James
Dickey, John
Dickey, Rev. & Mrs. Howard
Dickson, Lois
Dickson, Louis
Dickson, Patty
Diefenbaugh, Sophia
Dille, Geneva Opal
Dilley, Jesse
Dillon, James (Jim)
Dillon, Mrs. Ralph
Dinius, Melvin (Mel)
Dinius, Mildred
Dinius, Sandra
Dinius, Sharon
Dolby, Myrtle
Doren, John J.
Douglas, Barbara
Douglas, Rosemary
Draper
Duhammel, Cheryl
Dunn, Howard
Dunn, John
Durfee, Maurice F.
Durflinger, Louis L.
Dyer, Jesse
Eagleson, Thurman
Earley, Marvin
Eastes, Bessie
Eastes, Leroy H. (Roy)
Eberhart
Eckman, Charles
Eckman, Junior
Egolf, Roger Lee
Eisen, Rev. T.
Eldon, Miss
Eller, Gale
Ellerman, Ruth A.
Ellet, Asa
Ellet, Carolyn

Ellet, Earl E.
Ellet, John
Ellet, Luke
Ellet, Wilbur
Ellison, Annice (Annis)
Ellison, Avis
Ellison, Homer
Ellison, Mary Margaret
Ellison, Richard
Ellison, Ruth Ellen
Ellison, S. E.
Ellison, Samuel (Sam)
Ellison, Treva
Elward, J. E.
Elward, Robert
Emley, Judy
Endicott, Carl (C. E.)
Endicott, Elizabeth
Endicott, J.
Endicott, Jack
Endicott, Mary Ellen
Endicott, Mrs. C. E.
Ervin, Myrtle
Ervin, Sarah Elizabeth
Evans, Paul
Everhart, Arthur
Everhart, Herman E.
Everhart, Loretta
Everroad, Dian
Everroad, Donna
Everroad, Edith Ruth
Everroad, Jean
Everroad, Peggy
Farthing, Jesse R.
Fast, Mary Helen
Favorite, Herman
Favorite, Wallace
Fearnow, Camella
Fearnow, Cathy
Fearnow, Emma Holbrook
Fearnow, Gary

Fearnow, John
Fearnow, Margaret
Fearnow, Phyllis
Fearnow, Ray
Fearnow, Steve
Ferguson, Kay
Ferguson, Russell
Ferguson, Sue
Ferrara, Joseph (Joe)
Ferrell, Darlene
Ferrell, Jack
Ferrell, Jackie
Ferrell, Robert
Ferris, A.
Ferris, Arthur
Ferris, Nora
Fields, Carolyn
Fields, Ernest
Fields, Frances
Fields, James (Jim)
Fields, Raymond (Ray)
Fields, Richard (Dick)
Fields, Ruth
Finkle (Finkey), Elmer
Finlayson, Don
Finton, Jesse
Finton, Laban
First, Emory
Fisher, Clifford
Fisher, Elaine
Fisher, Judy
Fisher, Loretta
Fisher, Mark
Fisher, Mary Lou
Fitch, Charles
Fitch, Delbert
Fitch, DeWayne
Fitch, Kenneth
Fix, Charles
Fix, Mrs. Charles
Flaugh, Charlie

293

Flaugh, Dennis
Flaugh, Jill
Flaugh, Lloyd
Flaugh, Sharon
Fleckinger
Flemming, Bert
Flickinger, Leland
Flickinger, Mrs. Leland
Flora, Carl
Flora, Ferrel
Flora, Joan
Flora, Judy
Flora, June
Flora, Kenneth
Flora, Robert (Bob)
Fluke, Richard
Follis, Ralph (Mr. & Mrs.)
Ford, Tennessee Ernie
Forrest, Mary
Forrest, Spencer
Forst, Alice
Forst, Bert
Forst, Donal L.
Forst, Donat
Forst, Georgia
Forst, Mary
Forst, R. H.
Forst, Ruth
Foster, Oren B.
Foust, Thelma
Fox, Eugene
Fox, Mrs. V. T.
Fox, Nyle
Frakes, G.
France, Mike
France, Terry
Frazee, Veva
Friedman, Maurice
Fritz, Rick
Frushour, Donna

Frushour, Roy; Mr. & Mrs.
   Roy Frushour
Fry, Dr.
Frybarger, Dr. Samuel (S. S.)
Frybarger, Mary
Fryer, Wendy
Fulhart, Gail
Fulhart, Mary
Fulton, Bernice
Fulton, Lucille
Fulton, Robert
Fults, Arthur
Fults, Betty Lee
Fults, C. E.
Fults, Charles
Fults, Dr. G. B.
Fults, F. E.
Fults, Frank E.
Fults, J. Arthur
Fults, Mr.
Fults, Mrs. A. J.
Fults, Mrs. F. E.
Fults, Mrs. Frank
Fults, Mrs. J. Arthur
Funderburg, Max
Galey, Donald
Gallaspie, Roy
Gard, Mildred
Garretson, A. (Ari) O.
Garretson, Ben
Garretson, Claude
Garretson, Claudia
Garretson, E.
Garretson, Emery C.
Garretson, Lawrence
Garretson, Linda
Garretson, Lyle
Garretson, Michael
Garretson, Mickey
Garretson, Mrs. A. O.
Garretson, Mrs. Ben

Garretson, Mrs. Claude
Garretson, Mrs. Lawrence
Garretson, Sally
Garretson, William
Garrison, Angela (Angie)
Garrison, Anna
Garrison, Carol
Garrison, Carolyn
Garrison, Charles
Garrison, Claude
Garrison, Delana
Garrison, Dorothea
Garrison, E.
Garrison, Ella
Garrison, Esther
Garrison, Halen (Haley?)
Garrison, Harry (Mr. & Mrs.)
Garrison, James (Jim, Jimmy);
    Mr. & Mrs. James Garrison
Garrison, Joan
Garrison, John
Garrison, John W.
Garrison, Lana
Garrison, Larry
Garrison, Linda
Garrison, Madonna
Garrison, Maria
Garrison, Marie
Garrison, Mrs. Charles
Garrison, Mrs. Paul
Garrison, Pat
Garrison, Pauline
Garrison, Phil
Garrison, Phyllis
Garrison, Richard (Dick)
Garrison, Sandra
Garrison, Shirley
Garrison, Vivian
Garshwiler, Guy
Gaskill, W. H.
Geiger, Lawrence

Gephart, Arlo
Gephart, Orlo
Gerard, L. M.
Gerard, Lloyd
Gerard, Samuel
Gerdes, Mary
Gerdes, Mrs.
Gilbert, Eunice
Gillmore, John
Glass, Charlotte
Glass, Claude; Mr. & Mrs.
    Claude Glass
Glass, Clyde
Glass, Duane
Glass, Frances
Glass, Francis
Glass, Sharon
Glass, Shirley
Glaze, Bruce
Glaze, Charles
Glaze, Fanny
Glaze, Henry Miller
Glaze, Mrs. Bruce
Glaze, Olive ("Allie May")
Gleason, Elizabeth
Gleason, Mary Elizabeth
Gleason, Mrs. O. K.
Gleason, Otto K. (O. K.)
Goebel, Carrie
Goebel, Ella
Goebel, Gertrude
Goebel, Harry
Goebel, John
Goebel, Katherine
Goebel, Louis
Goebel, Mrs. Carl
Goebel, Roderick
Goebel, Sam
Goebel, Sharon
Goebel, Velma J.
Goebel, Wallace

Goebels, Gertrude Peting
Goings, Elaine
Goings, Everette D.
Goodale, Ford N.
Goodmiller, Lawrence R.
Goodmiller, Rev. L.
Goodrich, Edwin (Ed)
Goodrich, Huel E.
Goodrich, Rosemarie
Gordon, Clyde
Grace, John W.
Grade, Dale
Gradeless, Walter
Gray, Forrest (Forest)
Gray, George (Mr. & Mrs.)
Gray, Marie
Gray, Mrs. Forrest
Gray, Wilma
Green
Gressley, Ival, Jr.
Gretsinger, Betty
Gretsinger, Edith
Gretzinger, Betty
Gretzinger, John J.
Griffith, Fred (Mr. & Mrs.)
Griggs, Louis
Grimes
Grimm, Gene
Grodian, Jeffrey
Groscost, Kaye
Groscost, Marilyn
Groscost, Ray
Groscost, Sue
Groscost, Willia
Grossnickle, Billy
Grossnickle, Dixie
Gurtner, F. L.
Habegger, Rev. Homer
Hacker, Carol
Hacker, Steve
Hackworth, Hubert (LeRoy)

Hackworth, Linda
Hackworth, Mrs. Leroy
Hackworth, Susan
Hahn, A. C.
Hahn, Charles
Hahn, Mrs. John
Hahn, Robert J.
Hahn, Susie
Haines, Lee
Haines, Mary
Haley, Amy
Haley, Bob
Haley, Dr. Louis E. (Louis)
Haley, James (Bill)
Haley, Jerry
Haley, Jim
Haley, Joan
Haley, Mary
Haley, Michael (Mike)
Haley, Norma Whinery
Haley, Richard
Haley, Udah B.
Haley, William (Will)
Hall, Albert
Haller, Louis
Haller, Paul; Mr. & Mrs. Paul
   Haller
Hamer, Barbara
Hamer, Darlene
Hamer, Roy
Hamman, Evangeline
Hamman, Janice
Hamman, Robert
Hammel, Don
Hammel, Mrs. Don
Hammon, Janice
Hanselman, Arden
Hanselman, Meredith
Hanselman, Mrs. Roy
Hanselman, Ruth Ann
Harrell, Bob

Harris, E. L.
Harris, Irene
Harris, Lily
Harris, Lynn
Harris, Marvin
Harshbarger, Alma
Harshbarger, John
Harshbarger, Marcia
Harshbarger, Mary
Hart, Mrs. F. W.
Hart, Mrs. Thad
Hart, Thad
Harvey, Charles, Sr.
Harvey, Charles (Chuck)
Harvey, Hale
Harvey, Jerry
Harvey, Lonna
Harvey, Mildred
Harvey, Mrs. Charles
Harvey, Mrs. Gus
Harvey, Mrs. Hale
Harvey, Robert
Harvey, Ronald (Ronnie)
Hass, Rev. Lonnie
Haupert, Mary
Hausman, Roy
Hawes, Sarah
Haynes, Mrs.
Haynes, Ruth Ann
Heater, Patricia
Heck, Loyd
Heck, Mrs. Lloyd
Hefner, C. E.
Hefner, Ila
Hefner, John L.
Hefner, Richard
Hefner, Ruth M.
Hefner, Tommy
Hefner, Treva
Hegel, Charles
Hegel, Clarence

Hegel, Mrs. Charles
Heitz, Frank
Heitz, Vera
Helvie, Charles
Helvie, Harold
Helvie, James
Helvie, Lettie
Helvie, Lewis
Helvie, Reuben
Helvie, Reverend Otto
Helvie, Zachariah
Hemmick, John E.
Hendricks, Dennis
Hendricks, Gerald
Hendricks, Jimmy
Hendricks, Marlene Dickson
Hendricks, Mildred
Henson, John
Herman
Heslet, Chester
Heslet, Eva
Heslet, Mrs. Chester
Hethcote, Connie
Hethcote, Dea C.
Hethcote, Max
Hethcote, Merritt
Hetler, Donald R.
Hetler, Donna
Hetter, Pat
Hiatt, Dan
Hoch, George
Hodson, George
Hoffman, Severin
Holbrook, Wendell
Hollowell, Alan
Hollowell, Allen
Hollowell, Boyd
Hollowell, Donna
Hollowell, James E.
Hollowell, Joyce
Hollowell, Larry

Hollowell, Laverne
Holmes, Lawrence
Holmes, Mrs. Richard
Holmes, Richard L.
Homier, Charles F. (Charlie)
Homier, Mandy
Hoover, Carl
Horrell, Corinne
Hosler, Glen
Hostetler, Richard
House, Agnes
House, Nellie
Householder
Howell, John
Howes, Harold
Hubric, Mary
Huffman, Clarence
Huffman, Scotty
Hughes, E. V.
Hughes, James J. (Jim)
Hughs, Earl
Hummer, Arthur
Hunnicutt, Barbara
Hunnicutt, Joann
Hunnicutt, Ralph C.
Hunter, Helen
Huston, Alvin
Huston, Barbara
Huston, Frank C.
Huston, J.
Huston, Mrs. Roy
Huston, Nancy
Huston, R.
Huston, Roy
Huston, Sally
Hyman, Philip (Phil)
Hysong, Jerry
Inyart, Ron
Iry, Alice
Iry, Clarence
Isenbarger, Alda

Isenbarger, John R.
Isenbarger, Pearl
Isenberger, John
Jackson, Fern
Jacobs, Charles L.
Jacoby, Allen
Jacoby, Harry
James, Mrs. Pearl
James, Pearl
James, Richard T.
Jeffrey, Charles
Jeffrey, Eldon
Jeffrey, Howard; Mr. & Mrs.
    Howard Jeffrey
Jeffrey, Lloyd
Jeffrey, Marguerite
Jeffrey, Mark
Jellison, Eugene
Jennings, Cecil
Jennings, James (Jim)
Jennings, Leona
Jennings, Lowell
Jennings, Max
Jennings, Myron
Jersey, Ann
Johnson, Diana (Dianna)
Johnson, Eugene
Johnson, Fern
Johnson, James
Johnson, Mrs. Arlin
Johnson, Ronald (Ron, Ronnie)
Johnson, Wayne
Jones, Billy
Jones, Frances
Kahl, John
Kahlenback, Betty
Karst, Clarence
Karst, Judy
Kaufman, Gene
Kaufman, Tracy
Kautz, Henry

Keefer, Charles H.
Keefer, Clarence; Mr. & Mrs.
  Clarence Keefer
Keefer, DeWayne
Keefer, E. H.
Keefer, Eddie
Keefer, Edgar R.; Mr. & Mrs.
  Edgar Keefer
Keefer, Floris (Mrs. Edgar)
Keefer, Flossie
Keefer, Harold
Keefer, John
Keefer, Lester (Les)
Keefer, Mrs. Ned
Keefer, Ned
Keefer, Noel
Keefer, Phillip (Phil)
Keefer, Rosemary
Keefer, Steve
Keel, James
Keel, Leonard
Keel, Monroe (Mr. & Mrs.)
Keel, Mrs. Garnett
Keel, Ray
Keffer, Joe
Keiser, Coelestine
Kellam, Ann
Kellam, Bobby
Kellam, Everett
Kellam, George
Kellam, Georgia Ann
Kellam, Jackie
Kellam, Jerry
Kellam, Jon
Kellam, Kathy
Kellam, Mrs. George
Kellam, Ralph
Kelley, Ed; *see also* Ed Kelly
Kelley, Estella; see also Estella
  Kelly
Kelley, F. A.

Kelly, Ed; *see also* Ed Kelley
Kelly, Estella; *see also* Estella
  Kelley
Kelly, Jannetta
Kelly, Karin
Kelly, Marshal Ed
Kelsey, V. R.
Kendall, R. Clayton
Kennedy, H. Glenn
Kennedy, Larry
Kennedy, Lawrence
Kennedy, Rol
Kennedy, Sharon
Kern
Kester, Cheryl
Kilby, D. C.
King, Anna
King, Benjamin J.
King, Daisy
King, Delbert
King, Elizabeth
King, James
King, Mabel
King, Nina
King, Richard (Rich)
King, Wilson
Kingsley, Henry
Kitt, Edgar
Kitt, Esser (E. M.)
Kitt, Jay
Kitt, Mrs. Jay
Kitt, Norma Krile
Kitt, Renee
Kline, Don
Kline, Homer
Kline, Jane
Klotz, Prudence
Klotz, Richard
Knee, Archie; Knee, Mr. & Mrs.
  Archie Knee
Knee, C. E.

Knee, Elva Fults
Knee, L. E.
Knee, Margaret
Knight, "Rip"
Knight, Ben F.
Knight, Gege
Knight, Inez
Knight, Lewis
Knight, Mrs. Gene
Knight, Roy J.
Knight, Ruth
Knight, Willard
Kocher
Kohr, Joann
Kohr, Max
Korrecht, Michael
Korreckt, Frank
Krautz, Roy
Kreigh, Esther
Kreigh, Peggy
Kreigh, Steve
Krieg, Otto H.
Krile, Carol (Carole)
Krile, Earl
Krile, Gloria
Krile, Isabelle
Krile, Jean (Jeanne, Jeannie)
Krile, Linda
Krile, Lindal
Krile, Mrs. Earl
Krile, Norma
Krile, Norman
Krontz, Roy
Krumanaker, Andrew
Kuchel (Kuschel?), Helena
Kulb, Pamela
Kuschel, Charles (Chuck)
Kuschel, Kathy
Lakey (possibly Leakey?)
Lamprecht, Paul
Lamprecht, Paul, Jr.

Lamprecht, Thelma
LaRue, W. A.
Lasalle, Dr. G. M.
Lassiter, Donald (Don)
Lassiter, Donna
Latta, Nelson
Laugle, Judy
Laugle, Randy
Laymon, Debbie
Laymon, Earl
Laymon, Evelyn
Laymon, Helen
Laymon, Lyle
Laymon, Maxine
Laymon, Mrs. Earl
Laymon, Phyllis
Leaf
Leakey, Dale
Leakey, David
Leakey, Ersell
Leakey, Lawrence
Leakey, Mrs.
Leakey, Mrs. Ersel
Leakey, Roger
Leakey, Russel
Leakey, Ward
Leaman, Francis M.
Lease, Kathryn
Leedy, John
Lesh, Eben
Lesh, Joseph H.
Leverton, George G.
Lewis, Frances
Lewis, Lucile
Lewis, Luella
Lewis, Nancy Casey
Lewis, Ned
Liggett, Paul
Lindbergh, Charles
Little, Adrian
Long, Arthur

Long, Barbara
Long, Charles M. (C. M.)
Long, Harold
Long, James (Jim)
Long, Joyce
Long, Lessel
Long, Mrs. Charles
Long, Mrs. Lessel
Louis
Louthan, Elsa
Lowther, Dr. Wirt
Loy
Ludwig, Don
Luker, J. Forrest
Luker, Larry
Luker, M. J.
Luker, Mike
Lynn, Carolyn
Lynn, Clair
Lynn, Richard
Lyons, C. H.
Lyons, Earl A.
Lyons, Mary
Lyons, Max
Lyons, Mrs. Earl
Mahan, Pamela
Mahoney, Donald; *see also*
  VanDolson
Mahoney, James
Mahoney, Sarah
Malone, Donald
Malone, Mrs.
Manley, Rev. George
Manning, Ray
Mansbarger, Dale
Manson, Andy
Manson, Harry
Markle, J. W. (John); Mr. &
  Mrs. Mrs. John Markle
Marshall, Hugh
Martin, Betty

Martin, C. H.
Martin, Charles, Jr.
Martin, Charles J.
Mathews, Nancy
Mattern, A. E.
Maxton, Alan
Maxton, Carol
Mayne, Robert
McBride, Carolyn
McBride, Deanna
McBride, Inez
McClanahan
McClennahan
McCreary, June
McCullough, Barbara
McCullough, Bonnie
McDaniel, Clarence
McDaniel, Ellen
McDaniel, Eugene
McDaniel, Ivan E.; Mr. & Mrs.
  Ivan McDaniel; Mrs. I.
  McDaniel
McDaniel, Jane
McDaniel, Kate
McDaniel, Larry D.
McDaniel, Mary Edith
McDaniel, Opal
McDaniel, Sandra
McDaniel, Saundra
McDaniel, Terry
McDaniel, Tom
McDaniel, W. A. (Mr. & Mrs.)
McIlrath, James
McIlrath, Willard (Mr. & Mrs.)
McIlravy
McKeever, Mrs. Samuel
McKeever, Samuel
McKenzie, Maurice
McNabb, C. E.
McPherran, William (Bill
  McPherren)

Meadows, James (Jim)
Meredith, Richard J.
Merriman, Lawrence
Meter, Esther Van
Meter, Evelyn Van
Metz, Basil; Mr. & Mrs. Basil
   Metz
Meyer, Maxine
Meyers, Margaret
Meyers, Matilda
Michaels, Norma
Michaelson, Alberta
Middleton, Dennis
Middleton, Mrs. Hilbert
Milican, Daryl
Miller, Arnold
Miller, Bud
Miller, Earl
Miller, Evelyn
Miller, Frances
Miller, Harold
Miller, Henry, Jr.
Miller, Henry (Perk)
Miller, J. D.; Mr. & Mrs. J. D.
   Miller
Miller, James (Jim, Jimmy)
Miller, Josephine
Miller, Keith
Miller, Lydia
Miller, Mary
Miller, Mrs. Henry
Miller, Richard
Miller, Roger
Miller, Teresa
Miller, Wilma
Millican, Bettie
Millican, Bruce
Millican, Edward M.
Millican, Irene
Millican, Mrs.
Millican, William

Milliner, Jacob (Mr. & Mrs.)
Millman, "Dutch"
Millman, B.
Millman, Burl
Millman, H. Burl
Millman, Hollis
Millman, Holly
Millman, Jack
Millman, Karen
Millman, Laurence
Millman, Lawrence
Millman, Marian
Millman, Shelbylynn (Shelby,
   Shelbylyn)
Millman, Tim
Miltonberger, C.
Miltonberger, Charles
Miltonberger, Suzanne
Minnich, Elizabeth
Minnich, S. M.
Misner, Lucile
Mitchell, Virginia
Mohler, Ruth
Montel, Donald
Montel, Elizabeth
Moore, Albert (A. E.)
Moore, Diann
Moore, Elizabeth
Moore, Eugene
Moore, Gene
Moore, John C. B.
Moore, Lamonte H. (Mr. &
   Mrs.)
Moore, Mary (Mrs. Mary M.
   Morehead)
Moore, Mrs. Albert
Moore, Mrs. Gene
More, Gene
Morford, Russell
Morris, Dessie
Morris, John (Mr. & Mrs.)

303

Prilliman, Lucile
Prilliman, Mrs. B. E.
Prillman, Benjamin
Primmer, Donna
Priser, Floyd
Proffitt, James
Props, Earl
Pugh, Helen
Purcell, Elizabeth
Purcell, Mrs. Marvin
Putterbaugh, Gladys
Quakenbush, Ken
Quakenbush, Raymond
Quakenbush, Rosemary
Quinn, Kenneth
Quinn, Larry
Quinn, May
Quinn, Myrtle
Quinn, R.
Quinn, Ray
Quinn, Richard (D., Dick)
Quinn, Sam
Quinn, William
Ragan, Arretta
Ramer, "Bill"
Randall, Allen
Randolph, George
Randolph, Joann
Raney, Karen
Raney, Nancy
Raney, Rev. Glenn
Ray, Frank
Reamer
Rector, Flossie
Reed, Mrs. Don
Reemer, Betty
Reemer, Clyde
Reemer, Colleen
Reemer, Edward (Ed)
Reemer, Marcia
Reemer, Marjorie

Reemer, Mildred
Reemer, Nancy
Reemer, Robert (Bob, Bobby)
Reemer, William (Mr. & Mrs.)
Rees, Orville
Reid, Minnie
Reiff, Edith
Reiff, Hazel
Reiff, Lewis
Resler, Mrs. John
Reust, Alfred (Al)
Reust, Robert
Richards, Bonnie
Richards, Carl E.
Richards, Julia
Richardson, Darl
Ricks, Luther
Rider, Jewel
Riggars, Adolph
Riggars, Johnny
Riggers
Riley, Jean
Ripplinger, Dave
Ripplinger, Rhett
Riseborough, Mark C.
Rittenhouse, David
Rittenhouse, Edith
Rittenhouse, Glen (Glenn)
Rittenhouse, J. D. (Jay Dee)
Rittenhouse, Kenneth
Rittenhouse, Shirley
Rittenhouse, Ted
Rittenhouse, Terry
Ritter, Clement V.
Robb, Annabel
Robb, Geneva
Robb, Wilma
Roberts, Alta
Roberts, Clarence
Roberts, E. H.
Roberts, James

Roberts, Janice
Roberts, Jean
Roberts, Margaret
Roberts, Mrs. E. H.
Robison, George Harold
Robrock, Anna
Rockwell, Mrs. Thomas R.
Rockwell, Tom
Rodeheaver, Homer
Rodenbeck, Don
Rodocker, Darlene (Daleen, Dalene)
Rodocker, Donna
Rogers, Charles
Rogers, John
Rogers, Mike
Rogers, Mrs. Charles
Rogers, Walter
Rose, Kathryn
Rose", "Mary A.
Roser, Dan
Roser, Irene
Ross, Albert
Ross, Bert
Ross, Dessie
Ross, Ethel
Ross, Homer C.
Ross, Kathryn
Ross, Maymie
Ross, Ora A.
Ross, Richard
Ross, William
Rougeau, James
Roush, J. Edward
Rudicel
Rudig, Beulah
Rudig, Enid
Rudig, Frank
Rudig, Glynn
Rudig, Jake
Rudig, Julius

Rudig, Lou Ann
Rudig, Malinda Pauline
Rudig, Mary Margaret
Rudig, Mrs.
Rudig, Mrs. Frank
Rudig, Mrs. Jacob
Rudig, Nellie
Rudig, Tom
Rudig, William
Rupel, Gene
Rupel, H. R.
Rupel, Hildra
Rupel, Joe
Rupel, Mrs. H. R.
Rupel, Orville
Ruppert, Phil
Ruppert, Ron
Ruppert, Yetive
Rusher, Ed
Rusk, Walter
Russel, Joan
Russell, J. M.
Russell, James
Russell, JoAnn
Ryan, Dan
Ryan, King
Salisbury, Madeline
Saluke, Mrs. Don
Sandlin, Mary
Sandlin, Maurice
Sandlin, Morris
Sandlin, Mrs.
Sandlin, Mrs. Raleigh
Sandlin, Raleigh
Sandlin, Roy
Sandlin, Sharon
Sands, Dorothy
Sands, Mary Lee
Sands, Merrilee
Sands, Patricia (Pat, Patty)
Sapp, Arthur

Sapperstein, Abe
Satchwill, Betty
Satchwill, Herbert
Satchwill, Raymond
Satchwill, Walter
Satterthwaite, Myrneth
Schaefer, Gordon
Schaefer, Lucian C. (L. C.)
Schaefer, Mary
Schaefer, Michael (Mike)
Schaefer, Mrs. Gordon
Schaefer, Mrs. L. C.
Schaeffer
Schaeifer, Mrs. L. C.
Scharding, Nancy
Schenkel, Adam
Schenkel, Alvin
Schenkel, Elaine
Schenkel, Elnora
Schenkel, Ernest
Schenkel, Isabelle
Schenkel, Joyce
Schenkel, Kenneth
Schenkel, Marion
Schenkel, Mary
Schenkel, Monte
Schenkel, Richard (Dick)
Schenkel, Sue
Schenkel, Tom (T.)
Schery, Florence
Schilling, Lois
Schilling, Philip
Schlemmer, Harold
Schlemmer, Mrs. Ira
Schmalzreid, Mamie
Schmalzreid, Mrs. John
Schmalzried, Ethel
Schmalzried, Jake
Schmalzried, Joseph
Schmalzried, Pauline
Schmalzried, Raymond

Schneider, Edna
Schneider, William A.
Schoeff, Max
Schoeff, Mrs. Max
Schoolman, Adia
Schultz, Junior
Schwartz, Billie
Scott, Bonnie
Scott, Byron
Scott, Devota
Scott, Doris
Scott, Guy
Sees, John
Sellenberger, Paul
Sellers, David
Sellers, Don
Sellers, Orth
Sewell, Wayne
Shaeffer
Shaffer, Catherine
Shaffer, Kenneth
Shaffer, Mary Jane
Sharp, Laura Ellen
Sharp, Marie
Sharp, Opal
Sharp, Will
Shaw, Richard E.
Shearer, Firmer
Shellenbarger, Fred
Shenefield, Nina
Shenefield, Ray
Shepler, Moses
Shideler, Gilbert
Shinkel, Edna
Shinkel (Shinkle), Mrs.
   William
Shinkel (Shinkle), William
Shoemaker, B.
Shoemaker, Carl
Shoup, Edw. E. (E. E.)
Shoup, Mrs. E. E.

Shultz, Virgil
Simon, Marvin
Simons, Lavana
Simons, Marvin F.
Skinner, Lou
Slagel, Dean
Slagel, John (Mr. & Mrs.)
Slagel, Joseph
Slagel, Kenneth
Slagel, Louis
Slagel, Oscar
Slagel, Russell
Slagle, Hazel
Slagle, Joan
Slayton, William
Small, Carol
Small, Edwin
Small, India
Small, James R. (J. R.)
Small, Mrs. James
Small, Shirley
Small, William
Smart, Bob
Smart, Dan
Smart, Jim
Smart, Mary Ann
Smith, Alvin Eugene
Smith, Carl C.
Smith, Dan (Danny)
Smith, Devota
Smith, Dorothea
Smith, Eugene
Smith, Faith
Smith, Fred
Smith, James L.
Smith, Joann
Smith, Kathryn
Smith, Lawrence
Smith, Leon
Smith, Leroy
Smith, Loretta

Smith, Maurice F.
Smith, Miriam
Smith, Mrs. Eugene
Smith, Mrs. Pete
Smith, Pete N.
Smith, Rodger (Rod)
Smith, Roy
Smith, Ruth
Smith, William (Bill, Billy,
    Billy Joe); Mr. & Mrs.
    William F. Smith
Smuts, Bob
Smuts, Donna
Smuts, Doris
Smuts, Herbert
Smuts, Peggy
Smuts, Rex
Snider, C. Dean
Snider, Johnny
Snider, Mrs. Lewis
Snow, Delbert
Snyder, Barbara
Snyder, Charles
Snyder, Esther
Snyder, George
Snyder, John
Snyder, Marguerite
Snyder, Mrs. Bill
Snyder, Mrs. John
Snyder, William (Bill)
Snyder, Wilma Dean
Speicher, Roger
Speicher, Ruth Ellen
Spencer, Arnold P.; Mr. & Mrs.
    Arnold Spencer; Mrs.
    Arnold Spencer
Spencer, Douglas
Spencer, Robert (Bob)
Springfield, Billy
Sprowl
Spry, John

Stalling
Stallings, B.
Stallings, Bertha
Stallings, C. R.
Stallings, G.
Stallings, George William
Stallings, Lawrence
Stallings, Les
Stallings, Mrs. Clarence
Stallings, R.
Stallings, Robert L.
Stallings, Wilbur
Stambaugh, Ron
Starbuck, Terry
Steele, J. L.
Stensel, Harmon
Stensil, Helen
Stephan, Carl
Stephan, David (Dave)
Stephan, E. H.
Stephan, Earl
Stephan, Eldon
Stephan, Emanuel
  (Emmanuel) H.
Stephan, Frank
Stephan, George
Stephan, James (Jim)
Stephan, Lester
Stephan, Mae
Stephan, Marcella
Stephan, Margaret
Stephan, Mrs. & Mrs. John
Stephan, Mrs. Elmer
Stephan, Mrs. George
Stephan, Mrs. Howard
Stephan, Mrs. Lester
Stephan, Robert L.
Stephan, Rose Mary
Stephan, Shirley
Stephan, Vernice
Stephan, Walter

Stephen (Stephan?), David
Stephens, Carl R.
Stevens, Ethel
Stevens, Homer
Stevens, Newton
Stewart, Carl
Stewart, Lloyd
Stoeppelwerth, Paula
Stoffel, Kenneth
Stookey, Ruth
Stouder, A. R.
Stouder, Art
Stouder, Charles
Stouder, Dean
Stouder, Earl L.
Stouder, Eldon
Stouder, Harold
Stouder, J. Frank
Stouder, Judith (Judy)
Stouder, Kyle
Stouder, Nancy
Stouder, Neva
Stouder, Norman D.
Stouder, Sue
Stouder, Suzette
Stouffs, Arthur
Stouffs, Dan
Stouffs, Mrs. Arthur
Stout, Claude L.
Stout, Mrs.
Strange, Arthur
Strange, Frank
Street, Christina
Streit, Ersell
Streit, Leslie G.
Strevey, Lewis A. (L. A.)
Strevey, Lewis H.
Strevey, Mrs. Lewis
Strickler, John
Sunday, Billy
Sunderman, William

Sutton, Andy
Sutton, Evelyn
Sutton, Hugh
Sutton, Jacqueline
Swearingen
Tackett, Raymond
Taylor, Charles
Taylor, Charlotte
Taylor, Earl
Taylor, Edward (E. L., Ed)
Taylor, Lulu
Taylor, W. O.
Taylor, William Earl
Teague, Jim
Teague, John
Tester, Bob
Tester, David
Theobald, Carlene
Theobald, Chauncey R.
Theobald, Dallas; Mr. & Mrs.
    Dallas Theobald
Theobald, LaMoine
Theobald, Mary
Theobald, Nondas
Thomas, Velma
Thompson, Carolyn
Thompson, Clyde
Thompson, Mrs. Graham
Thompson, Professor
Thorn, Pam
Thorne, Richard
Thornsburgh, Donald W.
    (D. W.)
Thurman, Lucile
Tibbals, Sheridan
Tidrick, John William
Tidrick, William
Todd, Frank
Toerpel, Ernest
Toilolo, Jessie
Toilolo, Juliana

Tomlinson, Letha
Tommason, James
Tourfille, George
Trucks, Virgil
Truitt, Garl
Truitt, Homer
Truitt, Howard
Tucker, John W.
Tuggle, Donna
Tuggle, Doris
Tuggle, Garry
Tuggle, Walter
Tullis, Aldah
Tullis, Bud
Tullis, C. M. (Mr. & Mrs.)
Tullis, Jack W.
Tullis, James
Tullis, Janis
Tullis, Robert (Bob)
Tullis, Sam
Tullis, Tom
Turner, Beverly
Turner, Carl W.
Turner, Diana
Turner, Linda
Turner, Sharon
Turner, Steve
Turpin, John
Tuttle, Ida Mae (nee Pattison)
Tyner, Bernice
Ulery, Dorothy
Ulrey, Mary
Urbanek, Mary Sue
Urschel, Howard
Urschel, Norman
Urschel, Orville
Urschel, Roland
Van Dolsen (misspelling of
    VanDolson)
VanDolson, Donald; see also
    Mahoney

VanMeter, Robert, Jr.
Vaught, Ed
Verbeck, David
Vickery, Clyde
Wade, Cathlyn
Wade, Clara
Wade, Franklin (Frank)
Wade, Joyce
Wade, Kathryn
Wade, Lawrence
Wade, Morris
Wade, Oliver; Mr. & Mrs.
  Oliver Wade
Wagner, Clayton
Waid, O. (Oliver Wade?)
Walker, William
Wall, Doris
Wallace, Charles
Wallace, Earl
Wallace, Eva
Wallace, Margaret
Wallace, Marilyn
Wallace, Marjorie
Walsh, James R.
Walter, Doris
Walters, Kay
Walton, Doris
Walton, Jack
Ward, Howard
Ward, Susan
Ware, A. B.
Ware, Brice
Ware, Dr. Roger
Ware, H. Kenneth (H. K.)
Warfel, Frederick (Fred)
Warfel, Howard
Warfel, Mrs. Fred
Warfel, Mrs. Robert
Warfel, Phyllis June
Warfel, Robert Howard (Bob)
Warschko, Elizabeth

Warschko, Mrs. Paul
Warschko, Paul
Wasmuch, John
Wasmuth, A. D.
Wasmuth, A. E.
Wasmuth, A. F.
Wasmuth, A. W.
Wasmuth, Allen
Wasmuth, Arthur
Wasmuth, D. A.
Wasmuth, Daniel
Wasmuth, David
Wasmuth, E. M.
Wasmuth, Edmund
Wasmuth, Elizabeth
Wasmuth, Harry R. (H.R.); Mr.
  & Mrs. Harry R. Wasmuth;
  Mrs. Harry (H. R.) Wasmuth
Wasmuth, Hazel
Wasmuth, John
Wasmuth, Margaret Ann
Wasmuth, Mrs. Arthur
Wasmuth, Philip
Wasmuth, Robert E. (R. E.)
Wasmuth, Samuel H. (Sam)
Wasmuth, William (Bill, Billy)
Wasson
Watson, Ed
Way, Thelma
Weber, Robert
Weesner, T. D.
Wegmann, Jim
Wegmann, Joe
Wegmann, John
Wegmann, Judith (Judy)
Wehr, Mary
Weisse, M. G.
Welch, Marcella Marie
Wendell, Fannie
Wenter, R. L.
Weyler, Mark

311

Whinery, Norma
Whitacre, Richard
White, Jacob
Whitesell, Bob
Wiedenhoet, Elizabeth
Wiley, Abbie
Wiley, Irvin M. (I. M.)
Wiley, Max
Wiley, Mr.
Wilkerson, Rick; *see also* Wilkinson
Wilkinson, Elizabeth
Wilkinson, Mrs. Richard
Wilkinson, Rick (Ricky); *see also* Wilkerson
Wilkinson, Rod
Willets, C. A. (Mr. & Mrs.)
Willets, Clarence
Willets, Frank
Willets, Pearl
Willets, Vanis
Williams, H. G.
Williams, Lura
Williams, Mrs. D. V.
Williams, Ray
Wilson, Ann
Wilson, C. C.
Wilson, Claude
Wilson, Clyde R.
Wilson, Eugene (Gene)
Wilson, Keith
Wilson, Lowell
Wilson, Maydean
Wilson, Nancy
Wilson, Pamela (Pam)
Wilson, Paula
Wilson, Pauline (Toddie)
Wilson, R. Lowell
Wilson, Ratio
Wilson, Thelma
Winkler, Arlena

Wintrode, Blanche
Wintrode, Charles C.
Wintrode, Daniel
Wintrode, Dean
Wintrode, Diane
Wintrode, George
Wintrode, H. R.
Wintrode, Helen Farhnow
Wintrode, Herbert D.
Wintrode, Jacob
Wintrode, James
Wintrode, Jeff
Wintrode, John
Wintrode, June
Wintrode, Lottie
Wintrode, Maxine
Wintrode, Mrs. George
Wintrode, Mrs. Samuel
Wintrode, Norman
Wintrode, Robert (Bob); Mr. & Mrs. Robert Wintrode
Wintrode, S. Rollin
Wintrode, Verland
Wintrode, W.
Wintrode, Waymond
Wire, A. E.
Wire, Eugene
Wire, James
Wire, Mrs. Jeff
Wire, Paul
Wischmier, Rev. C. C.
Wise, William F.
Wisner, Clarence
Wisner, Howard
Wisner, Thelma
Withers
Wolverton, Estella
Wolverton, Laura
Wolverton, Wesley
Woodward, Jane
Woodward, Marilyn

Wright, Betty
Wright, Doyal
Wright, Helen
Wright, Howard; Mr. & Mrs.
  Howard Wright
Wright, John E.
Wright, Joyce
Wright, Kenneth (Kenny)
Wright, Mary
Wright, Mrs. Lavern
Wright, Ronald
Wright, Wilma
Wyatt, Robert
Xickery, Mrs. Warren
  (probably should be
  Vickery)
Yahne, Bill
Yake, Herbert
Yeiter, Ethel
Yeiter, Flossie
Yeiter, Larry
Yeiter, Walter
Yenter, Herbert

Yentes, G.
Yentes, Gerald
Yentes, Gilbert
Yentes, H.
Yentes, Henry
Yentes, Herbert E.
Yentes, Mary
Yentes, Mildred
Yentes, Nelson
Yentes, Wallace
Yentis
Young, Carol
Young, Dr. J. P.
Young, Stanford
Ziegler, Dwayne
Ziegler, Rex
Zimmerman, (?) B.
Zimmerman, Bernice
Zimmerman, Charles; Mr. &
  Mrs. Charles Zimmerman
Zimmerman, Mr.
Zintsmeister, Minnie
Zoll, Gladys

Made in the USA
Coppell, TX
12 January 2024

27520336R00184